Wedding Feng Shui

Laura Lau and

Theodora Lau

Calligraphy by Kenneth Lau

Illustrations by Michele Fujimoto

WEDDING FENG SHUI

*The Chinese Horoscopes Guide
to Planning Your Wedding*

HARPER

NEW YORK . LONDON . TORONTO . SYDNEY

HARPER

WEDDING FENG SHUI. Copyright © 2011 by Laura Lau aka Laura Lau Karmarkar and the Estate of Theodora Lau. All rights reserved. Printed in the United States of America. No part of this book may be used or reproduced in any manner whatsoever without written permission except in the case of brief quotations embodied in critical articles and reviews. For information address HarperCollins Publishers, 10 East 53rd Street, New York, NY 10022.

HarperCollins books may be purchased for educational, business, or sales promotional use. For information please write: Special Markets Department, HarperCollins Publishers, 10 East 53rd Street, New York, NY 10022.

FIRST EDITION

Designed by Betty Lew

Library of Congress Cataloging-in-Publication Data

Lau, Laura.
    Wedding feng shui : the Chinese horoscopes guide to planning your wedding / Laura Lau and Theodora Lau ; calligraphy by Kenneth Lau ; illustrations by Michele Fujimoto. — 1st ed.
        p. cm.
        ISBN 978-0-06-199053-3
        1. Astrology, Chinese. 2. Weddings—Planning—Miscellanea. 3. Feng shui. I. Lau, Theodora.
II. Title.

BF1714.C5L3645 2011
133.5´9251—dc22

2010038513

11 12 13 14 15   OV/RRD   10 9 8 7 6 5 4 3 2 1

For Harsh

and

Kenneth

Contents

PART III: *A Time and a Season to Get Married*

Since *The Handbook of Chinese Horoscopes* was published in 1979, the number one question asked in fan mail has been about picking an auspicious day to get married. In *Wedding Feng Shui*, we cover this important question—but many other aspects of Chinese astrology can improve your wedding planning as well, from compatibility based on your Chinese zodiac sign and the signs of your loved ones, to creative ways of weaving Chinese cultural traditions and symbolism into your wedding day.

We have assembled what we think is one of the most unusual books on the topic of weddings. Through the lens of the Chinese zodiac and our own application and interpretation of Chinese culture and folklore, we touch every aspect of planning a wedding. We talk about managing the many relationships that come together with a marriage—the interaction of the couple, in-laws, bridesmaids, groomsmen, vendors, and guests. We explore how your sign interacts and changes as a bride. To the delight of many of our readers, this book also recommends auspicious times and dates to get married over the next couple of years. We offer up the color and symbol palette of each animal sign and offer creative ways to mix and match these individual items to create a unique style signature to your and your fiancé's big day. We call this process of introspection, exploration, and creativity *Wedding Feng Shui* and hope you find our book to be one of inspiration on your wedding journey.

China's history, folklore, and mythology captivate many and have given us a rich set of traditions. In this book, we share with you our family's knowledge of Chinese weddings—which includes traditions that many brides and grooms still observe today in both the East and the West, as well as some that are lesser known. We advise you to engage your families in asking about what traditions they have kept alive and perhaps some you would like to bring new life to. Not only is this a fascinating family discussion topic, it's especially important when planning a cultural wedding ceremony, no matter which culture—or cultures—your family has roots in. We share our family knowledge in *Wedding Feng Shui* and encourage you to research and add your unique touch to your wedding with your families' history and your personality as a couple.

We wish you a long and happy marriage. "May your hair grow gray together."

—*Laura and Theodora*

PART I

How to Use This Book

Wedding Feng Shui was written to inspire and provide practical advice for brides. As you read through this book, we hope that you come across new ideas and have some fun learning about yourself and your loved ones along your road to the big day.

There are three categories we'd like you to reflect on when reading *Wedding Feng Shui*—relationships, Chinese tradition, and symbolism.

Relationships: Finding relationship harmony comes from the compatibility of your birth sign and your fiancé's, and how they interact with the signs of the other key members of your wedding, from attendants to in-laws. As described in Chapter 2 "Reference Dates and Tables on the Chinese Zodiac, East-West Sign Combinations, and Animal Hours," a different animal governs each time component of your birth.

We've provided the Wedding Feng Shui worksheets at the end of the book to assist in your planning and promote some self-discovery and inspiration through Chinese horoscopes.

We've outlined the bride and groom worksheet in the most detail and provided an example. Start with you and your fiancé, and then repeat the process for your bridesmaids, groomsmen, family members, and anyone else who will have an important role in your wedding, using the blank templates we've included in the back of the book. Once you have completed each person's Wedding Feng Shui Worksheet, you can better concentrate on the most relevant chapters for you. Keep in mind each person's strengths and weaknesses to create the most compatible wedding planning situation for yourself.

Tradition: In this book, we discuss a number of Chinese rituals and traditions. From post-engagement to post-wedding, there are many Chinese traditions that you can integrate into your wedding plan.

We suggest you read and reflect on how (or if) you are going to incorporate each event. Below are some important questions to discuss with your families and to consider when planning the timeline of events. Share the information with your vendors and bridal party, so they can prepare as well.

- Will you follow all Chinese traditional events or take an à la carte approach? Which events?
- What will be the location for the event?
- What will you wear for each ritual?
- How would you like these moments to be photographed?
- Who will take part in each ceremony?

Symbolism: Chinese weddings are rich with symbolism and can inspire a unique theme or touch to your wedding. From color, imagery, and food, there is room for a lot of creativity in planning weddings. Look back on your Wedding Feng Shui Worksheet to discover your animal's signature color, element, flower, and Western gemstone. Do the same investigation into other key players in your wedding and those you hold dear. You can honor a family member or friend who is important to you through a symbolic gesture like wearing his sign's flower in your hair or finding inspiration for appreciation gifts through her year of birth.

One

EAST MEETS WEST WEDDING PLANNING CALENDAR AND HELPFUL TIPS

Twelve months before your wedding

- Share news of your engagement and enjoy being engaged.
- Start thinking about wedding themes and styles that appeal to you as a couple.
- Determine your wedding and honeymoon budget.

Eleven months before your wedding

- If hiring a wedding consultant or *da ling jie* (Chinese wedding traditions adviser), meet to discuss details.
- Set a theme for your reception.
- Discuss with your fiancé and families what customs or rituals you would like to integrate into your wedding weekend.
- Research and meet with florists, caterers, musicians, and photographers/videographers.
- Reserve locations for your wedding ceremony, reception, and family rituals such as the tea ceremony and wedding banquet. Remember to include rehearsal times.

- Start researching wedding gowns and reception outfits, if applicable.
- Select your wedding party members and ask them to be a part of your big day. Get together and complete each person's Wedding Feng Shui Worksheet.
- Select an officiant, start discussing the ceremony, and begin any religious preparation.

Ten months before your wedding

- Choose and order your wedding gown.
- Set expectations with your maid of honor and bridesmaids on each person's responsibilities. Get them up to speed on any Chinese rituals you want to include and how they can help you prepare.

Nine months before your wedding

- Create gift registry and add new bedding to be used for *an chuang* (seating the new bed).
- Share detailed plans of your theme and chosen Chinese rituals with your vendors, so they can tailor their services.
- Determine the menu and drinks to be served at your reception, including wedding banquet. See symbolic foods for inspiration (pp. 22, 42).
- Purchase or order veil, shoes, and other bridal accessories.
- Start shopping for your *qi pao* or cheongsam, find a place to rent a wedding day outfit or have one tailor made (pp. 26–27).
- Research and book group discounts for flights and accommodations.

Eight months before your wedding

- Book photographer and entertainment.
- Go to first gown fitting and bring along a friend for her opinion.
- Select bridesmaids' dresses or accessories. For inspiration see p. 27.
- Start thinking about your wedding ring style.
- Select florist and incorporate wedding theme and style (try integrating your animal's symbolic flower).
- Launch your wedding Web site.

Seven months before your wedding
- Select outfits for flower girl and/or ring bearer.
- Choose and purchase wedding invitations and investigate Chinese stationers if you are interested in bilingual invitations.
- Determine order of wedding weekend activities, including all Chinese rituals and ceremony events. Prepare the proper wording for programs; include background of chosen rituals so your guests can follow along.
- Order your wedding rings and remember to order any special engravings.
- Purchase bridal accessories such as jewelry, lingerie, and pre-wedding day sleepwear for *shang tou* (p. 36)

Six months before your wedding
- Review and confirm wedding invitation proofs; be sure to ask your maid of honor, who can view the material with a fresh set of eyes.
- Research honeymoon spots.
- Reserve transportation for your wedding day.

Five months before your wedding
- Order or start planning how you will make your table cards and programs.
- Go to wedding cake tastings and select a bakery. Read about symbolic shapes and auspicious flavors and share with your baker (p. 22)
- Make reservations for wedding rehearsal dinner and reconfirm time and location of the wedding rehearsal.
- Make reservations for the wedding banquet, if not included at your wedding reception.

Four months before your wedding
- Have groom try on tuxedos and any other wedding day outfits (p. 27)
- Remind groom to start coordinating groomsmen's attire.

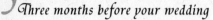

Three months before your wedding

- Plan a post-wedding brunch if applicable.
- Talk to your maid of honor and bridesmaids about your bachelorette party.
- Plan a bridesmaids' thank-you event—lunch, dinner, or spa day.
- Make an appointment with your hairstylist to discuss your wedding hairstyle.
- Add information on hotel, maps, and directions to your wedding Web site and include in your invitations.

Two months before your wedding

- Make plans for a wedding day dressing room for attendants to get ready and secure their belongings.
- Prepare and mail wedding invitations (weigh and include additional postage for square invitations and international addresses). Add a special note for people invited to take part in additional rituals with cultural background to help them prepare.
- Attend final gown fitting and organize pickup or delivery date.
- Have final fitting for groom's formal wear.
- Purchase attendants' appreciation gifts (ideas on p. 33).

Six weeks before your wedding

- Send out invitations to rehearsal dinner.
- Start writing thank-you notes as you receive gifts.
- Select food and drink for post-wedding brunch, if applicable.
- Start shopping for a gift for your fiancé and advise your parents on custom for new son-in-law gifts (p. 35).
- Shop for or start thinking about making wedding favors (ideas on pp. 23–24).
- Purchase or register for honeymoon travel needs—special clothing, luggage, and accessories.
- Schedule a day-of-wedding hair appointment and a practice run.
- Arrange gift exchange for groom's family and bride's family—can occur two to three weeks before the wedding (see p. 41).

Four weeks before your wedding
- Discuss delivery times and confirm order with florist.
- Meet or e-mail with ushers about individual duties.
- Review the details of your ceremony with your officiant.
- Determine seating arrangements for guests.
- Schedule a day-of-wedding appointment with a makeup artist and a practice run.
- Schedule a nail appointment for the day before your wedding and treat your mom or maid of honor to a manicure/pedicure as well.
- Finalize details and list of wedding shots with photographer and videographer.
- Confirm reservations for honeymoon.
- Discuss table card setup for wedding reception.
- Deputize a person to pick up or return groom's formal wear.

Three weeks before your wedding
- Call anyone who has not yet RSVP-ed and determine final list of reception guests.
- Send final headcount to the caterer and review any special dietary needs for guests.
- Pick the date for *an chuang* (seating the new bed; see p. 43).

One week before your wedding
- Start packing for your honeymoon.
- Pick up your wedding dress.

Night before your wedding
- Bride and groom have *shang tou* hair-combing ceremony and blessing with families (p. 36).

Wedding day
- Your wedding day!
- The traditional wedding tea ceremony also occurs on this day (see p. 40).

After your wedding

- Arrange for transport of wedding gifts.
- Send out thank-you notes and wedding announcements.
- Clean and preserve wedding gown and return any rented garments.

Two

REFERENCE DATES AND TABLES ON THE CHINESE ZODIAC, EAST-WEST SIGN COMBINATIONS, AND ANIMAL HOURS

LUNAR YEARS

Sign	Start Date	End Date	Element
Rat	February 18, 1912	February 5, 1913	Water
Ox	February 6, 1913	January 25, 1914	Water
Tiger	January 26, 1914	February 13, 1915	Wood
Rabbit	February 14, 1915	February 2, 1916	Wood
Dragon	February 3, 1916	January 22, 1917	Fire
Snake	January 23, 1917	February 10, 1918	Fire
Horse	February 11, 1918	January 31, 1919	Earth
Sheep	February 1, 1919	February 19, 1920	Earth
Monkey	February 20, 1920	February 7, 1921	Metal
Rooster	February 8, 1921	January 27, 1922	Metal

LUNAR YEARS

Sign	Start Date	End Date	Element
Dog	January 28, 1922	February 15, 1923	Water
Boar	February 16, 1923	February 4, 1924	Water
Rat	February 5, 1924	January 24, 1925	Wood
Ox	January 25, 1925	February 12, 1926	Wood
Tiger	February 13, 1926	February 1, 1927	Fire
Rabbit	February 2, 1927	January 22, 1928	Fire
Dragon	January 23, 1928	February 9, 1929	Earth
Snake	February 10, 1929	January 29, 1930	Earth
Horse	January 30, 1930	February 16, 1931	Metal
Sheep	February 17, 1931	February 5, 1932	Metal
Monkey	February 6, 1932	January 25, 1933	Water
Rooster	January 26, 1933	February 13, 1934	Water
Dog	February 14, 1934	February 3, 1935	Wood
Boar	February 4, 1935	January 23, 1936	Wood
Rat	January 24, 1936	February 10, 1937	Fire
Ox	February 11, 1937	January 20, 1938	Fire
Tiger	January 21, 1938	February 18, 1939	Earth
Rabbit	February 19, 1939	February 7, 1940	Earth
Dragon	February 8, 1940	January 26, 1941	Metal
Snake	January 27, 1941	February 14, 1942	Metal
Horse	February 15, 1942	February 4, 1943	Water
Sheep	February 5, 1943	January 24, 1944	Water
Monkey	January 25, 1944	February 12, 1945	Wood

LUNAR YEARS

Sign	Start Date	End Date	Element
Rooster	February 13, 1945	February 1, 1946	Wood
Dog	February 2, 1946	January 21, 1947	Fire
Boar	January 22, 1947	February 9, 1948	Fire
Rat	February 10, 1948	January 28, 1949	Earth
Ox	January 29, 1949	February 16, 1950	Earth
Tiger	February 17, 1950	February 5, 1951	Metal
Rabbit	February 6, 1951	January 26, 1952	Metal
Dragon	January 27, 1952	February 13, 1953	Water
Snake	February 14, 1953	February 2, 1954	Water
Horse	February 3, 1954	January 23, 1955	Wood
Sheep	January 24, 1955	February 11, 1956	Wood
Monkey	February 12, 1956	January 30, 1957	Fire
Rooster	January 31, 1957	February 17, 1958	Fire
Dog	February 18, 1958	February 7, 1959	Earth
Boar	February 8, 1959	January 27, 1960	Earth
Rat	January 28, 1960	February 14, 1961	Metal
Ox	February 15, 1961	February 4, 1962	Metal
Tiger	February 5, 1962	January 24, 1963	Water
Rabbit	January 25, 1963	February 12, 1964	Water
Dragon	February 13, 1964	February 1, 1965	Wood
Snake	February 2, 1965	January 20, 1966	Wood
Horse	January 21, 1966	February 8, 1967	Fire
Sheep	February 9, 1967	January 29, 1968	Fire

LUNAR YEARS

Sign	Start Date	End Date	Element
Monkey	January 30, 1968	February 16, 1969	Earth
Rooster	February 17, 1969	February 5, 1970	Earth
Dog	February 6, 1970	January 26, 1971	Metal
Boar	January 27, 1971	February 15, 1972	Metal
Rat	February 16, 1972	February 2, 1973	Water
Ox	February 3, 1973	January 22, 1974	Water
Tiger	January 23, 1974	February 10, 1975	Wood
Rabbit	February 11, 1975	January 30, 1976	Wood
Dragon	January 31, 1976	February 17, 1977	Fire
Snake	February 18, 1977	February 6, 1978	Fire
Horse	February 7, 1978	January 27, 1979	Earth
Sheep	January 28, 1979	February 15, 1980	Earth
Monkey	February 16, 1980	February 4, 1981	Metal
Rooster	February 5, 1981	January 24, 1982	Metal
Dog	January 25, 1982	February 12, 1983	Water
Boar	February 13, 1983	February 1, 1984	Water
Rat	February 2, 1984	February 19, 1985	Wood
Ox	February 20, 1985	February 8, 1986	Wood
Tiger	February 9, 1986	January 28, 1987	Fire
Rabbit	January 29, 1987	February 16, 1988	Fire
Dragon	February 17, 1988	February 5, 1989	Earth
Snake	February 6, 1989	January 26, 1990	Earth
Horse	January 27, 1990	February 14, 1991	Metal

LUNAR YEARS

Sign	Start Date	End Date	Element
Sheep	February 15, 1991	February 3, 1992	Metal
Monkey	February 4, 1992	January 22, 1993	Water
Rooster	January 23, 1993	February 9, 1994	Water
Dog	February 10, 1994	January 30, 1995	Wood
Boar	January 31, 1995	February 18, 1996	Wood
Rat	February 19, 1996	February 6, 1997	Fire
Ox	February 7, 1997	January 27, 1998	Fire
Tiger	January 28, 1998	February 15, 1999	Earth
Rabbit	February 16, 1999	February 4, 2000	Earth
Dragon	February 5, 2000	January 23, 2001	Metal
Snake	January 24, 2001	February 11, 2002	Metal
Horse	February 12, 2002	January 31, 2003	Water
Sheep	February 1, 2003	January 21, 2004	Water
Monkey	January 22, 2004	February 8, 2005	Wood
Rooster	February 9, 2005	January 28, 2006	Wood
Dog	January 29, 2006	February 17, 2007	Fire
Boar	February 18, 2007	February 6, 2008	Fire
Rat	February 7, 2008	January 25, 2009	Earth
Ox	January 26, 2009	February 13, 2010	Earth
Tiger	February 14, 2010	February 2, 2011	Metal
Rabbit	February 3, 2011	January 22, 2012	Metal
Dragon	January 23, 2012	February 9, 2013	Water
Snake	February 10, 2013	January 30, 2014	Water

ASCENDANTS:
THE TWELVE ANIMAL SIGNS AND THEIR HOURS

Start	End	Animal
11 P.M.	1 A.M.	Rat
3 A.M.	5 A.M.	Tiger
5 A.M.	7 A.M.	Rabbit
7 A.M.	9 A.M.	Dragon
9 A.M.	11 A.M.	Snake
11 A.M.	1 P.M.	Horse
1 P.M.	3 P.M.	Sheep
3 P.M.	5 P.M.	Monkey
5 P.M.	7 P.M.	Rooster
7 P.M.	9 P.M.	Dog
9 P.M.	11 P.M.	Boar

EAST-WEST COMBINATIONS: HOW MONTH OF BIRTH CORRESPONDS TO THE CHINESE ZODIAC

Sign	Sun Sign	Start Date	End Date
Rat	Sagittarius	November 22	December 21
Ox	Capricorn	December 22	January 20
Tiger	Aquarius	January 21	February 19
Rabbit	Pisces	February 20	March 20
Dragon	Aries	March 21	April 19
Snake	Taurus	April 20	May 20
Horse	Gemini	May 21	June 21
Sheep	Cancer	June 22	July 21
Monkey	Leo	July 22	August 21
Rooster	Virgo	August 22	September 22
Dog	Libra	September 23	October 22
Boar	Scorpio	October 23	November 21

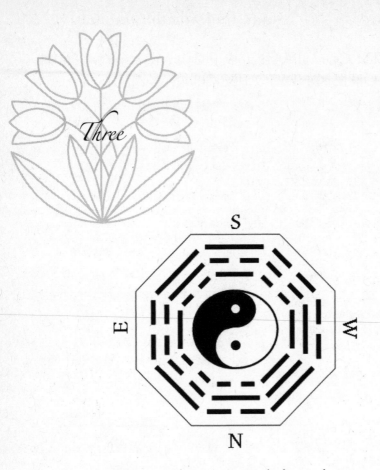

Three

S

E

W

N

The image above represents the *hou tian ba gua,*
which feng shui practitioners use in home environments.

WHAT IS WEDDING FENG SHUI? INSPIRATION
FOR YOUR WEDDING THEME AND DECOR

Feng shui, literally translated as "wind" and "water," has been most commonly
known in the West for informing our living environment. Using the *ba gua,* the
feng shui symbol, as a guide, feng shui is the art of placing objects in harmony
with *qi,* our natural energy or flow of life itself. The result is a feeling of peace in
our homes, offices, and gardens through simply being observant and thoughtful
of how we work with our environment. An area should have a continuous flow, by
keeping clutter at a minimum and placing objects in a harmonious way. For ex-

ample, when selecting a place for a bed, one should not choose a location below an exposed beam. The beam disrupts *qi*, and many believe that this can cause marital unrest. Doorways are of the utmost importance, and special consideration should be made when placing objects with respect to them. Feng shui experts discourage placing beds facing doorways, while desks should always be oriented so that a seated person can see a doorway.

The art of feng shui can also be used to plan a peaceful, calming, and positive wedding. *Wedding Feng Shui* combines Chinese astrology and the basic principles of feng shui to inform us of ways to add beautiful and symbolic style touches to weddings, while also creating harmonious relationships. Anyone who has ever planned or seen someone else planning a wedding knows that it's a challenging ceremony to coordinate. A wedding is a catalyst for many life-changing events: families begin to merge, cultures blend or are rediscovered, friendships become working relationships, and so on. Too often, we focus on the visible event details— the colors, the dress, the location. But the relationships are even more important— the relationship between bride and groom, family and in-laws, friends giving time, money, and energy. *Wedding Feng Shui* balances these two aspects.

On a symbolism level, *Wedding Feng Shui* outlines a style sheet for each animal sign—colors and natural elements. Each animal rules a direction of the *ba gua*, the principal feng shui symbol. We have added to this by sharing with you symbolic flowers, the governing elements, and Western birthstones. We offer creative ways to add these details into your own personal wedding style, creating a rich palette of design elements to plan a wedding that is filled with personal meaning.

Wedding Feng Shui for the Elements

While we may not think of it as feng shui, wedding planners of all cultures have been creating a harmonious blend of elements and guests for as long as we can remember. Guests' eyes are treated to beautiful wedding locations, luscious centerpieces, and the beauty of the happy bride and groom. The all-important selection of music invigorates the party, sumptuous cuisine and flowing libations feed our taste buds, and the powerful ambiance setters of fragrant flowers and luxurious fabrics please our senses of smell and touch.

A great visual metaphor for everyone's quest for balance is the tai chi symbol, better known as yin and yang. Presented as dark and light twins coming together in a circle, it signifies how opposites must coexist. Darkness and light, female and male, the Phoenix and the Dragon, each pairing has a relationship. You'll notice that each half possesses a dot of the opposite color. This is to remind us that nothing is ever completely good or bad. Nothing is ever perfect, and we can take solace in knowing that there is beauty in life's sum total.

To better understand how to achieve a harmony of the elements, we must talk about the cycle of construction and the cycle of destruction. The positive cycle of birth involves placing elements so that they nourish one another. Fire creates Earth, which births Metal, which holds Water that gives life to Wood. The negative cycle originates from how elements can harm one another. Fire melts Metal, Metal can be forged into a tool to cut Wood, Wood consumes the nutrients of Earth, Earth soaks up Water, and of course, Water extinguishes Fire. Knowing these cycles will help you pair or group items in a harmonious way. Look for nurturing relationships from the cycle of construction.

The two key tools used by feng shui practitioners are the *ba gua* and the *luo pan*, the feng shui compass. The first *ba gua*, called Xin Tian or Early Heaven Ba Gua, dates back over five thousand years ago to the San Huang period. It wasn't until two thousand years later in the Zhou dynasty that the Hou Tian or Later Heaven Ba Gua was created. At this time, the I Ching or Book of Changes assigned the *hou tian ba gua* to use for the living and the *xin tian ba gua* to the dead. When a feng shui practitioner assesses a location, he or she evaluates the environment based on the octagonal *ba gua*, which places our key wishes in life by direction. You'll notice in the *hou tian ba gua* illustration above that south is at the top of the octagon, according to feng shui convention. Family and Health are ruled by the east, Marriage lives in the southwest, and Children in the west.

But let's be practical: many factors go into wedding and reception location choices, and often every element can't conform to every rule of feng shui. There are countless things to take into account, from your own personal preferences to unique family traditions to budget and timing limitations. So we will concentrate on wedding feng shui elements and symbolism that can easily be a part of any wedding location.

Double Happiness by Kenneth Lau

The Wedding Location

Just as the entrance to a home is of crucial importance in feng shui, so is your wedding location entrance. It should be unobstructed and decorated with prosperous colors like red, pink, or gold to invite good energy. Hanging wedding banners is a traditional and attractive way of adorning an entrance. Red banners are painted with the Double Happiness sign or traditional four Chinese character sayings that are wishes for prosperity, longevity, and happiness. The character *fu*, which stands for prosperity, is also a common symbol for celebrations. Floral arrangements are also prosperous entryway decor.

Natural light or brightness is also a good element of feng shui. Like honoring the *li chun* (the eye of spring) in choosing a wedding date, a wedding should have good visibility to represent the clarity of sight for the future. While it's romantic to have a dimly lit ceremony, it is considered inauspicious to not have a well-lit environment when exchanging vows. For evening weddings, consider adding more light or candles to brighten the scene when you are exchanging your vows. The presence of light is powerful and is symbolic of a clear path in your marriage.

The Wedding Cake and Flavor Inspiration

There's an incredible amount of creativity in the wedding cake art form today. From sky-high wedding cake towers to a delightful selection of miniature cupcakes, variety is the spice of the wedding reception. Feng shui and Chinese wedding symbolism favor symmetrical shapes because they naturally speak to the balance we aspire to have in our lives and marriages.

In addition, a strong theme of Chinese wedding traditions and symbolism is the idea of an unbroken bond between husband and wife. We suggest extending the same element to your cake. Even if you're planning on having wedding cupcakes, cookies, or other small treats, it is bad wedding feng shui to have only a cake split in pieces because it is representative of your marriage to come. Many couples these days have a small cake for the cutting ceremony. This can be a simple and symbolic moment that observes wedding feng shui with a round or square shape. The circle is a symbol of unity and perfection in feng shui. It is the most auspicious shape for a marriage because it represents an unbroken bond for a relationship. The circle shape also represents the Metal element and fertility—a good choice for those who hope to start families soon after the wedding. A square cake is an equally appropriate choice for a wedding cake because it represents the Earth element, a stabilizing force. The Earth's energy can nurture a new relationship to grow.

Another way to inspire some creativity in your wedding cake bakery is by integrating some symbolic Chinese fruits into flavors and decoration to really bring wedding feng shui to life. Peaches, plums, and ginger represent longevity; tangerines are a symbol of good luck; kumquats and oranges symbolize gold and prosperity; lychee fruit connotes family; coconuts symbolize togetherness and continuation of generations; and apricots and cherries celebrate women's beauty. You can use some of these fruit flavors as inspiration for a creative signature cocktail for your reception or bridal shower. One should avoid using pears because the word *li* is associated with parting or divorce. While it's customary to favor lighter colored cakes for Chinese weddings, you can apply wedding feng shui by balancing a light cake with a darker cake, such as vanilla and chocolate or dark red velvet. Chinese tradition favors less sweet desserts, which are typically lighter in color and texture.

Love by Kenneth Lau

Using the Elements as Symbolic Wedding Favors and Decor Inspiration

The section below talks about the elements and how they correspond to the seasons in the Chinese zodiac. Each sign has a ruling element and season. Additionally, depending on the year you were born, your sign will have another related element. Make sure to use the chart on pp. 11–15 to look up the elements associated with your and your fiancé's birth years.

Water Element: The signs of the Rat, Ox, and Boar share the element of Water and the winter season. A dark, sophisticated color palette of dark blues, such as navy, as well as black and gray represent the water element. Scarves and other objects that mimic the movement of water represent this element. A creative centerpiece idea is floating flowers in lucky numbers such as three, eight, or nine.

Wood Element: The Tiger, Rabbit, and Dragon come together in the season of spring and are represented by Wood. Green represents Wood's energy. Plants, trees, and long thin shapes are symbols of Wood and can be easily integrated into centerpieces, wedding favors, and bouquets. Bamboo is a good wedding favor idea because it also represents good luck and long life.

Fire Element: The Snake, Horse, and Sheep belong to the summer season and are represented by Fire. Its core color is naturally red. Pink and orange are also associated with Fire, as they emanate off the primary color of red. Red is an especially auspicious color, which symbolizes good luck and is believed to chase away evil. Fire is already well integrated into many ceremonies, most commonly through the Unity Candle. It's easy to integrate the Fire element through lanterns, candles, and sparklers.

Metal Element: The Monkey, Rooster, and Dog are all autumnal animals and are represented by Metal. The metal color palette possesses white, which symbolizes pureness and femininity as well as the dramatic accents of silver and gold. Many Chinese families favor off-white when a part of a wedding because white is the traditional color of mourning in China. Traditionally, gold is a common theme in a Chinese wedding, symbolizing prosperity for the new couple. You can represent the metal element through color or material. Cloisonné objects are beautiful representations of Chinese art as well as of the Metal element. Items like chopsticks and small decorative boxes are unique wedding favors. Just remember to fill the boxes with something, like candy or a small coin, because it is considered unlucky to give an empty gift.

Earth Element: The Earth is common to all seasons and animals. Earth tones such as browns and yellows represent this element. Wooden and ceramic items are good candidates for interesting wedding favors and centerpieces. Lots of carved wooden objects make great gifts, from carved boxes (again, make sure they are filled) to chopsticks. Small ceramic vases are nice foundations for your centerpieces.

In addition to the wedding favors and centerpieces mentioned, one of the most traditional wedding gifts and favors to give is tea, or *cha*. Symbolic of family continuity, it is a gift often given between families. Lychee tea is one of the most popular options for weddings. Other options to explore are blacks teas, green teas, white teas, and infused flavored teas.

Traditional Chinese Wedding Decor and Themes

While there are some variations for each sign, as explained in the individual chapters, many traditions are the same for all. The traditional color for Chinese weddings is red. Red is an auspicious color that the Chinese believe invites good fortune and repels evil. The bridal suit called a *hong qua* or the long fitted dresses known as cheongsams and *qi paos* are usually red for its positive meaning. Pink, a more feminine shade of the color red, is also a common choice. Gold and silver as metallic accents are a common theme through wedding wear and decorations, symbolizing wealth and prosperity. The peony is a popular flower at Chinese weddings because it is known as a royal symbol of elegance. Butterflies are symbolic of joy and are commonly a part of traditional Chinese wedding art. Wedding banners with good wishes for the bride and groom are traditionally written in gold ink on a red background.

The quintessential symbol for Chinese weddings is the character for Double Happiness. You'll be hard-pressed to find the word in a standard Chinese-English dictionary but it is a symbol that everyone knows. It speaks to the synergy of pairing two compatible people and the happiness that comes with it. Perhaps the most well-known symbol of the union of the new couple is the image of the Dragon and the Phoenix. The Dragon symbolizes the strength and power of the yang, or male personality, joining with the Phoenix, the grace and longevity of the yin, or female personality. The Dragon and Phoenix motif adorns wedding garments, bedding, and other items like candles that are used in ceremonies such as the *shang tou*, the pre-wedding day ritual described later in this book.

While registries are popular, giving cash at a Chinese wedding is the most common practice. Crisp, new money is placed in red envelopes, called *lai cee* in Cantonese or *hong pao* in Mandarin, and given at the wedding as gifts. Red envelopes allow monetary gifts (large or small) to be given discreetly. Have your wedding coordinator, maid of honor, or mother bring extra red envelopes so that guests have one handy in case they have forgotten or are unaware of the tradition. Red envelopes are also expected from honored elders at the tea ceremony (p. 40). Be sure to designate a person responsible for the red envelopes. You can never be too careful with your first home's down payment. When you do register for items for your home, you should avoid signing up for a clock. The word for "clock" is *zhong*, which sounds like the word for "the end" and can be interpreted as a gift giver wishing the new couple ill will. It should never be given, no matter the occasion. But watches make fine gifts and are traditional for weddings.

Wedding Formal Wear

Today's weddings in the West and the East integrate wedding fashions from both cultures. Chinese brides often favor the Western white wedding gown, while many brides in the West like to include a cheongsam or *qi pao* for its grace and form-fitting drama. Chinese weddings receptions have had a fashion show element woven in for as long as anyone can remember. A bride typically changes into multiple dresses throughout the reception. This tradition started as a way for families to communicate their wealth and prosperity through a bride's brag-worthy closet and lives on today.

For the wedding ceremony, modern Chinese brides wear an off-white gown, because white is seen as a color of mourning in China as well as much of the Far East. Since it is worn for only part of the day, the Chinese believe it is counteracted by the other outfits the bride will wear throughout the big day. The *hong qua* or wedding suit is the traditional wedding ceremony outfit. It is a two-piece garment, adorned with the Dragon and Phoenix motif, that pairs a long skirt with a short jacket. The bride can wear the outfit for the wedding ceremony as well as the tea ceremony. These garments are often difficult to find or quite expensive, so it is fairly common to rent or borrow them. The Chinese believe that if you do borrow an item to wear for your wedding, it's best to do so from someone who has a happy marriage. Similar to the Western tradition of having "something borrowed, something blue," it is seen as a lucky charm. However, if you have rented or bought a vintage dress or accessory and do not know its provenance, we would advise you bring the item to your *shang tou* ceremony (described in a later section) to be blessed for your wedding day.

The Chinese favor wearing wedding dresses that have the fewest cuts of the fabric possible to emphasize the importance of wholeness to a new marriage. Look at the figure-flattering cheongsam or *qi pao*, a form-fitting Chinese wedding garment with only one major seam. Today, ceremony dresses range in color and style, though the cheongsam or *qi pao* are popular choices. High collars are seen as the most formal, and updo hairstyles are the best complement to show them off. Cheongsams are also an investment piece that can be worn many times after your wedding. We'd also argue that the cheongsam is the most effective motivator for a bride to get in shape. The ultra-feminine dresses embrace every curve of a woman's shape. Therefore, a woman should temper her diet to complement the abilities of her tailor.

Brides often try in vain (or claim to try) to choose a bridesmaid dress that their attendants can wear again in the future. We recommend cheongsams as a bridesmaid dress or mother or mother-in-law fashion—not only are they a visual honoring of the Chinese culture but they are also a welcome addition to any fashionable woman's wardrobe well past your wedding. For those who would prefer a more conservative cut, ask about two-piece pantsuits, which will keep the Chinese fashion element consistent, while providing more comfort for the long wedding day. Assuming the cost and effort to coordinate finding these perfect outfits, it would be a generous attendant gift, to say the least.

Unlike the bride, the groom does not do multiple dress changes, with the exception of perhaps wearing traditional robes for the ceremony and a tuxedo for the reception. The bride is the belle of the ball, after all. Modern Chinese grooms favor the classic tuxedo for the wedding and reception. Men take the lead from their brides, complementing their chosen outfit with traditional robes to go with their bride's wedding suit. Another culturally inspired formal wear option is a mandarin-collared suit, which is both understated and a nod to Chinese style. An East-West style combination we suggest is unifying the bridal party's look through fabric. Matching cummerbund, vest fabric, or pocket squares are all possibilities.

Four

YOUR PERSONAL WEDDING ATTENDANT PLANNER

When you become a bride, you are thrust into a leadership role with many hats. Whether it's boss, negotiator, or designer, it's all in a day's work for the bride-to-be. You can do yourself a big favor by choosing the right backup in the form of the right attendants. Oftentimes brides pick their bridesmaids by envisioning their wedding day pictures and who will be smiling right beside them. This is a great way to honor the most important people in your life. However, the best friendships are not always the best working relationships, especially when you are now in a position of authority.

Think of your bridesmaids as your Bridal Cabinet, in which each member possesses a particular expertise. They are there to support you on your wedding journey. When assigning a task, ask yourself whether the job fits the person. The biggest opportunities for bridal disappointment occur when you ask for something that goes against a person's nature. A future sister-in-law born in the year of the Tiger makes a natural publicist, with her gift of gab—but perhaps she's not the person to share any top-secret gossip with. An old college roommate born in the year of the Horse has circumvented the globe a few times and can certainly give you excellent pointers on planning your honeymoon, but may not have the patience for stuffing your wedding invitations. Your wonderful sister born in the year of the Sheep will pick up the phone no matter the hour to commiserate with you about the wedding headache of the moment, but her forgetful nature makes her the worst person to hold on to Grandma's pearl earrings on the big day.

When you know each attendant well and understand how to best use or sometimes diffuse each person's strengths and natural personality, the team you assemble can result in great wedding feng shui. Below is a snapshot of how friends of each animal sign fit in the role of bridesmaid. Make sure to also read each animal's chapter in more detail to get better acquainted with each person.

Your Bridesmaids' Personality Profiles

BORN IN THE YEAR OF THE RAT
Gets along best with: Dragon and Monkey.

Finds challenges with: Horse.

She's your best: Photographer. She always has a camera and the knack for putting together the best photo slide shows—something to think about when putting together yours.

Most likely to: Sweat the small stuff. With her critical eye, she cannot hold back comments that can be viewed as nitpicky.

Recommended attendant gift: The Rat is sentimental. Find a meaningful picture of the two of you together, and frame it.

BORN IN THE YEAR OF THE OX
Gets along best with: Snake and Rooster.

Finds challenges with: Sheep.

She's your best: Project manager. You can depend on her to follow through on any project to the very end; she is highly unlikely to ask for last-minute deadline extensions.

Most likely to: Hold a grudge, especially if her work has gone unthanked. She is more sensitive than she comes off.

Recommended attendant gift: A book that's been on her list for a while. The Ox prefers to spend time with the classics.

Born in the Year of the Tiger

Gets along best with: Horse and Dog.

Finds challenges with: Monkey.

She's your best: Motivational dancer. She's confident and will be the first person to get out on the dance floor and get the reception into full swing.

Most likely to: Spill the beans. She's prone to emotional outbursts, which can make secrets tough to keep.

Recommended attendant gift: A vibrant-colored wrap or clutch. The Tiger likes to make a statement.

Born in the Year of the Rabbit

Gets along best with: Sheep and Boar.

Finds challenges with: Rooster.

She's your best: Etiquette consultant. She's known for her prompt thank-you notes and her way of treating people with style and grace.

Most likely to: Avoid bad news. She's the sensitive type who cannot stomach sad stories or criticism.

Recommended attendant gift: Monogrammed stationery or handkerchiefs. The Rabbit enjoys being proper and elegant.

Born in the Year of the Dragon

Gets along best with: Rat and Monkey.

Finds challenges with: Dog.

She's your best: Shopping buddy. Unfailingly honest, she will always give you her true opinion and will be your ally in the quest for the perfect dress.

Most likely to: Overstep. The Dragon is inclined to take her role as maid of honor too seriously, and she's prone to power trips.

Recommended attendant gift: Think rainy day comforts like a plush robe or a throw for the Dragon, who prefers to curl up with soft fabrics.

Born in the Year of the Snake

Gets along best with: Ox and Rooster.

Finds challenges with: Boar.

She's your best: Confidante. You can feel confident that when you share with her, it's in the vault.

Most likely to: Give the cold shoulder. While always polite, she can be slow to warm up to strangers, and often shuns small talk at parties.

Recommended attendant gift: Look around for a perfume or sultry accessory that heightens the Snake sign's natural sex appeal.

BORN IN THE YEAR OF THE HORSE

Gets along best with: Tiger and Dog.

Finds challenges with: Rat.

She's your best: Partner in crime. She's the most adventurous, and always ready to jump in the car and go location scouting.

Most likely to: Multitask and lose focus. She is the eternal optimist who can sometimes bite off more than she can chew.

Recommended attendant gift: Athletic gear. Whether it's yoga or running, the Horse is known for an active lifestyle.

BORN IN THE YEAR OF THE SHEEP

Gets along best with: Rabbit and Boar.

Finds challenges with: Ox.

She's your best: Listener, who will always have a kind ear for the trials and tribulations of being a bride.

Most likely to: Procrastinate. She'll need constant reminders to send in her dress measurements on time and is a good candidate for showing up fashionably late.

Recommended attendant gift: Lotions and potions. The Sheep enjoys pampering herself with spa goodies.

BORN IN THE YEAR OF THE MONKEY

Gets along best with: Rat and Dragon.

Finds challenges with: Tiger.

She's your best: Brainstormer. Spontaneous and creative, she's a great person to invite when imagining a new project.

Most likely to: Compete with other bridesmaids. She is by nature a go-getter who always has to be number one.

Recommended attendant gift: The newest gadget or the book that everyone's talking about. The Monkey enjoys anything cutting edge.

BORN IN THE YEAR OF THE HEN

Gets along best with: Ox and Snake.

Finds challenges with: Rabbit.

She's your best: Event planner. Amazingly efficient, she'll keep you on track on a day where there is a lot to do.

Most likely to: Say "I told you so." And she absolutely hates admitting when she's wrong.

Recommended attendant gift: Hens loves scene-stealing accessories—bracelets, earrings, and other jewelry, the more unusual the better.

BORN IN THE YEAR OF THE DOG

Gets along best with: Tiger and Horse.

Finds challenges with: Dragon.

She's your best: Mediator. She's an excellent impartial judge who gives fair and balanced advice.

Most likely to: Need the most hand holding. She works best when given clear direction. If you're too vague, she'll feel uncomfortable doing it all on her own.

Recommended attendant gift: A Dog sign likes things to have purpose. Look for something that supports a charity or make a donation to her favorite cause.

BORN IN THE YEAR OF THE BOAR

Gets along best with: Rabbit and Sheep.

Finds challenges with: Snake.

She's your best: Cheerleader. She's the eternal optimist who will always find the silver lining amid wedding chaos.

Most likely to: Overindulge. She just cannot pass up ordering one more cocktail at last call.

Recommended attendant gift: Fine chocolate or a bottle of dessert wine. A Boar is a connoisseur of life's treats.

Attendant Gifts

Being a bridesmaid is a special gift one gives to a bride, and a bride should acknowledge and thank each one well. Finding attendant gifts can be challenging, but making them personal and unique is a great source of inspiration, so we hope the recommendations based on each animal's personality are helpful! Still, when in doubt, jewelry is always a safe bet. We've paired East with West and suggest using birthstones as an individual guide for gifting jewelry to accompany bridesmaid dresses.

Sign	Sun Sign	Gemstone
Rat	Sagittarius	Turquoise
Ox	Capricorn	Garnet
Tiger	Aquarius	Amethyst
Rabbit	Pisces	Aquamarine or Bloodstone
Dragon	Aries	Diamond
Snake	Taurus	Emerald
Horse	Gemini	Pearl or Moonstone
Sheep	Cancer	Ruby
Monkey	Leo	Peridot or Sardonyx
Rooster	Virgo	Sapphire
Dog	Libra	Opal or Tourmaline
Boar	Scorpio	Topaz

Five

Three radicals come together in the Chinese character for wedding—
woman, person, and day, which can be interpreted as the woman's day.
Wedding Calligraphy by Kenneth Lau

Love as rare as twin lotus on a single stalk.
—BEST-LOVED CHINESE PROVERBS

CHINESE WEDDING RITUALS AND CUSTOMS

Marriage is a rite of passage. When you get married, you have ascended into adulthood in a Chinese family's eyes. You are starting a new home and your own branch of the family. A good wedding is meant to give you the best start possible because you will eventually become caregivers to the new as well as the older generation.

With this in mind, there are a number of Chinese traditions associated with this rite of passage. For Chinese brides who have attended traditional weddings, many of these will be familiar. For brides looking for inspiration for a wedding based in any culture, we hope that these ceremonies will inspire you and that you will find new traditions that can be tailored to be meaningful to you and your family.

Engagement Gift Exchange

In Chinese culture, the groom's family assumes the costs of the wedding and many key responsibilities, including picking a wedding date and paying for the honeymoon. The origins of this practice are linked to the groom's family honoring the bride's family's loss of a daughter and showing their appreciation for the bride's family's trust in her becoming a member of the groom's family. Above all, the Chinese believe that a good marriage is smoothed with the support of both families. The long road of married life is always easier with both families in agreement from the beginning.

To represent the promise of both families' commitment to the marriage, a gift exchange takes place. The groom's family starts the gift exchange by sending a traditional gift basket to the bride's family home.

The traditional gift basket can be quite elaborate. This list includes coconuts, palm fruit, dried lychee, longan, walnuts, red beans, green beans, water lily seeds and peanuts (still in their shell), loose tea, candles, wedding calligraphy banners, two pieces of red silk cord, wine, fish, roast chicken, live fish, and *tai bing* cakes. The items are highly symbolic of wedding wishes. The word for "water lily" is *bai he*, where *bai* means "one hundred" and *he* means "together," offering a wish for the couple to be together for a hundred years. Coconuts symbolize the continuity for family because the word for "coconut" in another tone in Mandarin means "son." Palm fruits symbolize fertility, and tea is one of the most traditional wedding gifts of all. Tealeaf trees are difficult to replant. They reproduce and build on each other in the same location for generations. Tea has come to symbolize the promise of a new generation and the closeness of family. All the gifts are given in pairs or good supply and are accompanied with a cash gift in a traditional red envelope—called *hong bao* in Mandarin or *lai cee* in Cantonese.

After the bride's family receives the gift, they acknowledge the gesture by split-ting it in half and sending back half with some additional gifts. The gesture of sharing represents closeness between families. The additional gifts usually placed in the groom's family gift basket are water lily roots, ginger roots, pomegranate, cy-press pine, coconut leaves, and pastries. Also rich with symbolism, the pomegran-ate represents fertility and the water lily roots are especially romantic in nature. If you try to cut a lotus root in half, it's very difficult. The roots are so intertwined that they are practically inseparable. Chinese give these roots to symbolize a mar-riage in which nothing can pull you apart.

> *May your hair grow gray together.*
>
> —BEST-LOVED CHINESE PROVERBS

The Pre-Wedding Night Ritual of *Shang Tou*: The Hair-Combing Ceremony

The night before the wedding, the bride and groom prepare themselves through *shang tou*, or hair combing, a ritual that incorporates prayer and relaxation. *Shang tou* is a blessing that families give to their children the night before the wedding. Performed separately, the ritual is to bless the new couple with a happy marriage, where they grow old together with their children and grandchildren. This ritual helps usher the bride and groom into adulthood, so it only needs to be performed once in a person's life. Therefore, if a person is entering into a second marriage, the *shang tou* ceremony does not need to be performed. As you'll see from the symbolic items involved, the idea of continuation is strong. When preparing the ceremony, first a specific hour is selected. Some couples still observe the tradition of consult-ing a Chinese astrologer to select an hour that works well with both the bride and groom's birth signs; others simply choose a convenient hour to observe this lovely tradition. You can select your own hour by researching which animal hours work well with your and your fiancé's signs with this book. Animal hours are given on p. 16.

In advance, the bride and groom each select an older friend or family member to act as the *hao ming gong* (male) or *hao ming po* (female). This person performs the hair-combing ritual. The bride and groom should each choose a person who has been "lucky" in life: someone who has had a long and happy marriage, is a parent to a son and a daughter, and has the pleasure of grandchildren. The Chinese believe you're very fortunate to have both a son and a daughter, especially when they come as a set of twins, which is referred to as *long feng tai*—a Dragon and a Phoenix. As you and your husband grow older, your children will take care of you. If a couple lives long enough to have three generations in one household, it is considered a great blessing. The Chinese believe that the most fortunate people have five types of blessings bestowed upon them: a long and healthy life, prosperity and wealth, a peaceful mind and body, the opportunity to help those less fortunate and earn the respect of their community, and a harmonious life with children and grandchildren. It's believed that a person who has achieved all these things has a complete and fortunate life. By presiding over the *shang tou* ceremony, the *hao ming gong* or *hao ming po* rubs off good luck onto the new couple. By the same token, brides and grooms invite friends and family who are single and hoping to get married to be a part of the ceremony so that they can share in the presence of good fortune. Unlike your bouquet, you can share your wedding luck with more than one unmarried friend.

Before the ceremony begins, each family says a prayer for a good and happy wedding and lights a candle. Then, with lit incense in hand, the bride and groom bow three times to begin the evening. The incense is placed at an altar of symbolic items, many of which were a part of the gift exchange baskets, such as coconuts, apples, red dates, lily seed, and a pair of Dragon and Phoenix candles. In addition to these items, the bride and groom each has a mirror to symbolize a happy marriage that is bright and long lasting. The groom's items also include a ruler, *zi sun chi*, which represents family posterity and wishes for children, while the bride's should include scissors, which resemble a butterfly in shape, which stand for happiness and a lasting marriage. The Dragon and Phoenix and Double Happiness motifs are often a decorative part of many items purchased. *Tang yuan* (round rice dumplings) in numbers of six or nine in each bowl await the bride, groom, and their families as an evening snack before bedtime. The dumplings' round shape represents wholeness and perfection.

Before the hair combing, the *hao ming gong* or *hao ming po* assists the bride and groom with pouring water over their hair in preparation. The water passes through a collection of coconut leaves and cypress sprigs, to cleanse and relax the mind before the wedding day. The coconut leaves represent family continuity, and cypress represents peace and longevity. After the bath, each puts on new red pajamas to prep for the hair combing and for a good night's rest. Pajamas are commonly sold with the popular Dragon and Phoenix motif on them, which not only are meaningful keepsakes, but also photograph beautifully. The structure of the pajamas should be as simple as possible—a sheath for the bride and simple shirt and pants for the groom. As mentioned earlier, the garment is also a symbol of marriage, so the fewer the seams the more whole the marriage will be.

When all the preparation is done, it is time for the hair-combing ceremony. (Traditionally, the groom completes the ceremony before the bride, approximately a half hour to one hour before.) The sponsor for the bride or groom will comb her or his hair, passing through the entire length of the hair four times. We've written the poem below, which encapsulates the traditional Chinese blessing and can be used as an accompaniment to the ritual.

Shang Tou Blessing

I comb your hair to wish you a marriage that is as happy as it is long
May your hair grow gray with your love and
bring the blessings of children and grandchildren into your home.
I wish you a life of prosperity
where your love and success will be so abundant
that there will always be plenty to share.

After the bride's hair is combed, she ties a sprig of cypress on the left side of her hair with red silk cord to bring about peaceful sleep. It is also believed to repel evil and discourage jealousy. The groom's cypress is also tied with red cord and is placed in his pocket.

In ancient times, a woman would wear a cord made of red silk in her hair. It functioned like an engagement ring, letting others know that she had found her husband. In modern times, this is no longer observed, and many Chinese women have adopted wearing the traditional Western engagement ring. The symbolism of tying red cord still exists in the *shang tou* ritual as well as in a less-commonly practiced hair-tying promise act between the bride and groom. Occurring after the engagement, brides and grooms each cut a lock of their hair and tie it with red cord. The couple keeps this as a symbol representing how they will remain one until their hair turns gray.

The Dragon and Phoenix are symbolic of weddings.
The Dragon symbolizes the groom, and the Phoenix symbolizes the bride.
Drawing by Michele Fujimoto

The Day of the Ceremony

The morning of the wedding day, the bride's family meets the bride and prepares for the groom's arrival. The most traditional brides and grooms wear their traditional Chinese wedding garments, saving white dresses and tuxedos for the wedding ceremony. A bride's area is decorated as a public space, where many of the day's activities will take place. Whether this is her hotel room or home, it is understood that this area will be well trafficked throughout the wedding day. The first activity is where the groom earns entrance into the bride's quarters. His groomsmen accompany him for support, but the groom's family does not participate. The bride's family and friends place a red ribbon barrier at the entrance of her room. In order for the ribbon to be cut for the bride's fiancé to enter, he has to win the privilege through an interview. Almost the equivalent of "speak now or forever hold your peace," this time can be as easy or as brutal as the bride's family and friends want to make it. How will he provide for her? Will he be faithful? How can he prove his love and devotion? Almost any question is fair game, but people are often on good behavior because the bride is present to hear all the answers. One traditional way to grease the wheels is for the groom to come bearing red envelopes for your friends and family. It's seen as a gesture of commitment.

Tea Ceremony and Gift Exchange

Next, the bride and groom serve tea to their elders. The most traditional families have a tea ceremony for the bride and groom's families separately at each family's respective homes or hotel rooms during the wedding. The bride's family tea ceremony occurs first. Modern weddings often integrate the tea ceremony into the wedding day, after larger wedding ceremony, as a way of sharing Chinese culture more publicly and bringing the two families together. Bridesmaids assist in preparing the tea ceremony and are on hand during the event to help the bride and groom.

Whether public or private, the ceremony begins with the bride and groom bowing three times. According to tradition, the woman stands to the left of the man. The first bow honors heaven and earth, the second bow is done in respect for parents, and the third bow is for the couple to honor each other. Recipients of the tea sit in chairs, while the new couple kneels and presents tea to their elders from oldest to youngest. It's expected that each person honored will say a short speech and give a red envelope to the couple. (Here's where having lots of red envelopes comes in handy.) Both families will give gifts to their new daughter-in-law or son-in-law. Traditional gifts for the bride are gold or jade jewelry. Gift ideas for the groom include a new suit, belt, cuff links, watch, or wallet. If a wallet is given, the gift giver should put a coin or dollar bill inside. It's seen as unlucky to give a gift that is empty. Also, don't forget to thank your bridesmaids for their help in the tea ceremony. It is customary to give tea ceremony helpers each a red envelope that contains new money or jewelry in appreciation.

Fortune by Kenneth Lau

Wedding Ceremony and Wedding Banquet

In ancient China, the veiled bride was ceremoniously brought to her husband's home on a red marriage chair, carried by four men, one at each corner. Musicians and lanterns, decorated with the bride and groom's family names, drew attention to the bride's processional to the happy groom. On her arrival, the bride would be carried by the groom into the house under a red parasol—the color red serving as both protection and celebration. Inside the home, the wedding ceremony took place. The couple sealed their union by drinking wine and honey from two cups joined by a red silk string. It is said that the God of Marriage matchmakes humans in heaven and records couples' names in a book. He then connects their feet with an invisible red silk thread, so they find each other. This is why wedding cups were symbolically tied together with red string. After the drinking of the wine, the new couple went to the family ancestral altar and bowed three times to honor the family past and present. This ceremony is no longer commonly practiced, since most couples now opt for religious or non-denominational ceremonies. While the sharing of wine is uncommonly practiced, families still have ancestral altars in their homes and still honor them when getting married.

The wedding banquet is a time-honored tradition of a wedding celebration. Traditionally, it is composed of eight dishes to symbolize prosperity. There is some variation in the selection of dishes, but some common dishes are roast pig, duck, fish, lobster, and chicken. Lobster represents the Dragon and chicken represents the Phoenix. A sweet dessert ends the meal as a final wish for a blessed life to the new couple. Traditional wedding cakes are served in addition to other Chinese desserts such as dumplings, sweet sticky buns, and red or lotus seed soup. No celebration would be complete without libations. Many Chinese favor whiskey and cognac for after-dinner drinks, in addition to the popular toasting champagne. When raising a glass, the Chinese say *gan bei*, which literally means "empty your glass."

The Wedding Bed

The wedding bed is a very symbolic element of the marriage. For the wedding night, friends and family have young girls and boys jump on the bed to wish the new couple the happiness of many children. Afterward, friends or family sprinkle lotus seeds, red dates, cypress sprigs, and lily bulbs on the bed. These represent long life, happiness, and fertility in marriage.

After the Wedding

As in Western traditions, the groom traditionally carries the bride over their new home's threshold. The origins of this tie back to maintaining spiritual order and energy in your new home. The Chinese believe there is a House God that rules the new home. A new member to the household has to ease her way into the home environment. By stepping on the threshold, the new bride would anger the House God, so to keep the peace, the groom carries the bride over the threshold.

The first three days following the wedding, the bride is expected to relax and decompress after all the stress. The new bride should abstain from cooking, cleaning, or writing thank-you notes. Three days after the wedding or after returning from the honeymoon, the new couple traditionally visits the bride's family. The new Mr. and Mrs. should bring gifts to her family. Fruit baskets, liquor, and sweets are all appropriate gifts.

An Chuang, Seating a Peaceful Bed

Traditionally, Chinese couples consult an astrologer for a harmonious time to set up their new bed in a home. Called seating the bed, this is a very important event in a new couple's life. The gift of new sheets and bedcoverings is an important gift for a new marriage, so be sure to register for some and have them accessible for setting your bed as newlyweds. Like wearing new clothes at your *shang tou*, new bedcoverings are only fitting for a new marriage to start off clean and with a good foundation. The Chinese believe that seating the bed well can help a couple have fewer arguments and have an easier time having children. Couples choose a date that works well with their birth signs to seat the bed to have a prosperous beginning to their new married life. You can consult the suggested wedding dates in the back of this book as options to consider for seating your wedding bed.

During this time, a couple's new home entrance is decorated to invite good luck. The Double Happiness symbol is placed above the front door, and red banners with happy wishes for the new couple are hung alongside. Outside the front door, three symbolic items are placed to bring good luck to a couple's new house: a mirror to ward off evil, a ruler to represent abundance and plenty in a couple's life, and scissors to symbolize that a couple will always be together. These items are also symbols used in the *shang tou* hair-combing ceremony.

PART II

The Chinese Zodiac

The Chinese zodiac is composed of twelve animals, each with its own year of the twelve-year lunar cycle. You might wonder why these animals in particular were selected. The legend goes that the Lord Buddha summoned all his animals to visit him before he left Earth. Only twelve gathered to give him a proper farewell. To show them how much their efforts meant to him, Lord Buddha named a year of the zodiac after them, in the order in which they arrived. First came Rat, then Ox, Tiger, Rabbit, Dragon, Snake, Horse, Sheep, Monkey, Rooster, Dog, and last but not least, Boar. Each animal has certain characteristics, skills, strengths, and weaknesses, and each sign relates to the other eleven differently. In the charts below, keep an eye out for triangle symbols, which denote trios of animals that get along particularly well, and ×'s, which indicate animal opposites, who will struggle to find common ground.

However, your sign is affected by more than just the year of your birth. Other factors include the reigning element of your birth year—Water, Wood, Fire, Metal, or Earth—and the animal ruling your birth hour which we refer to as your ascendant. We also believe in pairing lunar (Eastern) and solar (Western) signs in a marriage of Eastern and Western astrology, first published in the *Handbook of Chinese Horoscopes* in 1979.

In the charts that follow, you'll be able to look up your animal sign, the animal ruling your birth hour or ascendant, and the Western zodiac sign that relates to your animal. You can also look up the signs for your future spouse, wedding party, family, and friends—and especially anyone else involved in planning the wedding. The worksheets in the back of the book will be helpful for keeping track of the many signs and elements that will be interacting in your wedding— fill them out using the charts at the end of this book so that they are an easy reference as you plan your wedding.

Six

BORN IN THE YEAR OF THE RAT

Here Comes the Initiator Bride

Lunar Years of the Rat	Elements
January 24, 1936, to February 10, 1937	Fire
February 10, 1948, to January 28, 1949	Earth
January 28, 1960, to February 14, 1961	Metal
February 16, 1972, to February 2, 1973	Water
February 2, 1984, to February 19, 1985	Wood
February 19, 1996, to February 6, 1997	Fire

Initiator Bride Details

Birth Hours (Ascendant): 11 P.M. to 1 A.M.

Western Sign: Sagittarius

Western Gemstone: Turquoise

Symbolic Color: Blue

Flower: Chrysanthemum

Season: Winter

Element: Water

Famous Initiator Brides:

Lauren Bacall, Doris Day, Queen Elizabeth, Scarlett Johansson, Julianne Moore, Mary Tyler Moore, Gwyneth Paltrow, Gloria Vanderbilt.

The Dress:

As a sentimental soul, you'll take pleasure in wearing a dress that has special meaning to you. Perhaps you'll wear your mother's dress or your grandmother's veil. You're also a fan of being creative to stretch your budget and be original. You may rent a showstopping gown, for all the drama at a fraction of the cost. Vintage is also one of your secret tricks to a unique dress choice.

The Rat Sign: The First Bride of the Chinese Zodiac

As the first sign of the Chinese zodiac, the Rat is a natural self-starter. You are a part of what we refer to as the Doers group. There are four groups: the Doers, the Thinkers, the Protectors, and the Catalysts. The groups are made up of the three animals that have a natural affinity to one another, referred to as a Triangle of Affinity. Each set of three animals has a social connection—a kind of chemistry that is connected to each zodiac sign.

The Doers group is made up of the Rat, the Monkey, and the Dragon. No surprise, people with these birth signs or ascendants are your most natural friends and working partners. In fact, it's likely your fiancé has strong ties to this group as well. As their team name suggests, these ladies don't like to stand still—they are the ones who make things happen. Those born in the year of the Rat have the mantra "I do." She is the bride voted most likely to be a wedding planner, not need a wedding planner. Here comes the Initiator Bride.

The Initiator Bride—Born in the Year of the Rat

As brides go, those born in the year of the Rat are part of a select group who are well-suited to the planning and partying ahead. You're a natural planner who enjoys bringing people together and chasing down a deal. No surprise, your wedding is a welcome challenge for you. And not only will it be beautiful, but you'll be asked about your creative additions and amazing finds. You like to be original. Post-wedding, you'll be flattered that friends and guests have copied some of your best ideas.

With your vast network and knack for communication, you'll keep everyone in the loop. While others lament the pressures of wedding planning, you'll excel at nailing down the details. People will wonder how you found the time to put up a Web site so fast or make calls to friends and family far and wide in such a short amount of time. But, as they say, it's only work if you feel like it is. The Initiator Bride doesn't consider any of this work. You take pleasure in staying busy. The joy you bring to your wedding and your ability to keep everyone connected is a delight to many. And, in many ways, each conversation you have is an investment. Each e-mail or phone call is like planting a seed. All this goodwill will bloom with love and support around you, through good times and bad. Close friends and family all feel like they are an important part of your wedding because you've made them feel like they each played a small part along the way. Your ability to bond so easily with people is rare and makes you an especially gracious bride.

So, charm and organization you have in spades. You're also a gifted hostess. But how does your passion for getting things done extend to the other parts of your wedding journey? After all, it is a long road. Well, the truth of the matter is that your management and leadership skills may be a mixed blessing for your wedding planning. Your clear vision of your wedding is a great strength, but you will need to balance your sometimes demanding standards against your relationships with those who are involved. Be thoughtful and kind to all your bridesmaids and wedding party. You can be calculating at times, even selfish, and while you are due a certain amount of indulgence, those you love may grow impatient if pushed. One of your biggest challenges will be not doing *everything* yourself. You have to accept that you will be delegating many tasks to your family or bridesmaids because it is impossible not to employ the aid of other people. Remember, it's not a question of whether you are capable of taking care of everything, but whether you need to oversee everything. And if you really are in denial about touching every part of the planning process, reflect on the twelve animals of the Chinese zodiac and note that there is no year of the Octopus.

As the Initiator Bride, your quest is to accomplish things quickly and well. You tend to use a take-no-prisoners approach, and when things go awry, all hell can break loose. While the Rat tries to camouflage her feelings, one can always tell she is upset. You can become edgy and give yourself away. Inefficiency, idleness, waste, and tardiness go against your active and industrious nature and cause you to complain until things are done right. The Rat in you loves to run the show, and everyone and everything had better be on point. Make sure to listen to your practical side and think about what makes the most sense, then split duties among those who are most involved. You can ask for updates and share the choices you have made to give your team a good idea of your style and how you like things. While your friends, family, and even fiancé may not do it the way you would have, you need to give each of them a fair opportunity to finish the job. It helps everyone feel more connected, and when you look back, you will be happy you were able to integrate everyone. Think about your natural hostess personality, which makes everyone feel welcome and lively, and treat your friends and family as such.

Some other words of advice focus on one of your biggest inner conflicts—being thrifty and being generous. As your native sign suggests, you can be a bit of a pack rat, especially when it comes to finding a bargain. You are planning for only one wedding, so buy accordingly. It doesn't matter if it is the steal of the century. You won't have room for all your beautiful new wedding gifts if you stockpile a ridiculous amount of tulle and dove-themed place cards. Also, even though you are skilled at being thrifty, you have a tendency to become generous with those you love most. Therefore, you must be most careful when your emotions are running high. Be open to accepting financial help from family and friends and do not over-extend yourself (and your soon-to-be husband). Don't feel like you need to offer to pick up the hotel bill for every out-of-town family member or overtip your close friend who happens to be the florist. You can use your wedding to work on one of your biggest flaws, which is not being able to admit when you need help.

East Meets West: When Moon Signs Meet Sun Signs

Many people don't realize that each animal of the Chinese zodiac has a solar calendar connection. In our interpretation of Chinese horoscopes, the lunar calendar links into the solar calendar through the month and season, where the Rat's parallel sun sign is Sagittarius. But every Western sun sign has a different effect on the lunar moon sign.

THE SAGITTARIUS RAT

Sagittarius: November 22 to December 21

The Initiator Bride mixed with Sagittarius produces a vivacious and fascinating woman. You're one who takes life by the horns, enjoys its simple pleasures, and regularly takes the road less taken to satisfy your wild streak. Your strong sense of self will make a stylish mark on your wedding. You will be focused and direct with what you want. But be cautious about giving too much criticism too quickly or too often. Others may not have your thick skin for candor. Your creative and original style will be successful, whether it's taking the chance on an up-and-coming caterer that you hired on intuition or that vintage dress that you tailored on a whim. On your wedding day, you will be calm in the midst of the humming activity around you because your confidence always shines through.

THE CAPRICORN RAT

Capricorn: December 22 to January 20

Capricorn plus Rat produces a sensible and intelligent bride. While you tend to be more careful than some of your counterparts, this is a quality that you embrace and regularly use to your advantage. You are adept at managing your budget, consistently taking stock of your vendors, reviewing every quote line by line. Beware anyone who writes you off as one of those brides who will sign anything—nothing gets past you. It also wouldn't be a surprise if you took on an ambitious workout plan with stunning results. Your only Achilles' heel lies in your frugal nature and hoarding ability. Beware buying in bulk or extra items for all those what-if nightmares that go through your head. Two pieces of advice: poll your friends before you buy any additional things, and check your storage area to see if you have any treasures from past buying victories.

THE AQUARIUS RAT

Aquarius: January 21 to February 19

The mix of the flexible Aquarius with the industrious Rat produces a gal who loves variety and the feeling of freedom. Water makes emotions run high and low, and this can make wedding planning difficult at times. You embrace change better than most, which is a great quality, but often you can become distracted and less focused than the more traditional Initiator Brides. Don't indulge every whim or you will quickly blow through your budget. The good news is that your sweet personality can win over the most difficult of people, whether it is an overprotective mother-in-law or a high-maintenance bridesmaid. Use your skills of persuasion to get what you want.

THE PISCES RAT

Pisces: February 20 to March 20

The water of Pisces has a calming effect on the workaholic Rat. True to your lunar sign, you are extremely family-focused and look to your family for their opinion and approval. Since you are slow to trust, it may be difficult at first to come out of yourself and tell those outside your inner circle—like salespeople and vendors—your feelings, but this will only come with practice and support. If this is difficult for you, don't be afraid to bring backups such as your fiancé, mom, or best friend to your appointments. Buyer's remorse is a terrible thing, and your peaceful nature may sometimes encourage you to compromise too quickly.

THE ARIES RAT
Aries: March 21 to April 19

The Aries Rat is a woman in charge. Perhaps you are in a leadership role at work or just have always been the social queen bee. Aries brings out a showy, almost theatrical side in the Initiator Bride. Will it be a dazzling set of dress changes or an impressive routine on the dance floor? Maybe you will be head-to-toe in shiny jewels on your wedding day or you'll grab the mic and keep your guests entertained with captivating stories and heartfelt thank-yous. Either way, you will be the center of attention. While you may have to hold yourself back on other days of the year to be a team player, your wedding day gives you the right to show off your star power.

THE TAURUS RAT
Taurus: April 20 to May 20

The Taurus Initiator Bride is a traditional Rat at heart, with a little bit of flair. Both signs love security, not just in terms of financial security, but emotions as well. For you to feel at ease, your plans always have to be in order, and you are a stickler for being on time, even early. You are definitely a bride who will not procrastinate. In fact, the role of bride will bring out your studious side. Not long after you accepted your fiancé's proposal (or perhaps before), your nose is already buried in a bridal magazine or you are signing on to a wedding Web site for ideas. Wedding planning will put your work ethic into overdrive, and your loved ones will not be disappointed with your efforts. You'll be "on" in every sense of the word—on trend, on budget, and on time. Enough said.

THE GEMINI RAT
Gemini: May 21 to June 21

The twins bring exploration and energy to the naturally industrious Initiator Bride. While the Rat makes you a careful planner, the Gemini sisters are there to tempt you into changing your mind. This should make you cautious from the onset of your wedding plans. Your energy and creativity can actually create so many wonderful options that you are left overwhelmed or with a disjointed theme. Stay true to your original plans when tempted with something new and trendy. Bounce ideas off your fiancé or friends. Also, consider the time and trouble involved with changing direction. You have always been a thoughtful friend and daughter, so make sure to remind yourself of how changes can ripple into big waves.

THE CANCERIAN RAT

Cancer: June 22 to July 21

Cancer makes the already sensible Rat more cautious. This Initiator Bride does not give trust easily. You probably have a close-knit group of friends. Your inner circle is composed of family and childhood classmates. It probably took some time for you to really let go with your husband-to-be. Needless to say, you don't give up the reins very easily. Since you can be emotional, the best way to combat any of the unnecessary drama that comes with giving up control is to go with what is familiar or recommended by a trusted source. Don't feel the pressure to break the mold on your wedding. There's no harm in replicating something you saw in a magazine or even getting inspiration from a close friend's recent wedding. Most people will see it as a compliment, and you find solace in choosing something that has been road-tested rather than a bridal experiment.

THE LEO RAT

Leo: July 22 to August 21

The Leo Initiator Bride is a girl after anyone's heart. The cunning Lion and level-headed Rat combination creates a fun sense of humor with a strong sense of leadership. The Leo Rat also enjoys the thrill of the hunt. You love getting a good deal and will do the legwork necessary to make it happen. Also, your sense of humor will break the tension during stressful moments and quickly bond you with your new in-laws. On your wedding day, your magnetic personality will truly be electric. There is a regal quality that comes with Leo, which will make your wedding finery seem like a natural second skin. You will walk with the grace and integrity you've grown into as a lady.

THE VIRGO RAT

Virgo: August 22 to September 22

This Initiator Bride is like a double shot of espresso—double the energy with double the punch. Virgo and Rat both have an incredible amount of drive to make things perfect. You will have to be conscious of the fact that those around you may not have the same motivation for results. By the same token, try to hold back your desire to give constructive criticism too often. Either give specific direction or give a task to someone who knows your tastes exactly. Since you will have energy to spare, you may want to channel your efforts into a fitness program, so that you can look your best on your big day. The added activity will help relieve stress and give you a natural glow of health.

THE LIBRA RAT

Libra: September 23 to October 22

The scales of Libra mixed with the intelligent Rat produces the perfect mix of beauty and brains. The Rat's natural sense for finances still holds firm, but gets a style shot with Libra's good taste. This Initiator Bride will get the bargains through hard work and charm. Work your Rolodex and don't be shy about discounts and tips on where to get the truly unique items. Your social skills really pay off for getting your wedding details in order. The Rat and Libra both treasure harmony, and all your relationships are built on fairness and sensitivity. As a result, there will be no shortage of helping hands in your efforts. Your past good deeds will return good wedding karma when you need it most.

THE SCORPIO RAT

Scorpio: October 23 to November 21

The Initiator Bride's core is built on the hardworking nature of the Rat. Scorpio puts the Rat race into overdrive with the added love of competition. The result is an intense and driven bride who has tremendous willpower. You will definitely not struggle with setting goals and meeting or surpassing them. Whether it's losing those last ten pounds or doing the hand calligraphy for each of your invitations, you will take on challenging tasks with great ease. One of your true talents is the art of communication. You can harness this artistic gift into all sorts of beautiful expressions for your day. Perhaps you can write a poem for your wedding program or compose heartfelt dedications in journals to your bridesmaids. Everyone will appreciate a keepsake with your special touch.

Wedding Synergy: When Dragon Meets Phoenix

As you embark on your planning, check out the Wedding Relationship pairings below to see how your strengths and weaknesses come together during the planning process. These compatibility descriptions are based on year of birth combinations, which is the tip of the iceberg when it comes to each of your charts. As described in Chapter 2 "Reference Dates and Tables on the Chinese Zodiac, East-West Sign Combinations, and Animal Hours," a different animal governs each component of your birth date and time.

RAT HUSBAND AND RAT WIFE

The two of you should beware of your tendency to be too codependent. As a couple, you naturally fall into a routine very quickly and like to indulge each other's whims. He will be more flexible than you are. Keep in mind that he might have some secret wishes for the wedding, whether he is quick to share them or not. Guard your wedding dictator tendencies and find out what will make this his day as much as yours. Sharing the Rat sign focuses you both on the budget. If you two aren't on the same page about which details are important to the wedding, you could end up in frequent arguments.

OX HUSBAND AND RAT WIFE

Yours is a very satisfying and rewarding partnership. He is the strong and silent type, and you're the social butterfly. He loves being fussed over and admired by you, and you take comfort in his calm and stable nature. The challenge of wedding planning is that it acts like a third person in the relationship. Do not get lost in your planning so much that you forget to show him the attention he loves and has become so used to. His support for you comes naturally, so be sure to reach out to him for help or advice. Check out different wedding sites or go cake tasting together. Leaving him out of the wedding plan would just feel unnatural. It may surprise you, but you two could end up having a lot of fun in the process.

TIGER HUSBAND AND RAT WIFE

While the Tiger and Rat do not make the most common of pairings, your personality differences can create an interesting balance that keeps your relationship exciting. However, bear in mind that your differences will only be amplified by wedding planning. He may seem a little checked out of the wedding process. It's not his nature to embrace the details the way you do. You may end up feeling taken for granted and feel sore about your efforts not being noticed. Use your communication skills to get at what's important to him and his family for the big day. He may not be forthcoming with his wishes for the wedding, so get creative by talking to his friends, his siblings, or your future mother-in-law to sniff out the details of what will make the day memorable for both of your families.

RABBIT HUSBAND AND RAT WIFE

You two will be a team in the wedding process, much to the envy of other brides-to-be. He is forever admiring your innovative mind and energy. As a Rabbit, he may be on the calmer side, but these qualities are what make him a sweet and harmonious match. You will love sharing special finds for the wedding, and he'll be a good partner in investigating wedding sites and poring over details. He will carry through with all your wishes, so don't be afraid to delegate responsibilities. With your knack for organization and his dedication, he can really put those groomsmen to work. But be careful not to take advantage of him because (as you certainly know) he has trouble saying no to you.

DRAGON HUSBAND AND RAT WIFE

The best way to maneuver through the wedding planning process is by looking ahead and budgeting from the very beginning. Since this is the Rat's strong suit, know that you will be leading the process. It's a blessing and a curse, but it's your role in this relationship. Your couplehood is harmonious because of the balance you strike, having matched his yang with your yin. He's a spender. You're a saver. If you don't reel him in, no one can. You know him better than anyone else, so go with your instincts when it comes to delegation. If you don't, the Rat in you may be pinching pennies on centerpieces, while he's out there stocking a top-shelf open bar. Added up, that doesn't make a whole lot of sense.

SNAKE HUSBAND AND RAT WIFE

As the natural power couple, you two are not afraid of hard work and love to work alongside each other. Be sure to be up front about your wedding plans and come to an agreement early on about what you both want. Since you are two natural leaders, you both like to get a lot done at lightning speed. This can be dangerous if you both pick the same tasks. As a result, without good and constant communication, you two may have petty arguments and unnecessary drama. If you plan and communicate well, you can really take a lot off your shoulders with his flair for getting it done.

HORSE HUSBAND AND RAT WIFE

You two are an opposites-attract couple. He likes to blaze new trails, while you like the comforts of home. It works for you two, but, as the Chinese say, "Happiness is found with compromise." Wedding planning harmony comes from constant communication. That's not to say that pinning him down will be easy. A horse doesn't stand still. You'll have to keep his projects interesting to hold his attention. Perhaps you will find common ground in a destination wedding or a honeymoon that is off the beaten path. This is the type of new adventure he can sink his teeth into.

SHEEP HUSBAND AND RAT WIFE

You were drawn to his warm and generous nature. He was taken by your charm and interesting stories. No doubt you both love a good party. The challenge you will encounter in wedding planning stems from two different working styles. The Sheep has a short attention span and is blessed with a no-stress take on life—something that can drive the Rat type crazy. You not only deal with stress well, but somewhat thrive on it. Know that the Sheep has a tendency to procrastinate and overspend. You'll have to chart out areas where he can spend and play. Meanwhile, keep the really tempting projects for yourself, but get his input. There might be some nail-biting moments while he is finishing his projects, but the Sheep always pulls through. Luck seems to always be on his side.

MONKEY HUSBAND AND RAT WIFE

It's always nice to meet a couple who enjoy working together. You are very competent in executing any plan, while he is the great strategist. You charmed the Monkey in him to put down roots, and he adores your creativity and resourcefulness. This mutual respect encourages you to value each other's opinion. The wedding will be the ultimate project to tag-team because you each bring personal ways to make the day your own. Neither the Rat nor the Monkey is afraid of hard work, which makes the path so much smoother. The Monkey has a way of enjoying the back-and-forth of bargaining, so encourage your fiancé to take on the role of negotiator. He will see it as a game and push to get the deal.

ROOSTER HUSBAND AND RAT WIFE

He is analytical and a perfectionist; you are a practical go-getter. You two may be prone to public displays of affection or argument, so no one is disputing that passions run deep. This is a time where you may be emotionally vulnerable and need constant support, and since he can be insensitive and picky sometimes, you have to be thicker-skinned than usual if he puts down any of your ideas. It's his Rooster way to dig deep into the details, but there's an easy way to create a diversion. In your planning, identify the aspects he will be most passionate about and ask him to take the leadership role on these. Once his domain has been established, he can dig into his own planning, and you can get your things done without interruption or argument.

DOG HUSBAND AND RAT WIFE

You're a sociable and affectionate couple that everyone likes being around—whether together or separately. The wedding planning for you two will be smoother than for most. Yours is a relationship built on mutual respect and value placed on your own personal freedoms. Since the Dog husband is a reasonable and even-keeled partner, he will provide great support to you during the most stressful parts of the process. If you have drama with your bridesmaids or you don't get that amazing photographer you've had your heart set on, feel free to vent to him. He'll always take your side and provide a patient ear.

BOAR HUSBAND AND RAT WIFE

You have love and a shared passion for life. You are the sociable couple that single people still like hanging out with. Together you share hobbies and passions that have widened your circle of friends. When it comes to wedding planning, trust in your good judgment for big decisions and planning and take the project leader reins from the onset. Give him his homework, and he will follow through. The bigger challenge will be winnowing down the invite list. You know too many people, and your fiancé believes in "the more, the merrier." Perhaps a good alternative to having everyone at the ceremony is a low-key engagement party or housewarming that has a more reasonable price per head, to which you can invite everyone on both of your lists.

The Rat's Relationships with Friends and Family

Family and friends are an important part of most weddings. Since we all operate differently in our nonromantic relationships, the pairings of your Chinese zodiac sign will take a slightly different form. Knowing the compatibility of your animal sign with your family and friends is a real asset when planning and setting expectations for responsibilities. As you think about how best to integrate your vast network of friends, review the relationship overviews below. They will help cast light on your friends' and family members' strengths, weaknesses, and working styles.

Δ WITH ANOTHER RAT

Rat signs work well together and form quick friendships. This friend can easily become a person for gossiping, bouncing ideas around, and treasure hunting. Because you two share so many similarities, a bit of friendly competition comes up every once in a while. For your wedding planning, your Rat friend will be one of your planning confidantes. However, be sensitive to her luck in love. If she is single, envy may creep in on occasion, so don't rub your good fortune in too much. Your friend will work hard to make your event a success. Be sure to give her appropriate recognition at the reception, so she gets her moment in the sun.

WITH AN OX

Loyal and patient, your Ox friend is the ultimate listener. She will be there to support you through all the twists and turns of your wedding planning. While she may not be as fast as you are at getting tasks done, the Ox will make sure the job is done right. Be patient and trust in her work ethic. Depending on the Ox's ascendant, this friend may not have the natural gift for public speaking. She typically takes on work that is done behind the scenes. However, if she is up to the task of toasts and speeches, the Ox will plan, practice, and pull it off.

WITH A TIGER

The Tiger makes a fun and exciting friend. You two are thick as thieves, whether partying into the night or catching up over a quiet glass of wine. Since she may be a bit of a wild child, know that you may need to play project manager for any of the tasks assigned to her. If she is a maid of honor or bridesmaid, your friends may have to reel her in during the festivities. Whether it's the bachelorette party or the rehearsal dinner, she has to be careful not to overindulge. Be sure to give recognition for her hard work personally and publicly. You may be prone to small arguments, but it's amazing how far a thank-you goes with this friend.

WITH A RABBIT

The Rabbit and the Rat are not the most natural of friends. You had to work a little bit harder to appreciate each other's strengths. The Rat enjoys being in large groups and working in teams. The Rabbit may prefer to think about projects alone before sharing ideas with the rest of the group. The Rat in you produces high expectations, and you may be uncomfortable with your friend's desire to maintain a little bit of secrecy about your wedding. However, strange as it may be to let go of the reins, you need to respect the Rabbit's almost artistic process. Give this friend or family member some space and independence when helping you, and you could be pleasantly surprised. The more you try to control, the worse things could be.

Δ WITH A DRAGON

Because you two belong to the same Triangle of Affinity, you are well-suited to partner together in any project. A Dragon has incredible energy and charisma. Like you, she is great with a crowd and makes friends easily. Your Dragon friend or family member will be a great source for ideas, building on your creativity to make things even better. Through the years, this friend has been there time and time again. She is confident and inspires the same in you. The only watch-out for this team is the Dragon's boredom with the details. She can deliver results, but doesn't have your appreciation for reading the fine print.

WITH A SNAKE

While you and your Snake friend may seem very different at first glance, there are quite a number of similarities. Bright and resourceful, you are both clever and take on ambitious plans. However, the Rat and the Snake have very different work styles. You like to talk out loud and get other people's opinions about your ideas. The Snake thinks before she speaks, choosing to announce plans when everything has been tested and retested. Don't worry, though; the Rat and Snake end up with the same high-quality results. This is yet another opportunity for you to let others do the work with less of your input. The Snake's methods are mysterious, but focused.

× WITH A HORSE

You are fascinated by the Horse's exciting take on life—independent and full of spontaneity. Depending on the nature of this relationship, these are the very qualities that can drive the Rat up the wall when it comes to wedding planning. The Horse is an impulsive animal who is not a big fan of bureaucracy. People of the Horse sign like to jump in and see what happens, while you favor following the rules to the letter. You two have strong personalities and love to lead. Fortunately, in this situation, the bride's word goes. The Horse may not like following you, but she will cooperate. Remember to be gracious, as the Horse finds it difficult to take a backseat.

WITH A SHEEP

This friend or family member is charming and fun, but terrible with a budget. Even though they have a way of always landing on their feet, it's not a good idea to let this person do the spending for you. The Sheep will have the best of intentions, wanting to be generous and thoughtful. This desire may be at odds with your practical and thrifty side, so it is best to avoid these situations, rather than argue. Sheep can wear their hearts on their sleeves. Put on the kid gloves when giving criticism because when you are stressed, you start to get short with people. Compliments go a long way and can inspire some great help from the Sheep.

Δ WITH A MONKEY

As natural partners in the Triangle of Affinity, the Rat and the Monkey make up one of the best dream teams. You are both positive people who are not afraid of rolling up your sleeves and getting your hands dirty. She will be a great source of ideas. Also, the Monkey has a knack for the quick problem solving that every bride needs. The Monkey takes criticism well, so you don't have to worry about sugar-coating problems. One of the wonderful qualities of this relationship is the sense of humor you both share. You two complement each other well, and she will help keep up your spirits when times get tough.

WITH A ROOSTER

When seeing eye to eye, you two appreciate the qualities that you share—an appreciation for the details and a natural cleverness. When you disagree, it is because your love of debate and competition has gotten the best of you. The Rooster personality is a mixed blessing to a Rat bride. The Rooster loves to play the critic. Having another thorough eye is valuable, but your feelings can get hurt by too much criticism. Know that this is the way the Rooster thinks she can best help. With this insight, be careful when you open the door to be evaluated. If the Rooster is a family member, such as a parent or future mother-in-law, the best advice is to hold your tongue and let her say her piece. Oftentimes the Rooster just wants to be able to air her opinions without interruption.

WITH A DOG

A wedding is a great project for the Rat and the Dog to work on together. She will respect your position as bride and will want you to have things your way. The Dog is very rational and does her best to make things fair. She'll look through the lens of "What would I want if I was getting married?" You can entrust her with your wishes, and they will be carried out perfectly. This friend or family member is very dependable and has a warm personality. Also, the Dog's straight-arrow approach to work means results with limited drama. As long as directions are clear, the Dog will deliver to your wishes.

WITH A BOAR

This is a relationship that is built on a lot of common ground. Like you, the Boar is a charmer and can connect with most everyone. However, the Boar likes to live the good life, while the Rat likes to save for a rainy day. In short, don't leave any of your financial matters to Boar types because their generosity overpowers their better judgment. No doubt, without proper communication of responsibilities, small arguments can take place. This person is a great facilitator of large groups and should be given tasks that can take advantage of this talent. Perhaps she can spearhead the ultimate bachelorette party or bridal shower.

Seven

BORN IN THE YEAR OF THE OX
Here Comes the Enforcer Bride

Lunar Years of the Ox	Elements
February 11, 1937, to January 20, 1938	Fire
January 29, 1949, to February 16, 1950	Earth
February 15, 1961, to February 4, 1962	Metal
February 3, 1973, to January 22, 1974	Water
February 20, 1985, to February 8, 1986	Wood
February 7, 1997, to January 27, 1998	Fire

Enforcer Bride Details

Birth Hours: 1 A.M. to 3 A.M.

Western Sign: Capricorn

Western Gemstone: Garnet

Symbolic Color: Blue

Flower: Orchid

Season: Winter

Element: Water

Famous Enforcer Brides:
Joan Chen, Gloria Gaynor, Paloma Picasso,
Vanessa Redgrave, Meryl Streep, Margaret Thatcher,
Sigourney Weaver.

The Dress:

Simplicity and tradition draw you to elegant dresses that make strong foundations for great accessories or your grandmother's string of pearls. You especially like pieces of high quality and lasting style, so that you can pass on the investment to future generations.

The Ox Sign: The Second Bride of the Chinese Zodiac

The Ox is the second sign of the Chinese zodiac. She represents strength and integrity. She is also the first member of the Triangle of Affinity we refer to as the Thinkers group. There are four groups: the Doers, the Thinkers, the Protectors, and the Catalysts. The groups are made up of the three animals that have a natural affinity to one another, referred to as a Triangle of Affinity. Each set of three animals has a social connection—a kind of chemistry that is connected to each zodiac sign.

The Thinkers group is made up of the Ox, the Snake, and the Rooster. No surprise, people with these birth signs or ascendants are your most natural friends and working partners. In fact, it's likely your fiancé has strong ties to this group as well. As their team name suggests, these ladies are never ones to procrastinate. They are deep thinkers and planners who enjoy mapping out tasks, putting them on the calendar, and crossing off each one. One of their great strengths is that they do things from start to finish. They not only create a vision, but also put it in place. Those born in the year of the Ox have the mantra "I will." She is the bride voted most likely to come in on budget. Here comes the Enforcer Bride.

The Enforcer Bride—Born in the Year of the Ox

As a bride born in the year of the Ox, you've got some serious tools in your belt for the task at hand. You have the patience for the long road that is wedding planning, and you perform very well under pressure. Drawn to family tradition and classic styles, you will do your research, identify your preferences, and set the direction of your wedding very quickly. You are very unlikely to change your mind, and in fact, you might not even need to do a lot of research because you already have a gut feeling for what you want. Some may try to tempt you with switching up plans you've already set—perhaps something a friend has seen at a recent wedding or on TV. "You should experience the whole wedding thing, look around, visit lots of places," they'll say. True to your Thinkers foundation, you will stay the course with your original plan and politely decline. Your wedding will come together exactly the way you pictured it. Of course it will. It isn't every bride who can come up with a plan and patiently execute every last detail.

You're a bright woman, with a close inner circle of friends. Most likely a mixture of family and longtime friends, you've assembled a group of people that you trust and can depend on through thick and thin. Since you are a very fair-minded person and as dependable as the North Star, you naturally demand the same respect from others. You have little patience for drama and try to keep it at a minimum in your own life. You stayed clear of that kind of thing in high school and will try to

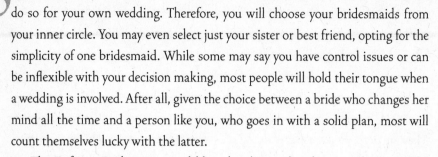

do so for your own wedding. Therefore, you will choose your bridesmaids from your inner circle. You may even select just your sister or best friend, opting for the simplicity of one bridesmaid. While some may say you have control issues or can be inflexible with your decision making, most people will hold their tongue when a wedding is involved. After all, given the choice between a bride who changes her mind all the time and a person like you, who goes in with a solid plan, most will count themselves lucky with the latter.

The Enforcer Bride may sound like a harsh moniker, but it makes sense for a strong-willed lady like you. Intelligent and very logical about how you make decisions, you will do everything in your power to make sure a task gets done. The tale of the tortoise and the hare comes to mind when thinking about the Ox. Your philosophy is: "If I put the time and work into something, I will complete the task." The hardest thing for you in coordinating your wedding will be sharing responsibility with others. Your inclination is to do things on your own and not ask for help, let alone accept it. Remember that because a wedding is the merging of two families—a mixture of family, friends, and obligations—it is more like a team sport than an individual race. Including members of your new family is equivalent to being gracious. Keeping in mind what is polite and proper may be helpful if you need to release some control and let some people in.

Depending on the sign of your future spouse, you may have to make more concessions than others. If your fiancé is born in the year of the Thinkers group or has a similar ascendant, you may both agree to have a simple wedding, with no fuss. However, if it's going to be a larger affair, you will embrace the planning and details, but as mentioned above, that will naturally be a challenge in accommodating more people and more outside opinions. Most importantly, as more people become involved and offer their assistance, you will need to learn to share the workload and communicate your wishes. With larger weddings, you cannot do everything yourself. You don't like to owe anybody anything, but as you may have guessed, weddings are exceptions to many rules. When friends or family offer their help, be open-minded. Whether it's time, money, or a special hookup to a wedding location or discount, these are all sincere gestures of love and friendship. If you do like the idea, go for it. Don't be tight-lipped about gushing if you really want to. However, if you don't like the idea, be polite in declining. Also, be sure to check with your fiancé to find out the long-term implications of saying no. Oftentimes, loved ones who want to have a more active role in your wedding are trying to send you a message by offering small favors.

The Enforcer Bride's strengths are honesty, dedication, and organization. Your biggest area to work on is communication. Since you have such a clear idea of what you want, it is easy for only criticisms to come out of your mouth. To others, that will become tiresome, especially since all they want is for you to be happy. So when things are done well, come out of your shell and give compliments and hugs as a means of support. While you are the type who doesn't need encouragement to do hard work, most people do, and a few kind words will smooth the way for the wedding and the years to come.

East Meets West: When Moon Signs Meet Sun Signs

Many people don't realize that each animal of the Chinese zodiac has a solar calendar connection. In our interpretation of Chinese horoscopes, the lunar calendar links into the solar calendar through the month and season, where the Ox's parallel sun sign is Capricorn. But every Western sun sign has a different effect on the lunar moon sign.

THE SAGITTARIUS OX

Sagittarius: November 22 to December 21

You are the dependable Ox, with added style and grace. While you are still the perfectionist who works late into the night, you are no drone. The presence of Sagittarius injects a certain amount of showmanship that others of your lunar sign may lack. Your Enforcer Bride instincts are sharp, with a keen eye for style and timing. You understand that you can be on budget and practical while still imparting a bit of entertainment to the party. Aside from added flair, Sagittarius enhances your strong beliefs in fairness as well as your desire to help others. One of your great joys is to try to understand people and look for the best in them. Understandably, it wouldn't be a surprise for you to see your wedding as an opportunity to back the causes you are most passionate about. This could include supporting a local family business you are loyal to or asking your guests to support a charity in lieu of gifts.

THE CAPRICORN OX

Capricorn: December 22 to January 20

You are a self-sufficient woman to begin with, and Capricorn encourages selfless-ness. Since you are strong and feel like you can shoulder any burden, you don't like to say no to the ones you love. Over time, you tend to amass quite the to-do list—and because you are not one to complain, people don't always pick up on when you have reached your limit. Weddings bring together a million little projects on the way to the big day. Stick to your guns, keep the wedding as simple as you like, and discourage needless changes along the way. If things cannot be helped, do not be afraid to ask for or hire help. While you may feel that this is equivalent to shirking your duties, know that no one will see it that way. In fact, people are probably wait-ing in the wings to come to your aid. Consider it reciprocation for all the times you have gone out of your way to help others.

THE AQUARIUS OX

Aquarius: January 21 to February 19

The Ox is known for being a bit stubborn at times. However, the influence of the Water Bearer's sense of calm creates a bride that is less of an enforcer and more of a cooperator. Water is symbolic of psychic ability and heightens your sense of intu-ition. When faced with a challenge, rather than charging forward with your point of view, you pause to ask questions and hear out your adversaries. This is a good quality, especially during wedding planning. There are so many types of commu-nication styles, your inquisitive nature may help curb any unfortunate misunder-standings. Your above-average ability to read situations extends to your keen sense of social graces. But you are still an Enforcer Bride at heart, which means that you will stick to your guns when it comes to how you want your wedding to come to-gether. It doesn't matter if it isn't fashionable or others recommend differently, you like things a certain way and you will be sure to get what you want.

THE PISCES OX

Pisces: February 20 to March 20

A luxe party on a budget can be achieved by the fancy but sensible Pisces Ox. You are drawn to gourmet items and will work your magic to plan a wedding that brings your impeccable taste to life. The Ox has an interesting way of being able to shape her environment as she sees fit. While outwardly you appear all buttoned up, inside you have adventurous dreams that would surprise even your closest friends. Try to fight your apprehensive nature and open yourself up to one of these fantasies. Maybe you are thinking about a daring dress or skydiving on your honeymoon. Share your dreams with your fiancé. Both Pisces and the Ox have a sensitive nature and do not like to expose their ego to any harm. Therefore, you may feel vulnerable with so much change occurring. Do not be afraid to come out of your shell a little, because this is your moment to be the belle of the ball.

THE ARIES OX
Aries: March 21 to April 19

The Ram and the Ox are both strong, confident personality profiles. Dissenters, be warned. You have the makings of a bridezilla if you do not know yourself and play to your strengths. On one hand, you are a member of the Thinkers group. You will map out what you want to do, and then you will attack it like going out to war. While this is all well and good, the challenge comes when you are met with questions and, dare I say, criticism. You can be stubborn and have a nasty temper when forced to put your opinions into words. It's strange, but even though you have a very good sense of direction, you are not the best communicator. Therefore, it's not a surprise that you are not always willing to ask for help. It is imperative for you to bring together a group of people that you trust and feel comfortable with supporting you. Otherwise you may grow tired of doing all the heavy lifting yourself.

THE TAURUS OX
Taurus: April 20 to May 20

The influence of Taurus makes you more guarded than your Ox sisters. You definitely have a great sense of self and approach life with great determination. Clearheaded and direct, you have a practical nature that will serve you well in your wedding planning. You are not the type to get sweet-talked into dresses or decorations through flattery alone; you are too down-to-earth and honest with yourself. Since you have no problem delegating tasks, your mother, bridesmaids, and fiancé will have plenty to do. Your good sense of discipline will make any money spent on diets or bridal boot camp workouts great investments. With your eyes on the prize, your own enthusiasm will carry you to your target weight. On the negative side, you're not one who likes to compromise. While brides are typically indulged in their planning, remember that you will have to make some concessions here and there.

THE GEMINI OX
Gemini: May 21 to June 21

Oxen are not typically known for their sense of humor, but the Gemini Ox is one of the exceptions. You have a fun-loving approach to life and try your best to look for the silver lining. Even the most mundane of activities will not bring you down. The iterative work of putting together your wedding invitations or putting together a seating chart that seems to take forever does not ruin your day. You have a healthy view of these activities as a means to an end. The Ox in you sees that schedule for what it is, and a set of tasks as the chores you have to do before heading to the party. While many native to your sign may have a hard time expressing their feelings, Gemini makes you an Ox with a gift of communication. You are very articulate and do not have a problem connecting with others. Naturally, you are also more inclined to public speaking and should show off this gift with mic in hand.

THE CANCERIAN OX
Cancer: June 22 to July 21

You are an Enforcer Bride in the truest sense of the word. Comfortable giving orders, you will have no problem sharing the wedding workload with your family and friends. Cancer's influence will help the tendency for the Ox in you to focus solely on work. While you are not afraid of rolling up your own sleeves, you are thoughtful about how others look at work and aren't always as motivated. You are a good listener who has the gift of being supportive, while knowing how to give good advice. Wedding work will hum along with you at the helm, but others should be careful of treading into your territory. You will guard yourself as Oxen do and are quick to fight when others challenge what you feel is sacred. Make efforts to be a gracious bride and engage people in conversation about ideas before balling up fists. Oftentimes a bit of discussion can prevent a fight and hurt feelings.

THE LEO OX
Leo: July 22 to August 21

Leo the Lion has a knack for adding a good dose of personality to the workaholic Ox. This combination of signs produces a beautiful bride indeed. You have the grace of nobility as well as the command that comes from a great deal of confidence. Needless to say, you fascinate people wherever you go, and you will not let your public down at your wedding. With a flair for drama, you'll treat your wedding like a red carpet affair and strut your stuff. The path to the wedding will have its ups and downs. Your strengths as a leader will bring everyone into line. Others respect your clear sight and will follow your plan as best they can. Beware of getting too caught up in being spoiled as the bride-to-be. Your ego can get overfed with all the compliments and favors bestowed on you. Look to your big heart to help temper any periods of inflated ego by saying your pleases and thank-yous to show your appreciation to your supporting cast.

THE VIRGO OX
Virgo: August 22 to September 22

The mixture of Virgo and Ox harkens back to the essence of the Thinkers group. You are the type who likes to have time to yourself to recharge and reassess on a regular basis. All the more so when it comes time to think not only of your wedding, but of the big evolution occurring in your life. You are a fan of learning and are forever trying to improve yourself. Therefore, you should be sure to maintain your own personal time amid all the craziness that is wedding planning. It will help you to de-stress. Your introspective qualities may produce a deep sense of faith and spirituality. The strong belief system you possess creates a sense of discipline that makes you an effective leader. With your sense of discipline, you rarely feel like you make mistakes. However, every bride learns that one cannot prepare for everything, as disappointing as that may be. So dig deep and learn from mistakes. Take them as a gift of seeing yourself from a different point of view.

THE LIBRA OX

Libra: September 23 to October 22

Libra tempers the traditional Ox method of all work and no play. In fact, your inner bride has used your Ox discipline to focus on work-life balance. You like the satisfaction of both a job well done and the celebration that follows. It's a good thing too, because it is always a shame to see a bride who puts in all the hard work and doesn't seem to enjoy it. You have a happy disposition that makes you an easy person to help and a fun customer to work with. While it's always nice to be popular, you have to be careful not to be well liked because you go along with everything. True to yourself, you work toward your high standards, but you're inclined to compromise to keep others happy and can even lose sight of your own plan. Stay motivated by working with people you respect and admire. If you plan ahead, you can get all your chores done and still have time to enjoy the good life.

THE SCORPIO OX

Scorpio: October 23 to November 21

You are not a bride to be trifled with. When you set a goal, you attack it like warfare. Your passion for realizing your dreams is known to everyone who is close to you. It's both your most attractive quality and your weakness because it is tied to your temper. Let's face it. Weddings bring out our egos. That's why they call it the bride's day. You will have to work on your patience, as others may not always achieve your standards of perfection. The Scorpio in you means that you have an especially pointy sword in battle. Do not strike until you give people a chance to right their wrongs and offer up new ideas. After all, anyone on the receiving end will understand that your intensity never lets up, so try a little graciousness before brute force. Tame your inner bridezilla and the path to wedding will be so much smoother.

Wedding Synergy: When Dragon Meets Phoenix

As you embark on your planning, check out the Wedding Relationship pairings below to see how your strengths and weaknesses come together during the planning process. These compatibility descriptions are based on year of birth combinations, which is the tip of the iceberg when it comes to each of your charts. As described in Chapter 2 "Reference Dates and Tables on the Chinese Zodiac, East-West Sign Combinations, and Animal Hours," a different animal governs each of the components of your birth date and time.

RAT HUSBAND AND OX WIFE

Rat husband and Ox wife make a happy pair because they are both honest and dependable people. Since each sign likes to play fair, they understand what it means to reciprocate. As healthy couples know, it's not an accounting of what is given and taken, but sharing each other's strengths and supporting each other's weakness. You can always depend on your husband to keep his word, and he knows that your loyalty is unwavering. You have found a sweet husband who isn't afraid of personal displays of affection and you won't be afraid of fawning over him.

OX HUSBAND AND OX WIFE

Your friends probably tell you that you both need to relax more often. Double the oxen means double the work ethic. It's a good thing that you decided to get married because a mandatory vacation is already built into your honeymoon. While you both like to do the responsible thing and save money all the time, don't get caught using all the fun money for something practical. You need to make a commitment to enjoying each other's company on a trip for just the two of you.

TIGER HUSBAND AND OX WIFE

Every girl loves a bad boy, but not as much when she's planning a wedding. Since your instincts draw you to be teacher's pet, choosing the safe and responsible path, you will be the consummate planner. Your wedding will have a strong sense of tradition and classic style. However, your husband-to-be can be stubborn about his likes and dislikes and may put up a fight for those things closest to his heart. Tigers take joy in breaking the rules. There will be many a heated argument between you two because neither of you backs down from a fight. With your Enforcer blood, you will most likely have the harder time in finding compromise.

RABBIT HUSBAND AND OX WIFE

You found a lover, not a fighter in your fiancé. While you can sometimes be too serious for your own good, he has a knack for putting things into context. Without fail, whether you like it or not, he always has a different perspective on your problems. He is the only person whom you can be weak in front of and come away stronger than before. In you he has found a woman who understands his softer side and can motivate him to realize his bigger dreams. In him you have found both a lover and a best friend.

DRAGON HUSBAND AND OX WIFE

Two strong personalities who both like to win amounts to some clash-of-the-titan moments, especially when it comes to planning a wedding. Neither of you is afraid of doing hard work and both can be depended on to get the necessary chores done. However, the ways you each like to be recognized are very different. Know that you can never lay it on too thick with a Dragon. And he should learn that a little bauble or fancy date night is the way to celebrate a job well done for the Enforcer Bride.

SNAKE HUSBAND AND OX WIFE

The Snake and the Ox may not sound like nature's most obvious partnership, but it works splendidly well. You both are driven to succeed, with the benefit of having a good sense of reality. The result is you will roll up your sleeves to get the job done together. With regard to your wedding, the two of you are committed to doing your homework. However, you may be especially careful before committing to your vendors, choosing to be very thorough in your searching and interviewing. Be sure to make decisions quickly, especially if you are getting hitched during the high wedding season.

HORSE HUSBAND AND OX WIFE

You two have very opposite tendencies and most likely have common ground in your birth ascendants. Where you can be a bit reserved and all work and no play, he is lighthearted and lives for high adventure. This means that you two have found a good balance. He can be too flexible and outgoing for the Enforcer Bride at times, who does her best to be proper and organized. However, he will encourage you to get out of your shell and to take advantage of the open bar when the wedding is in full swing.

SHEEP HUSBAND AND OX WIFE

This is a couple where emotions have to be just right to do work together. Your fiancé does not respond well to forced work. Instead, ideas will come to him through conversation and what seems to you like random inspiration. On the other hand, the Ox personality enjoys creating a list and going after it. There will need to be compromise to keep the peace. The biggest piece of advice for this bride is to do as much as you can when your guy's attention is given—there is no telling when you can get it back fully. Also, be sure to gush about the day because he responds well to positive reinforcement.

MONKEY HUSBAND AND OX WIFE

Just try to get the mic out of your fiancé's hand. The Monkey sign injects a master-of-ceremonies quality into people, and when it gets out, it's hard to put back in. It's not a bad match, though, as the Enforcer Bride likes to support and be behind the scenes. While you are planning the wedding, your future husband will have all sorts of preferences and opinions. Be ready to compromise on some, but be strategic about holding your tongue. He hates criticism, and silence is sometimes the best tool when getting your way.

ROOSTER HUSBAND AND OX WIFE

You two are a dynamic duo indeed. As the Enforcer Bride likes a good plan and balanced budget, he is there to support you with hard work and a positive attitude. You will enjoy choosing many of the details together and discussing how your family and friends will delight in the choices you have made. Fortunately for you, you can depend on your guy to take care of things he volunteers for or that you have artfully assigned to him.

DOG HUSBAND AND OX WIFE

The Dog and the Ox respond to clear rules and fair play, which can get complicated when planning a wedding. The Enforcer Bride has a natural tendency to be conscientious about her manners, but it doesn't hurt for you to ask for the Dog's opinion often when it comes to wedding aspects that involve his family. There is nothing like one small detail being overlooked and feelings getting hurt. Therefore, pave the road well with good communication when it comes to your future spouse and in-laws.

BOAR HUSBAND AND OX WIFE

The Boar's reputation for being a party animal is both famous and infamous. However, this is no surprise to you by this point! You both love and hate it. On one hand, he gets you out on the dance floor; on the other, you worry about him overindulging at the party. There is no getting around your future husband's love for life, so have some honest conversations in the planning process. Be sure to concentrate on financial matters and the planning of pre-wedding parties. When in doubt, don't be afraid to enlist the help of groomsmen and families.

The Ox's Relationships with Friends and Family

Family and friends are an important part of most weddings. Since we all operate differently in our nonromantic relationships, the pairings of your Chinese zodiac sign will take a slightly different form. Knowing the compatibility of your animal sign with your family and friends is a real asset when planning and setting expectations for responsibilities. As you think about how best to integrate your vast network of friends, review the relationship overviews below. They will help cast light on your friends' and family members' strengths, weaknesses, and working styles.

WITH A RAT

The Rat and the Ox make a pretty good team. While the Rat can sometimes be a bit chatty for the Ox's liking, the work gets done and few complaints are made. You, as the bride, have to remember that you are the leader. If you tell the Rat what you want and set the rules clearly, she will follow your wishes to the best of her ability. She might even be able to pull in a few favors, if she is so inclined. The Rat has a knack for charming people that Ox ladies do not, so take advantage where you can. Both the Rat and the Ox love a deal.

Δ WITH ANOTHER OX

Imagine a scene of two polite ladies having tea. There's one last confection on the plate, and inevitably, they agree to split it down the middle. That about sums up the double Ox relationship. Remember, the rules are very clear when it comes to weddings. As we all know, the bride *always* gets the last piece of cake. For the Enforcer Bride, your friend or future-in-law will be looking to do everything just right to win your approval. If you are not close, do not fear. An Ox is a person who gives her word and means it. She shares the same strong work ethic as you and will not let you down.

WITH A TIGER

The best part of having a Tiger in the mix is that there's always a bit of adventure. While those born in the Ox year are typically not fans of surprises, you have to both embrace and control your Tiger friend. Make a point of living up to the Enforcer Bride moniker and set the stage the way you want it. After you get control, make a point of maintaining it. Along the way, do not lead so strongly that you do not give the Tiger the opportunity to share ideas and have some flexibility. A different perspective is incredibly valuable. You may benefit by looking at some of the fresh ideas of the intriguing Tiger.

WITH A RABBIT

Whether you have been paired up with a Rabbit by friendship or obligation, you have to understand that the Ox and Rabbit have very different work styles. Namely, the Rabbit likes to enjoy life. That means procrastination creeps in every once in a while, which just isn't in the Enforcer Bride's vocabulary. Therefore, rather than trying to fight nature, be realistic in what you ask the Rabbit to do. Avoid assigning the heavy lifting, or you will be sorely disappointed.

WITH A DRAGON

You and the Dragon will make a good team planning the wedding. The Dragon and the Ox are both inspired by achieving big things. Not many people can visualize the benefits and get excited about the long road to get there, but you two can. Fortunately, there won't be many disagreements along the way because you are both too reasonable to bother yourselves with that nonsense. However, don't be too surprised if the Dragon is quick to grab some credit here or there. Dragons have bigger egos than Oxen.

Δ WITH A SNAKE

The Enforcer Bride will find smooth sailing with the Snake as a companion. The Snake shares your strengths in organization and a commitment to hard work. You can look at her as a partner rather than a helper. Snakes have excellent taste and are known to have a keen sixth sense about character. But, as much as you two are thick as thieves, understand that a person born in the year of the Snake is difficult to get to know and, as a result, may not be the most popular with newly acquainted bridesmaids.

WITH A HORSE

The Horse is not the most natural working partner for the Enforcer Bride. The Ox work ethic is to put your nose to the grindstone and get things done. The Horse favors shortcuts. There's nothing wrong with mixing the two approaches, but this won't happen unless a good habit of communication exists or can be established quickly between the two of you. If the working relationship doesn't happen naturally, don't worry about it. Tailor your Horse friend's duties or partner her with another friend who knows what your tastes and standards are.

× WITH A SHEEP

With the Sheep, you have to fight your tendency to want to do everything yourself. The two of you are in many ways polar opposites. The Ox is on time, hardworking, and not one to complain. The Sheep is often late, is a gifted communicator, and likes to avoid hard work. Therefore, to minimize any frustration, figure out the working relationship that you want. If you know each other well, that will be easy. If you are just getting to know this person, do not be afraid to ask people to work in teams to get the job accomplished.

WITH A MONKEY

When the Monkey is on board for our project, she will commit to the challenge. As the bride, you are the one in charge. Since the Monkey has a way of going off-script, you have to remember to be specific when necessary. Monkeys like to do things differently, for the sake of exploring new ground. While she may sincerely believe she is acting in your best interest, trust your responsible Ox instincts and draw clear lines if you do not know this person well to avoid any misunderstandings.

Δ WITH A ROOSTER

The Enforcer Bride and the Rooster have a lot in common. You both enjoy taking care of the details and will try your best to stay organized. Because you both can commit to new routines, this person may actually be the ideal workout buddy. She can motivate you by being on time and planning ahead, which can be a nice source of support. Having someone else keep you on track is actually a welcome change for you. And because the Rooster can be chatty when you are a bit reserved, don't be afraid to use this person as a messenger.

WITH A DOG

You will have a good working relationship with someone born in the year of the Dog. This sign very much understands what it means to work in teams and to take direction. You two might already be very close, considering you have a lot in common. Specifically for weddings, a Dog can be your ally. Even though you can be a bit stubborn at times, Dog signs are patient and do not like to cause trouble. You will get great help from this person in a very dependable way.

WITH A BOAR

Everyone likes the company of the Boar, but this may not be the most productive of pairings for wedding planning with the Enforcer Bride. Your standards can be a bit high for the Boar. Those born under this sign like to party and spend money freely—two things that Oxen are not exactly known for. These strengths are not without value, however. The Boar makes a great person for greeting and warming up the dance floor on the big day. This job will feel more like a joy than an obligation for the Boar.

Eight

BORN IN THE YEAR OF THE TIGER
Here Comes the Idealist Bride

Lunar Years of the Tiger	Elements
January 31, 1938, to February 18, 1939	Earth
February 17, 1950, to February 5, 1951	Metal
February 5, 1962, to January 24, 1963	Water
January 23, 1974, to February 10, 1975	Wood
February 9, 1986, to January 28, 1987	Fire
January 28, 1998, to February 15, 1999	Earth

Idealist Bride Details

Birth Hours: 3 A.M. to 5 A.M.

Western Sign: Aquarius

Western Gemstone: Amethyst

Symbolic Color: Green

Flower: Tulip

Season: Spring

Element: Wood

Famous Idealist Brides:
Agatha Christie, Ali MacGraw, Marilyn Monroe,
Beatrix Potter, Amber Valletta, Natalie Wood.

The Dress:

You're an entertainer—a scene-stealer in personality and in style. Always knowledgeable on trends, you're drawn to the newest fashions. Whether the dress is intricate or simple, you'll walk down the aisle like it's a runway. You'll put just as much care into choosing a hairstyle as a dress, if not more.

The Tiger Sign: The Third Bride of the Chinese Zodiac

The third sign of the zodiac, the Tiger is a fierce and loyal supporter of the loves in her life. She is a part of what we refer to as the Protectors group. There are four groups: the Doers, the Thinkers, the Protectors, and the Catalysts. The groups are made up of the three animals that have a natural affinity to one another, referred to as a Triangle of Affinity. Each set of three animals has a social connection—a kind of chemistry that is connected to each zodiac sign.

The Protectors group is made up of the Tiger, the Horse, and the Dog. No surprise, people with these birth signs or ascendants are your most natural friends and working partners. In fact, it's likely your fiancé has strong ties to this group as well. As their team name suggests, these ladies are loyal friends and champions of causes. Those born in the year of the Tiger have the mantra "I feel." She is the bride voted most likely to save the world. Here comes the Idealist Bride.

The Idealist Bride—Born in the Year of the Tiger

When you have a Tiger in the house, everybody knows it. Your energy is literally contagious. There is no halfway with the Tiger. You are a symbol of passion and confidence. With all these strengths channeled into one woman, the natural result is a dynamic bride indeed. You are called the Idealist Bride for the very passion you possess and the commitment you have to your dreams. Your wedding is special to you on a number of levels. First and foremost, it is a celebration of the love of your life and the sacred union you are making. Second, you get to deck yourself out in the outfit of your dreams and be the shining star of the day. Third, a wedding can help you shine the light on other passions in your life such as your family, friends, and perhaps a special cause that is near and dear to your heart.

Parties come naturally to you, but intense planning and details carved in stone do not. Tigers are known for a healthy dose of rebelliousness in their youth. You are one of those women that many girls look at and say, "I wish I could do that." You live in the now, which is a virtue. Trips to far-off destinations, interesting jobs (however temporary), or a dance card filled with fascinating guys are all a part of your coming of age. When you decide you want to do something, "now" is a better time than any other. So if you and your fiancé have agreed on a more traditional type of wedding, the idea of picking a location, photographer, caterer, etc. etc. does not particularly appeal. You'd rather skip the details and get to the celebration, where the role of "life of the party" comes so easily.

Whether you go with an off-the-beaten-path destination wedding or a ceremony close to home, one of your favorite parts of the wedding planning process will be deciding what you are going to wear. Idealist Brides are not known for being particularly materialistic, but they do like looking good. You will enjoy playing around with different kinds of hairstyles, shopping for that perfect dress, and shopping around for new ideas. You might want to observe a very traditional Chinese custom of having multiple dress changes. The idea of having a different dress for the ceremony and the reception is already quite popular. Having any number of dresses is not uncommon for Chinese weddings and is a great way for you to make multiple entrances and garner additional attention. It's also a great way of not having to decide on one dress. As Tigers go, if one beautiful dress is good, then a number of beautiful dresses is even better.

As a member of the Protectors group, you are a person who is not afraid of standing up for your loved ones and beliefs. Therefore, you plan your activities with your heart rather than your head. Weddings are about being proactive, so there is a shift in thinking that has to take place with you. You might want to think back to the last wedding you went to or, better yet, was a part of. What did you like and dislike, and how did those things happen? If they were intensely detailed and you do not have an ascendant that has an affinity for organization, you might want to think about enlisting the help of your family, friends, or even a professional. Too much busy work can make the Tiger native in you quite bored or even unpleasant. An impartial person like a planner may be an extremely valuable third party in the wedding process for you. You can be a bit of a moving target when it comes to decision making. Sometimes you can be incredibly decisive, maybe even rash. But often you may need some time to have conversations and really deliberate on what your heart is telling you. Since you like to go by intuition, it would not be a surprise if you make decisions for your wedding on a gut level. Therefore, try to meet people in person as soon as possible in the process. No matter how good the referral, you need to interact with people to really know if you connect. Most of all, you will need to resist your habit of procrastinating.

As mentioned before, emotions run very strong in you. You literally cannot hold your tongue when it comes to your feelings, both good and bad. This can create quite a roller coaster, if the people in your life take some of these extreme moments too seriously. Fortunately, anyone close to you knows that drama is a cycle for you: something goes wrong, you talk about it for hours, get the advice of many, cool down, and finally make a decision about what do next. The frustrating thing for those who don't know you so well is that at heart you always know what you want. You may like listening to advice, out of curiosity for other perspectives, but ultimately you steer your own life.

Because Tigers and passions are so synonymous, the Idealist Bride will celebrate all her loves during her wedding. Charitable causes quickly spring to mind because the Tiger's big heart and ability to empathize make connecting with a worthy cause a part of her DNA. Your generosity and the fact that you are not very materialistic indicate that you might want to consider asking for donations in lieu of gifts or supporting a cause rather than giving party favors. After all, you have a tendency to step away from tradition to do things the way you want them anyway. It's even better if you can help people and create visibility for something you are passionate about.

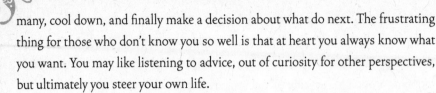

East Meets West: When Moon Signs Meet Sun Signs

Many people don't realize that each animal of the Chinese zodiac has a solar calendar connection. In our interpretation of Chinese horoscopes, the lunar calendar links into the solar calendar through the month and season, where the Tiger's parallel sun sign is Aquarius. But every Western sun sign has a different effect on the lunar moon sign.

THE SAGITTARIUS TIGER
Sagittarius: November 22 to December 21
You embrace life fully. With a curious mind, you like to explore and create your own adventures. Your friends look on in awe, as very little can hold you back. From these experiences you have refined your instinct for situations, which you should embrace in your wedding planning. When you have a feeling that something is wrong, do not ignore it. Your first instincts are very sharp. Your energy can also be a double-edged sword for your wedding journey. Your good sense of humor will come in handy to break tension when it arises. However, the Sagittarius Tiger's style of communication is very direct, and you should guard against being too combative during disagreements. While you have a refined sense of style, you

may not like to be formal when it comes to your wedding. Perhaps you will make use of an unconventional setting or wear an offbeat color. Breaking conventions can be lots of fun.

THE CAPRICORN TIGER

Capricorn: December 22 to January 20

Capricorn makes you a less stubborn Tiger than most. Also, while many Idealist Brides may make many decisions spontaneously, you will be more patient and do research when you can. But although you may be more balanced than other Tigers, your temper is still fiery. When someone has crossed you, the Tiger claws do come out. Still, Capricorn's influence helps your anger be focused on legitimate issues rather than random power trips. Fortunately for those around you, you are more inclined than other Tigers to want to get your details in order well in advance because you are not comfortable with changes, especially last-minute ones. You will need to become comfortable with the reality that where a wedding is concerned, there will always be something that goes wrong or happens unexpectedly.

THE AQUARIUS TIGER

Aquarius: January 21 to February 19

The Idealist Bride name is so apt for this combination. Communication flows like water with the Aquarius Tiger. Your loving heart enjoys expressing your feelings without hesitation. No bottling things up for you. Everyone will know your thoughts and hopes, including your big dreams for your wedding. Your fiancé and all those involved will find it hard to keep up with your whirlwind of a schedule, while you find it terribly difficult to stand still. Whether it's running off to meet with a dozen florists or an ambitious bridal boot camp, you will be keeping busy— all in the name of your upcoming nuptials.

THE PISCES TIGER

Pisces: February 20 to March 20

The influence of Pisces is a good one for the energetic Tiger bride. Your combined signs encourage a life with less drama than many other Tigers. While you may like a calmer-paced life, that doesn't mean you won't have the roar of the Tiger in you.

Pisces makes you a person of action who will fight for what you believe in. One of your greatest strengths is that you have a great talent for understanding people. You should draw upon your intuitive nature to maneuver through the many negotiation hurdles in your wedding planning. From balancing people's feelings with your wants to getting the best rates possible, approach problems by means of psychology and you will be better off.

THE ARIES TIGER
Aries: March 21 to April 19

This combination of sun sign and moon sign is a personality that makes a real impression. No one forgets you! You will enjoy the added attention and special treatment of being a bride. Your life story is a page-turner and people are naturally drawn to your dynamic nature. With such extreme actions come equally strong reactions. You will find, when working with people out of your inner circle, that people's attractions to you will be extreme and so will yours to them. You are best advised to let relationships exist naturally because compromise will not come easily to you during your wedding planning. Try to steer clear of relationships that you know or suspect will be challenging. After all, patience is not one of your virtues, so be realistic about how you will approach the wedding process.

THE TAURUS TIGER
Taurus: April 20 to May 20

Because you practice good planning and efficiency in your daily life, you will embrace wedding planning better than your sister Tigers. The balance achieved by Taurus and Tiger results in a very lovely combination of clear thought and a natural ease in working with people. You will know how to work with difficult people, opting for a tough but ladylike way of tackling problems. You are also inclined to champion causes that are important to you, and they will play a key part in your wedding. The wedding is a great venue to reflect all the things that are important to you, including spiritual things. Whether you prefer asking for charitable donations in lieu of gifts or you find creative ways of supporting people you believe in, each of your wedding actions will be carried out with a lot of thought.

THE GEMINI TIGER

Gemini: May 21 to June 21

With your bubbly personality, others know you as the life of the party. You are quick with a joke and bond with people very quickly. However, you may need to tone down your larger-than-life persona for some parts of the planning process. You are a very honest person—to the point of sometimes being brutal. Know that others may not have your thick skin and can take words very seriously. Another thing to be careful of is jumping too quickly into things. Remember that hassle-free returns and weddings rarely go together, so be sure to think through all your purchases. Finally, you have a strong competitive spirit. While the eye of the Tiger approach is good for getting fit, be aware that it can put a damper on your budget.

THE CANCERIAN TIGER

Cancer: June 22 to July 21

You are a sweet and romantic Tiger who has been dreaming of her wedding since she was a girl. You are a natural entertainer and hostess. All the help you have given your girlfriends with their weddings will come back to you via thoughtful brides-maids. The combination of your big heart and Cancerian personality produces a mixture of light and dark. Your feelings, whether happy or sad, show on your face. Since your wedding is very important to you, you can become defensive when you feel threatened. You can get very protective, even jealous of your husband-to-be. Perhaps it will be the idea of a wild bachelor party or the reemergence of your fiancé's ex-girlfriend—either way tears may flow. But don't worry too much; no doubt your fiancé has seen your emotional side before.

THE LEO TIGER

Leo: July 22 to August 21

Lions and tigers and brides, oh my. This Idealist Bride always makes an entrance. Your combination of Leo and Tiger makes you an especially devoted fiancée be-cause you feel your emotions so deeply. When you love, it is all encompassing. And when you hate, well, look out. Your wedding experience will be very emotional. From happy tears to ones of frustration, you may feel like you are all over the place, but your nature of taking breaks of thought and solitude can be very healing. One of your secret fears in planning a wedding may stem from the unknown. Because you like to be an expert in things, you may feel awkward if you have never planned a big event before. Don't be afraid to let some of your guard down and ask questions and, most of all, ask for help.

THE VIRGO TIGER
Virgo: August 22 to September 22

Where the Tiger is the gas, Virgo is the brakes. The result is a well-balanced lady Tiger. Added to the Tiger's naturally sophisticated ways, you find a strange calm in things being tidy. But Virgo's analytical eye will not dampen the Tiger's natural charisma. Where other Idealist Brides may be quick to rush into wedding decisions, the Virgo in you will encourage you to analyze situations before you sign on the dotted line. While you will still have the infamous Tiger's temper, you are more inclined to thoughtful communication, which will be a huge asset in dealing with new friends and family. As the Chinese say, "Kind words can be brief and simple, but they echo in our memories forever."

THE LIBRA TIGER
Libra: September 23 to October 22

After you make up your mind, you will be a Tiger off and running. However, your process of making decisions may cause many arguments between you and your fiancé. Both Librans and Tigers have the nasty habit of procrastination, born out of a curious nature that makes you think there is always more to be researched. It would be best to designate a date for the most important decisions because deadlines for you are crucial. Fortunately, once you have made a decision, your hardworking nature will kick in. Both your sun and moon signs have a good work ethic and like to see things get done well. As bride, you will be equal parts hostess with the most-est and party princess, as lady Tigers always are.

THE SCORPIO TIGER

Scorpio: October 23 to November 21

The scorpion and the tiger both get a bad rap in the animal kingdom. Even though they are more than deadly stings and treacherous bites, the vengeful streak is definitely real. Accepting this part of your passionate personality and learning how to manage it during wedding planning will be very important for you. Because weddings mean that you will have to deal with a diverse group, with undoubtedly a few you vehemently dislike, you must channel your Tiger actress to be artful in how you deal with others. After all, your natural sex appeal means that you do have the art of persuasion down pat. If you work on improving your emotional control, you can lay a better foundation for your married life to come.

Wedding Synergy: When Dragon Meets Phoenix

As you embark on your planning, check out the Wedding Relationship pairings below to see how your strengths and weaknesses come together during the planning process. These compatibility descriptions are based on year of birth combinations, which is the tip of the iceberg when it comes to each of your charts. As described in Chapter 2 "Reference Dates and Tables on the Chinese Zodiac, East-West Sign Combinations, and Animal Hours," a different animal governs each component of your birth date and time.

RAT HUSBAND AND TIGER WIFE

Your approach as a couple to the wedding will be different, but rooted in positivity. Inviting guests and planning the party details will be lots of fun because you share so many common interests. Struggles may lie in the area of finances and a breakdown in communication. The Rat is a strong provider and will do his best to keep his Tiger lady pleased. Be advised that if you two are paying a significant amount of the wedding bill, the Rat will be very watchful of spending and want to feel his fiancée is being responsible with their nest egg. The Idealist Bride also has a quirky way of getting things done and must remember it's best to keep surprises at a minimum for your planner of a future husband.

OX HUSBAND AND TIGER WIFE

From the outside this relationship may seem like an odd match, but a mixture of compatible ascendants is probably building a bridge between two very different animals. The benefit of an Ox and Tiger combination can be a very positive one indeed. Your fiancé approaches life in a no-nonsense kind of way, purposeful in planning with an eye for details. The Idealist Bride breathes life into any party through her spontaneous nature. Knowing this, dividing up responsibilities should be quite obvious.

TIGER HUSBAND AND TIGER WIFE

There's already been quite a lot of discussion about how one passionate Tiger can liven things up. Now, let's double the trouble. With so much passion in one house, there will be very heated discussions when it comes to wedding details. You are both stubborn and when opinions are at odds, there will be sparks. It would be best to carve out some independence in wedding planning early to diminish disagreement. Hashing out the wedding budget early and sticking to it will also be a struggle for you two. Try to curb your generosity where you can.

RABBIT HUSBAND AND TIGER WIFE

The Idealist Bride is the real assertive energy in this couple, as the Tiger likes to take center stage and the Rabbit chooses to be in the background. This combination in wedding planning can be a real asset, if you can share some of the responsibility and creative direction. Your husband-to-be has the Rabbit's keen eye for sophistication and good taste. Be sure to ask for his opinion and really listen to his perspective because he will definitely have some different ideas. Trust in his taste—after all, he did propose to you.

DRAGON HUSBAND AND TIGER WIFE

The marriage of a Dragon and Tiger is a pairing of two strong individuals. You two were drawn to each other's independence. Together, you like to trailblaze new territory and shake things up. As a result, your wedding approach may verge on unconventional. You may be drawn to an adventure honeymoon or having your wedding at a nontraditional place. However, with the Idealist Bride's need to be free, your fiancé should know that you will fight hard against anyone who tells you to tone down your wishes.

SNAKE HUSBAND AND TIGER WIFE

Your attraction has to be built on appreciating each other's differences; otherwise your relationship would not have progressed as far as it has. The pairing of Snake and Tiger is the partnership of introvert and extrovert. The Idealist Bride is full of energy and likes to live life out loud. The Snake chooses to keep many of his inner thoughts safely guarded away. You will have to pull teeth to get his views on many things, but you must struggle through it to keep arguments at bay. He is not forthcoming with information, but has a need to be involved.

HORSE HUSBAND AND TIGER WIFE

You two are a very active and charming couple. With an active social life and jam-packed calendar, the Horse and the Tiger like to keep busy. Both of you delight in exploration and can have lots of fun scouting out wedding venues and tasting the delicious treats you will be serving your guests. With such a lust for life, it wouldn't be surprising if you were both very tempted by the idea of eloping and forgoing tradition. Either way, you will find a way of adding some offbeat fun to your big day.

SHEEP HUSBAND AND TIGER WIFE

Let's face it, a Tiger wife is a lot of woman. Your larger-than-life personality may challenge the sometimes-quiet Sheep. Your attraction is most likely built on the Tiger's charisma (which always demands attention) and the Sheep's sweet and affectionate nature. You love that his eyes are always on you and that he provides comfort and stability. The Idealist Bride needs to be cautious about letting stress get the best of her. You may end up being too critical of your husband-to-be, when you should know that he is always trying to act in your best interests.

MONKEY HUSBAND AND TIGER WIFE

Wedding planning and certainly marriage demand a significant amount of compromise. Therefore, you should know from the onset that the Monkey and Tiger both like getting their way. Your planning will struggle as long as you think of yourselves as individuals rather than a couple. If you remain as separate units, you will struggle to agree on many key issues. Both of you are very clever and have a natural sense of competition. It would be wise to set a direction early and try to blend your tastes.

ROOSTER HUSBAND AND TIGER WIFE

Loving each other and working together can be two different things. The Rooster is an interesting guy. He is very particular and likes to go into a lot of detail about his opinions. You, the Tiger, have opinions of your own and like to get your way. You should both be prepared to up your patience for the long discussions ahead of you. Your bridal tendency is to charge forward with making your dreams come true, but you will need to integrate your Rooster's thoughts into the process to help keep the peace.

DOG HUSBAND AND TIGER WIFE

The strongest pairings bring out the best of each other, and that is what you get with a Dog husband and a Tiger wife. He will be very clearheaded and fair in how he approaches the wedding. Since your bridal tendency is to feel through decisions rather than think through every last detail, you would be wise to see your husband-to-be as good counsel. The always painful task of wedding invitations and seating charts comes to mind as a good team activity. You may cringe at the idea of inviting certain people, but your husband can see the big picture and help guide your thinking.

BOAR HUSBAND AND TIGER WIFE

Your relationship is very loving, since both animal signs are remarkably thoughtful to those they hold near and dear. As bride-to-be, you will experience the occasional emotional breakdown and cause the occasional fight, but the Tiger always makes it up to her loving partner. He understands you and will provide an affectionate safety net. The Idealist Bride knows how to persuade and will often get what she wants, but the Boar has similar skills. As a result, your wedding will come to reflect both of you when the planning is done.

The Tiger's Relationships with Friends and Family

Family and friends are an important part of most weddings. Since we all operate differently in our nonromantic relationships, the pairings of your Chinese zodiac sign will take a slightly different form. Knowing the compatibility of your animal sign with your family and friends is a real asset when planning and setting expectations for responsibilities. As you think about how best to integrate your vast network of friends, review the relationship overviews below. They will help cast light on your friends' and family members' strengths, weaknesses, and working styles.

WITH A RAT

This combination is not the quickest of friendships in the Chinese zodiac. The Rat and Tiger have different instincts. The Rat is more cautious and penny-pinching than the Tiger, who is more generous and grand with gestures. While the Rat may look at your wedding planning and think, "That isn't how I would go about it," the Rat will most likely bite her tongue because the bride's word goes. If a Rat has offered help, she is earnest and will follow through.

WITH A OX

The Ox and the Tiger both have strong opinions and tempers to match. If you have been longtime friends and find communication easy and natural, your working relationship can be compatible. The Ox is a hard worker once she has a clear sense of what needs to be done. You, as the bride, need to be specific about what kind of help you need and not change your mind; otherwise you will drive the Ox crazy. Your friend may also not find it easy to air her feelings like you and may hold a grudge over any misunderstandings.

Δ WITH ANOTHER TIGER

Two Tigers working together are likely to operate like siblings. They can be close friends, strong competitors, and prone to small arguments. Because you are united by friendship or perhaps linked by your fiancé, you can bond over a common goal, which is to have a happy and memorable wedding. Tigers do like to focus in on tasks and get them done. However, if there is past experience of petty rivalry, it's best to limit activities to those that will not fan the flame of your natural competition.

WITH A RABBIT

The Rabbit is a kind and good-natured assistant in a wedding. If you two are new friends, you are best advised to be careful with your at times brutally honest communication style. The Rabbit is gentler and can be very sensitive, especially if she does not know you very well. The Tiger can be a big personality and can learn a thing or two from the Rabbit's knack for diplomacy. This person may see your bridal ways as aggressive if you do not watch words and actions.

WITH A DRAGON

You both have strong personalities and a good amount of creativity. With all these skills, you can be a good team. There will not be a dull moment with you two. As your moniker suggests, you are an idealist, and so is the Dragon. This positive attitude will come in handy, as you may have some arguments along the way. The Dragon doesn't just follow blindly and will want her thoughts and work acknowledged. Your role as decision maker is clear, but getting the best out of the Dragon means working collaboratively.

WITH A SNAKE

The Tiger and the Snake can have an uncomfortable working relationship. Since free-flowing honesty is such a big part of who you are as the Idealist Bride, you can be uneasy with the Snake's introverted ways. The result will most likely be tiffs caused by simple misunderstandings. If you two are just getting to know each other, do not be offended if you do not become fast friends. Snakes are not known for being especially chatty, but thankfully for most brides, they are also known for not offering up unsolicited advice. A good piece of advice is to work through your wedding planner or limit intense discussions to reduce unnecessary stress.

Δ WITH A HORSE

The two of you will make a good team in wedding planning. You approach life in very similar ways. The Tiger and the Horse rely on instinct and are comfortable scrapping plans and just winging it. So you have your companion for pulling off the freeway to check out a random store or make the long drive to a sample sale. Your friend not only will go along with the idea, but also will actually enjoy the chance for uncharted adventure.

WITH A SHEEP

If you are close with this friend, the Tiger's protective spirit will come out. Because the Sheep does not usually have the same assertive nature as you, you are more careful with her feelings. If you two are getting to know each other, perhaps a future in-law or your fiancé's friend, a friendship can potentially blossom through the process. While the Sheep may not be the best planner, she is one of the best at being a kind ear during moments of stress.

× WITH A MONKEY

The Monkey and the Tiger have a natural conflict in the Chinese zodiac. The two of you have many things in common, and therein lies the root of many arguments that can take place. If you share compatible ascendants, a better communication link may exist. Your core animals will have extreme ups and downs when working closely together. The Monkey has many clever ideas, which you may benefit from if you don't rub each other the wrong way.

WITH A ROOSTER

Where the Tiger likes to jump into work, the Rooster likes to analyze and take stock of the situation. Therefore, this relationship can be very beneficial. The common tie between you two is a life of constant activity. The result can be either a very close friendship or a series of misunderstandings. As the bride, you should take the Rooster's critical opinion positively rather than defensively. Also, be prepared to give credit to your friend, whether her contribution is big or small, because the Rooster has a long memory for acknowledgment.

Δ WITH A DOG

As a Tiger bride, you will have strong opinions on how your wedding will be. As a sister from your affinity group, your friend born in the year of the Dog will be protective of you and your plans. Your friend knows how to present new ideas and challenge you for the better. Most times you respond well to her ideas, and this sharing can strengthen your wedding planning. When you two do have arguments, you are quick to get your feelings off your chest and do not hold on to grudges.

WITH A BOAR

The gregarious Boar is a fun friend to have on your wedding planning committee. Natives of this sign are drawn to the Tiger's charisma and creativity. If you chart the direction, the Boar is one hundred percent behind you. Since the Boar is known as the party animal of the zodiac, you should guard against her influence to spend lavishly and live in the moment. The combination of your inclination to choose on instinct combined with the Boar's vices may result in maxed-out credit cards.

Nine

BORN IN THE YEAR OF THE RABBIT
Here Comes the Harmonizer Bride

Lunar Years of the Rabbit	Elements
February 19, 1939, to February 7, 1940	Earth
February 6, 1951, to January 26, 1952	Metal
January 25, 1963, to February 12, 1964	Water
February 11, 1975, to January 30, 1976	Wood
January 29, 1987, to February 16, 1988	Fire
February 16, 1999, to February 4, 2000	Earth

Harmonizer Bride Details

Birth Hours: 5 A.M. to 7 A.M.

Western Sign: Pisces

Western Gemstone: Aquamarine or Bloodstone

Symbolic Color: Green

Flower: Peony

Season: Spring

Element: Wood

Famous Harmonizer Brides:
Drew Barrymore, Ingrid Bergman, Lynda Carter,
Stacy "Fergie" Ferguson, Billie Holiday, Angelina Jolie, Eva Longoria,
Sally Ride, Tina Turner, Queen Victoria, Kate Winslet.

The Dress:

Only the finest fabrics and highest quality materials will meet your standards. You favor soft and comfortable fabrics, so that your movements are always free and relaxed. You'll shy away from intricate beading and high drama color accents and choose elegance for your big day.

The Rabbit Sign: The Fourth Bride of the Chinese Zodiac

As the fourth sign of the zodiac, the Rabbit is one of the most sophisticated ladies of the cycle. She is a part of what we refer to as the Catalysts group. There are four groups: the Doers, the Thinkers, the Protectors, and the Catalysts. The groups are made up of the three animals that have a natural affinity to one another, referred to as a Triangle of Affinity. Each set of three animals has a social connection—a kind of chemistry that is connected to each zodiac sign.

The Catalysts group is made up of the Rabbit, the Sheep, and the Boar. No surprise, people with these birth signs or ascendants are your most natural friends and working partners. In fact, it's likely your fiancé has strong ties to this group as well. The Catalysts Affinity Triangle is made up of women who are skilled communicators and patrons of the arts. Those born in the year of the Rabbit have the mantra "I cooperate." She is the bride voted most likely to send off her thank-you notes in record time. Here comes the Harmonizer Bride.

The Harmonizer Bride—Born in the Year of the Rabbit

Your love of beauty and good etiquette will make your wedding a special labor of love. Some might say that the female Rabbit is a natural bride. Rabbits are lovers of the fine arts and seek out beauty in the world around them. Since you are an introspective soul, your true love most likely shares a passion you hold dear, perhaps a love of music, architecture, or theater. The Rabbit has an eye for good taste and likes to surround herself with beautiful things. You are a deep, psychological soul who thinks that although the world can be rude and ugly, you might as well try to focus on the things that make you happy. No surprise that your wedding and your honeymoon will be a reflection of elegance and peace.

The Harmonizer Bride is one of the ultimate power ladies of the Chinese zodiac. Fierce style and carefully chosen words are why you make friends easily and have an extensive network of contacts. The Rabbit is the natural peacemaker. Above all things, this may be one of the greatest assets that your fiancé should value. Diplomacy is a big piece of forming a family and keeping relationships smooth. You understand that first impressions carry a lot of weight and will make every effort to make his family your own. This will win big points with your husband-to-be and help cement bonds between families. As a Harmonizer, you are wise in knowing that peace does not come from liking everyone, but from knowing how to deal with people. While some people may drive you crazy on the inside, you treat each person graciously, choosing to vent only to your inner circle.

You probably have lots of experience planning parties; perhaps you have a few bridesmaid dresses in your closet yourself. The Rabbit makes a thoughtful friend who is not afraid of lending advice and a helping hand. With your very observant eye, you are a great planner and negotiator. You will do your research for market prices and are always sure to read the fine print. Where other brides may get flattered or manipulated, you are keen on getting exactly what you want. However, you don't achieve this by fighting—you are the Harmonizer, after all. Instead, you may back away from conflict by choosing another person or store to help you with your needs. This may be a challenge if you have your heart set on something specific. You may not be able to find a similar wedding venue or dressmaker, so be prepared to roll up your sleeves for a fight or bring reinforcements when you really want something.

As the consummate lady of the Chinese zodiac, you put up an almost perfect face to the world, but even you have a few flaws. The first is an inclination to being selfish at times. While this type of behavior is a risk of every bride, you should not think that you are an exception because of your impeccable manners and good taste. You observe a set of high standards that may come into conflict with your friends, family, and perhaps future in-laws. Compromise is the name of the game when talking about conflict-free wedding planning, and however painful it is to your sense of taste, it will be needed to maintain the tranquil life that you so cherish. Your sympathetic heart unfortunately gives you a weak stomach for criticism and unhappiness. When there is something that you do not like, you simply choose to ignore it. Whether you venture off to the spa or get lost in a book, you walk away from the scene of the crime and go somewhere more peaceful. Remember that while your methods may work for many things, marriage and wedding planning, for that matter, are about teamwork, not solitary pursuits.

As the Harmonizer Bride, your wedding will be your greatest work of art. Your love of elegance and tranquillity will be present in all your design and party decisions, much to the delight of everyone involved. If you can make peace with the reality that not everything will be perfect and that you will undoubtedly be inconvenienced in the course of your wedding planning, you can minimize any unpleasant feelings or stress. You carry the burden of noticing every detail and feel a duty to be courteous to everyone. You show respect by bestowing textbook-level etiquette to everyone, but consider that others will show their love for you in different ways. So let some people slide on being a little forgetful, and be gracious when getting those late RSVP cards. That's what maintaining harmony is all about.

East Meets West: When Moon Signs Meet Sun Signs

Many people don't realize that each animal of the Chinese zodiac has a solar calendar connection. In our interpretation of Chinese horoscopes, the lunar calendar links into the solar calendar through the month and season, where the Rabbit's parallel sun sign is Pisces. But every Western sun sign has a different effect on the lunar moon sign.

THE SAGITTARIUS RABBIT
Sagittarius: November 22 to December 21

Over the years, you have not been afraid to get to know a very diverse group of people, and you've stayed in touch with many of them. Your fiancé may be surprised to see the variety of people you call friend. If he balks at some, you can remind him that your friends helped you become the woman who fell in love with him. Sagittarius paired with the year of the Rabbit helps heighten your intuitive senses, which you should make sure to heed, especially in regard to negotiation. What will help you in getting your way is your genuine nature of trying to understand people, even those very different from you. Your sweet personality and poker face will make it hard for others to say no to you. The Harmonizer Bride always has a good strategy for getting what she wants and making both parties feel good about the end result. After all, everybody wants a happy bride.

THE CAPRICORN RABBIT
Capricorn: December 22 to January 20

The year of the Rabbit and the sign of Capricorn combine for an especially happy mix. While other Harmonizer Brides may err on the side of trying to please everybody, the Capricorn Rabbit has the knack for being more self-preserving, while maintaining fair play. This may be hard to believe, but it is a strength rooted in patience. Whether it is waiting out the perfect videographer, searching every sample sale for the dress of your dreams, or combing each estimate for any overages, you will eventually get what you want. Your luck in relationships will result in more than a good fiancé. Rabbits are good networkers, making strong connections along the way. Maybe you have an old college roommate who is a pastry chef? Don't be afraid to look her up and ask for some good advice.

THE AQUARIUS RABBIT
Aquarius: January 21 to February 19

Aquariuses are known for a cheery disposition and an open-minded perspective on life. This influence on the Rabbit bride is a very positive one. While some Rabbits may be overly emotional during wedding planning, the optimistic view of Aquarius will calm the Rabbit's sometimes-thin skin. You will be more balanced when it comes to many of the big decisions that come with wedding planning. Even though you have a sharp instinct for good deals and trustworthy people, you are more inclined to do your homework and sleep on your big decisions. This is a wise choice, since it is difficult to undo many things when it comes to planning a wedding. Trust in your almost psychic instinct and you will not be sorry. A tendency you should guard against is being too focused on others, rather than yourself. Remember that you are the star and others will find joy in making the bride happy.

THE PISCES RABBIT
Pisces: February 20 to March 20

As Pisces corresponds to the Rabbit, the Pisces Harmonizer Bride is a double sign of sorts. The combination makes for an even stronger focus on beauty and peace. You will find lots of joy in finding the perfect invitations, flowers, and other elements that will create an attractive wedding environment. While you have very strong instincts, you sometimes second-guess yourself and rely on others to help you make the difficult decisions. This helps you stay in your comfort zone. You may want to use your wedding planning as an opportunity to break with some of your habits and follow through with your first instincts. There is no harm in going after what you want and speaking on your own behalf. You need to get over viewing negotiation as conflict, when at its heart it's a conversation.

THE ARIES RABBIT

Aries: March 21 to April 19

You are a Harmonizer Bride with a very strong will and clear perspective. You are very decisive and like to get things done your way. Anyone dealing with you during your wedding planning will appreciate your strong opinions because there is nothing more frustrating than trying to help someone who doesn't know how to express what she wants. Fortunately, Aries honesty is paired with the Rabbit's gift for elegant communication. You will be able to deliver the hard messages while being seen as fair. Aries can sometimes be a hard person to deal with, but the Rabbit knows how to charm a competitor into giving you what you want. As the Harmonizer Bride, you will be a strong hostess and all smiles. Remember that whatever misunderstandings may occur, you should relax your razor-sharp memory to focus on the positive and not bring any grudges into your marriage.

THE TAURUS RABBIT

Taurus: April 20 to May 20

As always, the Harmonizer Bride is a lady to the extreme. You are drawn to elegance and conduct yourself with the best manners. The influence of Taurus is in most ways very positive. As Bulls like to follow the rules, your organizational skills will be sharper than some of your sister Hares. Taurus encourages you to find your inner confidence and stick to your guns with hard decisions. The combination of this tough work ethic with the Rabbit's keen observational eye means that little will get past you. And woe to the person who does try to cross you. Rabbits have a long memory and Bulls have a bad temper. While you may never lose your cool in public, you may hold on to grievances longer than you should. Just make sure that you don't let any unpleasantness take away from your special day.

THE GEMINI RABBIT

Gemini: May 21 to June 21

The Rabbit finds a good friend in the twins of Gemini. As a bride, you are well-suited to many decisions that other brides may find challenging. Your skill for communication will make negotiations and first meetings go smoothly. By making early connections, you can sweeten many deals and perhaps get some preferential treatment. You will also have a strong understanding of the areas in which you will need help in planning your wedding. This is not always seen as a strength, but it very much is, especially if you have never taken a big part in a wedding before. Since the Rabbit likes to enjoy life and seeks out life's shortcuts, it's a good thing that Gemini's two heads are better than one. Gemini is creative in finding solutions to problems. With the Rabbit's good fortune, you're really given a head start.

THE CANCERIAN RABBIT
Cancer: June 22 to July 21

You are a more private Rabbit than most, which can make the idea of getting married a difficult transition. However, your cautious nature and good communication with your husband-to-be will help smooth the path. You will try as best as you can to keep your wedding and life simple. This is a wise strategy, since the less complicated you can make the wedding, the better. Disappointment does not sit well with you. Lady Hares like to dwell on their problems in private and only come up once their private pity party is over. Once you are back in good spirits, it'll seem as if the event never happened. However, you tend to hold on to grudges. Because of your high standards you prefer to keep your inner circle small and intimate; thus, choosing your wedding party should be fairly easy.

THE LEO RABBIT
Leo: July 22 to August 21

This Harmonizer Bride brings together two charming signs that both like to enjoy the good life. With your strong leadership skills and natural hostess ability, no doubt you will throw an excellent and stylish party. The Leo Rabbit's ability to make fast friends comes in handy when picking excellent people to be involved with your wedding. You will make good decisions if you go with your instincts. However, your excellent taste could be one of your downsides in your wedding planning. The Rabbit has an attraction to all things beautiful and the Leo has a requirement to always look good. Therefore, it would be wise to watch your budget and not go beyond your means. Being born in the year of the Rabbit brings with it a good dose of luck, which is always helpful.

THE VIRGO RABBIT

Virgo: August 22 to September 22

The Harmonizer comes across to the outside world as a perfect bride, rarely exposing any wedding drama, even to her inner circle. The influence of Virgo is one of stability, helping to smooth out the emotional events during the wedding planning. You are not afraid of rolling up your sleeves and doing the hard work that comes with preparing for the party, especially if it is in the best interest of your budget. In fact, you will investigate all your options and keep good track of expenses. You will be clever about your deals and strategic about where you may ask relatives and friends for their assistance. The Harmonizer Bride's fiancé and inner circle will not hear much complaining about any wedding trials because you are someone who prefers to sort through difficult times by yourself.

THE LIBRA RABBIT

Libra: September 23 to October 22

The marriage of Libra and the year of the Rabbit is an elegant match. You will be especially thoughtful about your wedding planning, choosing to carefully evaluate the pros and cons of each event decision to make sure you are comfortable. Libra does not like making commitments unless absolutely positive. So one of your challenges in the beginning of wedding planning will be signing contracts to secure dates a year or sometimes two years ahead. You will feel uncomfortable signing on the dotted line when your wedding day feels so far away. However, once you learn that reservations are mandatory (not to mention few and far between), your Rabbit project leader skills will kick in. Since the Libra Rabbit is drawn to the arts, perhaps you will try to have your nuptials in a museum or historical landmark.

THE SCORPIO RABBIT

Scorpio: October 23 to November 21

This Harmonizer Bride has a cautious and graceful life philosophy. You will be very mindful of etiquette and careful about others' feelings when it comes to planning your big day. However, you may become quite guarded when sharing your wedding details. Just as some mothers-to-be don't like to share the name of their baby, you may not like to tell some people what your wedding dress looks like or maybe what your colors are. Whether it's to preserve the element of surprise or just to keep it your own little secret, the Scorpio Rabbit finds it fun to keep a few things under wraps. Pluto's influence on the Rabbit sign makes for a more affectionate lover than other Rabbits, and your fiancé should look forward to a few pleasant surprises from you during your engagement.

Wedding Synergy: When Dragon Meets Phoenix

As you embark on your planning, check out the Wedding Relationship pairings below to see how your strengths and weaknesses come together during the planning process. These compatibility descriptions are based on year of birth combinations, which is the tip of the iceberg when it comes to each of your charts. As described in Chapter 2 "Reference Dates and Tables on the Chinese Zodiac, East-West Sign Combinations, and Animal Hours," a different animal governs each component of your birth date and time.

RAT HUSBAND AND RABBIT WIFE

Quality time and compromise are the name of the game for you two. The year of the Rat offers you a husband-to-be who is romantic and very observant. He will want to spend lots of time with you, even though you may be very busy planning the big day. The Harmonizer Bride likes to get everything done to her exacting standards, so you may not be inclined to spend one-on-one time that doesn't include talking about the wedding. Be sure to include both your wishes and your family's wishes in your ceremony. You both care about representing your families well.

OX HUSBAND AND RABBIT WIFE

This relationship is positive because learning from your differences can enhance each of you as an individual. The Ox is as dependable as the North Star, and the lady Rabbit could be described as Miss Sparkle. Translate this to wedding planning, and the Ox will excel at holding the budget and making people honor timelines and agreements. The husband-to-be should be careful to not be too hard on the Harmonizer Bride. You are very sensitive to criticism, especially when it is about something like wedding details, which are so close to your heart. However, you must remember that the Ox is not malicious; in fact, he really does believe he is helping.

TIGER HUSBAND AND RABBIT WIFE

Your union is one of supermasculine and superfeminine, a good recipe for marital chemistry. Now, what kind of magic depends on how you two approach your wedding plans. The Tiger sign brings a lot of spontaneity and last-minute excitement. Therefore, long-term planning does not naturally come to your fiancé. You cannot ask for the same patient approach to poring over a hundred invitation samples for the perfect shade of pearl white. The Tiger just cannot handle it. You may get constantly frustrated when he brushes off your constant worries, but it really is a compliment. He knows that you will do everything perfectly in the end.

RABBIT HUSBAND AND RABBIT WIFE

The pairing of two common signs creates an instant connection in many ways, but requires compromise because you are so much alike. Since you both are inclined to be very visual people and art lovers, you will enjoy many wedding details. Music, food, and beautiful scenery have all been ingredients to fun dates in your past. It will be a treat to create your own special environment for your big day. However, finalizing the details and breaking down who owns what task will be the challenges for you as a couple. If you don't have a tortoise working constantly alongside you hares, you could be scrambling to get everything done in the final stretch.

DRAGON HUSBAND AND RABBIT WIFE

Both of your signs are known to be quite lucky, and your matching is compatible in many ways, especially when it comes to putting together a wedding. The Harmonizer Bride is a natural hostess and designer. Whether you lived together before engagement or spent lots of time at each other's homes, he is observant of your eye for style. Naturally, he will defer to you to lead most of the wedding decisions because it makes you so happy. Your base for companionship is strong, but many small irritations come up during your wedding planning. Try to be less concerned with petty arguments.

SNAKE HUSBAND AND RABBIT WIFE

The two of you like to enjoy the good life. With both of your signs being well-known for good taste and luxury living, your union is very compatible. You will chose personal details that will reflect your refined tastes at the wedding, from an elegant wedding gown to delicious cuisine. As in your daily lives, during wedding planning you will maintain your own separate lives and hobbies. This can be positive because many event details can be stressful. However, do not get so caught up in work that you do not make time to relax and enjoy a bottle of wine as a couple.

HORSE HUSBAND AND RABBIT WIFE

With two very different signs of the zodiac, wedding planning will be an adventure for you. The Harmonizer Bride is kind of a one-woman show who needs a devoted fan base. You can do it all, but you want to be acknowledged for your hard work and wise decisions. With making plans early and doing your research, you feel comforted to know that your event is in good shape. On the other hand, your husband-to-be likes to play things by ear, which will drive you crazy when getting him to make decisions. You should each try to be more understanding of the other's perspective. The bride in you can take occasional breaks and your Horse fiancé can be more attentive.

SHEEP HUSBAND AND RABBIT WIFE

Your relationship is one built on much love and support of each other. The Harmonizer Bride is the natural project leader for the wedding. Not only are you more inclined to break out the binder and maintain the spreadsheets, but you also care more about the artistic design of the big day. Your fiancé will be appreciative and applaud your hard work. His only Achilles' heel will be his generosity, which may get the best of him at times. However, if you maintain the budget, you can help hedge for a runaway open bar or crazy catering bill.

MONKEY HUSBAND AND RABBIT WIFE

Both of your signs are very enterprising and grounded in reality. This can make for some very efficient planning and heated discussions. However, since you have both committed to the long haul, you must appreciate the many strengths you each bring to the table. He will enjoy your eye for style and entertainment, while you appreciate his clever approach to solving life's puzzles. Remember that Monkeys love compliments, and doling out a few here and there can do wonders for putting your fiancé in an agreeable mood. To help smooth the road when the timeline becomes stressful, you will need to make efforts to be together as a couple and just relax. You'll also have to set aside some time to be by yourself to fully recharge, as the Rabbit needs her moments of solitude.

ROOSTER HUSBAND AND RABBIT WIFE

The Harmonizer Bride is a star in many subjects, from arts and culture to social etiquette and diplomacy, but where you may find the most trouble is in taking criticism. Fortunately or unfortunately, you have chosen a Rooster, who we think invented the term "constructive criticism." The combinations of your signs can be a great blessing. The Rooster is very dependable and detailed about hard work. He may question you on the whys and hows, but he truly is dedicated to making your wedding the best possible. While discussions may get heated, the result will be very positive and you can grow as a couple in the experience.

DOG HUSBAND AND RABBIT WIFE

The combination of the year of the Dog and the Rabbit sign is a very natural match. While you each have your quirks, they are complementary in many ways. Both of you are rooted in being fair, which will help make any difficult conversations more enjoyable and productive. Your more practical fiancé may occasionally sideline your love of luxury, but these are the compromises that will be hashed out on your journey to the big day. Fortunately, you each have your own interests and will give each other space when necessary.

BOAR HUSBAND AND RABBIT WIFE

Since the Boar and the Rabbit both share the same Affinity Triangle, your natural compatibility is very strong. Both of you enjoy the finer things in life, whether it is a wild night out or a luxurious dinner at the best restaurant. Your fiancé likes to show his love through indulging your desires. How lucky for you! You will enjoy making decisions and exploring your options together, with you taking the lead. However, with leadership comes the task of owning the budget, a responsibility that the Boar does not usually like to take on.

The Rabbit's Relationships with Friends and Family

Family and friends are an important part of most weddings. Since we all operate differently in our nonromantic relationships, the pairings of your Chinese zodiac sign will take a slightly different form. Knowing the compatibility of your animal sign with your family and friends is a real asset when planning and setting expectations for responsibilities. As you think about how best to integrate your vast network of friends, review the relationship overviews below. They will help cast light on your friends' and family members' strengths, weaknesses, and working styles.

WITH A RAT

The sign of the Rat brings a friend who will be very helpful with the minute details that you would not enjoy doing yourself. Harmonizer Brides are very good at coming up with the vision of something. However, imagination and execution are two different things. In addition to detailed tasks, this friend or family member can be depended on to handle money. In fact, like you, your friend has the ability to stretch a dollar until it practically cries out for mercy. Your struggles may lie in your approaches to communication. The Rat likes to be in constant contact, while sometimes you like to keep your distance.

WITH AN OX

While sometimes quiet, those born in the year of the Ox are some of the best people to assist in planning a wedding. The Ox's work ethic is well-known, and as long as you pay the proper respect and acknowledgment for this hard work, the road should be smooth. Your design choices may be a bit at odds with the Ox's sensible ways, so if this person is a parental figure or even a future in-law, take that into account. The Ox sign feels a sense of responsibility to guide people at times and will give advice with the best of intentions.

WITH A TIGER

What makes the Tiger such a fun and exciting friend is that she is an open book with her emotions. You can sit and people-watch, all the while knowing that the best observations will be from your friend the Tiger. The more devilish, the better. But where the Tiger lets her emotions run wild, the Rabbit likes to keep them wrapped up. The Harmonizer Bride will maintain the most harmony by avoiding heated discussions with the Tiger. If you know that you will disagree, it is best to sidestep the argument. You have a tendency to be thin-skinned, especially about precious moments like weddings.

Δ WITH ANOTHER RABBIT

Working together with a common sign is a great head start in many ways. You are drawn to similar styles and share the philosophy of keeping the peace. Since you are the bride, the chain of command should be fairly obvious to your friend or family member. However, if you are not confident about your direction, you should expect some suggestions from your elegant fellow Rabbit. Communication should flow easily, but disagreements throw you both for a loop. You avoid conflict, which sometimes works, but other times comes back to bite you. Air your feelings so you don't hold any grudges.

WITH A DRAGON

The Dragon and Rabbit can be a very synergistic combination, if you recognize that you approach life differently. The Dragon is a diehard competitor. Where you would call something a drag-out fight, she will just term it as a "discussion." With that in mind, don't ask for opinions on items you do not want to argue about. If you know you like the color purple and just want confirmation from a friend, avoid these topics with the Dragon. The Dragon is too honest a person to not give you her whole opinion. Another piece of advice is to give your Dragon friend lots of recognition for hard work, especially if she phoned in favors for your wedding. Like Rabbits, Dragons have long memories.

WITH A SNAKE

You will find that working with a Snake is pretty straightforward. Since Rabbits are fairly organized and have clear direction on how they like their environment, there will not be any vague subjects to cause problems. Snakes are grounded people who like to get their work done without much fuss. If you do not have close ties to this person, do not get your hopes up that the Snake will go above and beyond because it is your wedding. This sign is very practical, and without a close relationship, will not go the extra mile just for fun.

WITH A HORSE

The Horse and the Rabbit do not have the most compatible signs, but common ascendants can make the path smoother. While you two may not be the best work partners, it does not mean this person cannot peacefully help you with your wedding. Understand that you are a linear thinker and that like the majestic Horse, your friend sprints from thought to thought. Therefore, do not assign tasks that require a lot of detail. You are particular and the Horse may be too spontaneous for your tastes. To your advantage, the Horse can be very persuasive and may be able to negotiate some good deals, where you may be too timid.

Δ WITH A SHEEP

The Harmonizer Bride and people born in the year of the Sheep have good working chemistry because they share an Affinity Triangle relationship. In short, your approaches to life are very similar. You both like the finer things and will enjoy exploring all the beautiful luxuries of being a bride. Naturally, you may share complementary styles and find this friend a great sounding board when trying on dresses or creating the perfect centerpiece. Since the Sheep is too generous with her own finances, you will need to remain disciplined when shopping with this friend. She will always encourage you to buy.

WITH A MONKEY

The Rabbit and the Monkey have a lot in common, which can make for different challenges when planning a wedding together. The Harmonizer Bride can depend on the Monkey to offer up many creative ideas and be very quick with helpful tasks. However, there must be an established trust for more in-depth projects. The Monkey sign is often seen as being a little bit secretive, a quality that makes the

Rabbit's hair stand up in paranoia. If you are new to working together, understand that this is the Monkey's style and do not be afraid of questioning her. The Monkey is not afraid to communicate.

× WITH A ROOSTER

In the Chinese zodiac, the animals that are opposite each other have the most challenges in getting along. The Rooster and the Rabbit unfortunately tend to have this negative relationship. This does not need to be so for wedding planning. The Harmonizer Bride can avoid many challenges by understanding two key things with Rooster signs. The first is that they enjoy giving and getting criticism. Choose your battles, and you will be better off. The second is that the Rooster needs to be thanked and recognized for hard work, sometimes more than other people on the team. If you would like to tighten your future relationship with a Rooster, include her in a toast and lay it on thick.

WITH A DOG

Those born with the sign of the Dog are good team players. Since you are the bride, the chain of command is clear and your friend will not want to rock the boat. If you ask for help, you will get it from this person. While the Dog is not inclined to criticize, she will speak up when a problem is on the horizon. This is a great asset to you, since the Harmonizer Bride may favor shortcuts over tedious work. It may seem easier to turn a blind eye, but it would be wise to not ignore this friend because the sign of the Dog always has the best of intentions.

Δ WITH A BOAR

The Boar and the Rabbit share the same Affinity Triangle in the Chinese zodiac, which ensures easy communication and a natural friendship. Like you, the Boar enjoys a good party. You both like to indulge in all life has to offer and can be a great team. This friend may be one of your best candidates for a maid of honor or bridesmaid. Since you have a natural rapport, constant communication will be more fun than taxing. Also, since the Boar is a great communicator, she can spread the word to other bridesmaids and guests very easily and with a little bit of flair.

Ten

BORN IN THE YEAR OF THE DRAGON
Here Comes the Visionary Bride

Lunar Years of the Dragon	Elements
February 8, 1940, to January 26, 1941	Metal
January 27, 1952, to February 13, 1953	Water
February 13, 1964, to February 1, 1965	Wood
January 31, 1976, to February 17, 1977	Fire
February 17, 1988, to February 5, 1989	Earth
February 5, 2000, to January 23, 2001	Metal

Visionary Bride Details

Birth Hours: 7 A.M. to 9 A.M.

Western Sign: Aries

Western Gemstone: Diamond

Symbolic Color: Green

Flower: Jasmine

Season: Spring

Element: Wood

Famous Visionary Brides:

Courteney Cox Arquette, Shirley Temple Black, Julie Christie, Betty Grable, Marlene Dietrich, Isabella Rossellini, Amy Tan, Mae West.

The Dress:

Your wedding dress will reflect your practical approach to life. Clean lines with comfortable fabrics are the natural choice. You'll say no thanks to the glitter and gemstones and opt for a straightforward gown, and if it's something you could wear again in the future, even better.

The Dragon Sign: The Fifth Bride of the Chinese Zodiac

The fifth sign of the zodiac, the Dragon is a big dreamer. She is a part of what we refer to as the Doers group. There are four groups: the Doers, the Thinkers, the Protectors, and the Catalysts. The groups are made up of the three animals that have a natural affinity to one another, referred to as a Triangle of Affinity. Each set of three animals has a social connection—a kind of chemistry that is connected to each zodiac sign.

The Doers group is made up of the Rat, the Monkey, and the Dragon. No surprise, people with these birth signs or ascendants are your most natural friends and working partners. In fact, it's likely your fiancé has strong ties to this group as well. As their team name suggests, these ladies don't like to stand still—they are the ones who make things happen. Those born in the year of the Dragon have the mantra "I see." She is the bride voted most likely to set the highest standards. Here comes the Visionary Bride.

The Visionary Bride—Born in the Year of the Dragon

Blessed with great aspirations, you are a no-nonsense type of bride. Whether you have had your perfect wedding planned since childhood or are only starting to bring together your wedding concept, you will aim for the sky. Many Dragons are admirers of the outdoors, and one wonders if Mother Nature was a lady Dragon herself, grandly envisioning soaring mountains and powerful oceans. Ambition is the name of the game with you, and if your fiancé sighs at the thought or expense of your wedding musings, you can smile and assure him that he will never find your marriage boring. As you may already know, the Dragon is a symbol of strength and power in the Chinese culture, even representing the masculine side of a couple. The lady Dragon has every last ounce of the energy and willpower that made the Dragon sign famous. Your practical nature and passion for getting the job done well ensure that you will make your wedding dreams come true.

The Visionary Bride delights in the VIP status of being a bride. Most women find it fun, having others ooh and aah over the ring and find out you have gone from girlfriend to fiancé, but the sign of the Dragon puts a slightly different spin on it. You see the role of bride as leader. As the boss of a very important job, you expect anyone who will be a part of your big day to respect that you are the chief decision maker. It's very natural for you to get your way, and when you don't, there is hell to pay. All women must guard against the threat of bridezilla, and you should be especially careful not to fall into this unattractive territory. When you fall in love with an idea, you can become practically obsessed. Some may try to negotiate, but only a chosen few may even get your ear when you have your mind set on something. Not to mention you are competitive and can relish telling people what to do. It can be tough for you to acknowledge that compromise, love it or hate it, is a necessary ingredient in any successful marriage and wedding plan.

Your leadership qualities are second to none in the Chinese zodiac department. In addition to good strategy and vision, you have two great qualities in your bride tool belt—a thick skin and grace under pressure. Some women can fall over with the amount of stress they feel from planning a wedding. There is so much change, after all, and everyone is looking to you for answers. Well, the Visionary Bride always steps up to the challenge and does not shy away from getting honest feedback. Now, just because you take criticism doesn't mean you always like it. In fact, you have no problem pulling off the gloves to fight for what you believe in. But the benefit of always having the door open is that people will be honest with you and get things out in the open. You are a big fan of getting your feelings out, which is one of your biggest stress relievers. Your fiancé and friends will always get an earful of what's on your mind. You just hate how that elusive photographer keeps dodging you. And that amazing hairstylist you want is just so flaky. But while you may complain, you are not asking for someone else to sort things out for you. You are more than capable of fixing the problem. You just like to include some colorful commentary.

As a strong individual, the Dragon sign has to be especially confident about her future spouse in order to give up all the freedoms of the single life. You have cultivated a life of friends and work that you are proud of and could very happily exist on your own. But the love bug has bitten, and you are ready to share your life with someone who undeniably attracts you. He is fortunate to be partnering with a woman who knows how to take care of business and shoots from the hip. While you are a person of deep feelings and love, you are not the most romantic of the animal signs. Poetry and flowers are nice and all, but you are a person of action and respect the same qualities in your future husband. Dragon women think that it is better to get something you need than something you want.

The Visionary Bride is known for her honesty and vibrant personality. Your challenge will be to adjust the strength of your communication with all the different people you will be interacting with during the wedding. It may surprise some people that you can actually be quite naive when dealing with new people. You are an open book and assume that others give you the same courtesy, but unfortunately, some people play by different rules. Do not be hesitant to lean on your fiancé or friends when something smells fishy. A second opinion never hurt anyone! Another piece of advice when interacting with friends and strangers alike—don't forget your manners. You are probably not a fan of flowery talk, but trust us when we tell you that cultivating relationships should not be approached with a goal to be efficient. This goes against your practical programming, but open yourself up to some of the pleasantries of small talk and perhaps even some ego petting. You like to skip over these pesky pieces of etiquette, including apologies big and small. Remember that being a bride is a limited-time privilege for special treatment. Avoid any future problems and rack up the brownie points by going to the extra effort of acknowledging everyone for good deeds and kindness.

East Meets West: When Moon Signs Meet Sun Signs

Many people don't realize that each animal of the Chinese zodiac has a solar calendar connection. In our interpretation of Chinese horoscopes, the lunar calendar links into the solar calendar through the month and season, where the Dragon's parallel sun sign is Aries. But every Western sun sign has a different effect on the lunar moon sign.

THE SAGITTARIUS DRAGON
Sagittarius: November 22 to December 21

True to your native sign of the Dragon, you are a doer who would rather communicate through action than through words. The influence of Sagittarius makes you a particularly direct person, which means that you must be mindful of what you say. Lots of social interactions come about as the result of weddings. Whether it's an engagement party or a mini-celebration on short notice, you will be making all sorts of first impressions. Your warm and charming nature will make most of these meetings fun and enjoyable. However, even the most popular girl rubs some people the wrong way. You can be very opinionated when some people do not have the strongest stomach for criticism. Should the spirit sway you to be more honest than kind, take a moment's pause.

THE CAPRICORN DRAGON

Capricorn: December 22 to January 20

The Capricorn Visionary Bride combination is a recipe for a good general. You have the discipline, strong work ethic, and mind for strategy to get the most detailed of weddings accomplished with your small army. The Dragon is an exceptionally powerful sign, a symbol of strength and energy, but your expectations of others are too often the same as your expectations for yourself. The Visionary Bride's plans are the very definition of reaching goals. Remember to take a deep breath every once in a while because all your intricate plans can be taxing, not just for you but for your friends and family. You don't want your mother to cry out for mercy as you try on that hundredth wedding dress on a supposed short visit or have your fiancé collapse during a jam-packed agenda of florists and stationers. Rome wasn't built in a day and neither will your wedding be—not everyone has the Dragon's stamina.

THE AQUARIUS DRAGON

Aquarius: January 21 to February 19

Your role as a Visionary Bride is enhanced by the influence of Aquarius. The mixture of these two signs offers you an ability to focus in on what you want as well as the leadership skills to actually make it happen. Your wedding planning will have its share of stops and starts. You like to constantly improve on your work, always looking around for new and better ways to approach things. Therefore, you may change your mind quite suddenly or even choose a path that is very unconventional. Aquarius will help you be a gentler communicator than some of your Dragon sisters by connecting you with a diverse group of people. This is a blessing because there are always a few awkward moments associated with weddings, and they are rarely helped by poorly chosen words.

THE PISCES DRAGON

Pisces: February 20 to March 20

The sign of Pisces is a positive influence on the Visionary Bride. The Dragon makes your Pisces side feel like a big fish in a small pond and encourages your trailblazing spirit to come out to play. As a result, you have a well-balanced set of emotions, particularly when dealing with setbacks. The term "dragon lady" didn't come about without a small grain of truth to the legend. The sign of the Dragon does not bottle up her emotions; she lets them flow freely as a force of nature. The influence of the Pisces water sign encourages more restraint during those difficult moments. These moments of pause will give your fiancé or other close friends the opportunity to console you, which you crave but so often fight off.

THE ARIES DRAGON
Aries: March 21 to April 19

Blessed with natural charisma and megawatt star power, you are the Aries Dragon. One of your most attractive qualities emanates from your positive approach to life. If you have the will, you will accomplish your task. With all your past success, you have lots of confidence, and this may stray into overly ambitious projects. *You* have no fear of big projects, but your husband-to-be or family may be less sure of themselves. Do not react too forcefully when questioned about why you are choosing to bead your wedding dress yourself or make your wedding invitations by hand. You may see their words as an attack, when your loved ones are actually offering help or want to share their ideas. When stressed, you sometimes jump to negative conclusions and need to look before you leap.

THE TAURUS DRAGON
Taurus: April 20 to May 20

The work ethic of an Ox and the magnetic personality of the Dragon intertwine within this Visionary Bride. You are a very methodical person who likes to practice the old adage of measuring twice and cutting once. Some of your loved ones, perhaps even your fiancé, may not understand your process for everything and may mistakenly encourage you to hurry up and be more decisive. What they forget is that your thoughtfulness almost always pays off. Trust in your instincts, but put forth more effort in communicating your thoughts to others. When lost in your own head, you can shut out the world and become quite curt. Don't be so practical that you don't make time to shoot the breeze and gush a little about all the emotions you are feeling about your big day.

THE GEMINI DRAGON
Gemini: May 21 to June 21

If you can believe it, you are the type of bride who has even more energy than the average Dragon. The influence of the Gemini twins encourages you to be very hands-on with your ideas. When you are out and about, you don't just go shopping for things, you go shopping for ideas. Your inner craft goddess will come out and inspire you to create some beautiful things, helping you save money in the process. Be especially careful with taking on projects that are too intricate without the help of someone with more experience or an eye for detail. Both the Dragon and Gemini are so action-focused that they rush through the details on the way to the finish line. Remember to leave enough time to buy backup items if your experiment turns out to be a dud, or avoid projects that are just too ambitious.

THE CANCERIAN DRAGON
Cancer: June 22 to July 21

The natural force of the Dragon is tempered by the influence of the moon. Your demeanor is always pleasant, even regal, so everyone will have a good time at your wedding. You are an especially thoughtful bride who will take her time making decisions. Your fiancé and family can rest assured that your decisions are lasting ones. While you have a positive outlook on life, once you have passed judgment on someone, it will be hard to reverse. As a result, your fiancé may struggle to convince you to invite some of your past friends or family members that you would rather not be a part of the celebration. He may very well succeed in getting you to change your mind about invitations or even seating arrangements, but changing a Cancerian Dragon's mind is a process, not a discussion.

THE LEO DRAGON
Leo: July 22 to August 21

Both of your signs are strong, making the Dragon personality even more of a force to be reckoned with. You are blessed with the power of persuasion, which will help you get fair deals and some favors along the way. The influence of Leo's nobility also makes you an especially lucky bride, smoothing the way for your wedding planning and marriage. With all these gifts, you may find that you become a little too used to getting what you want all the time. In fact, others should beware when they break your lucky streak because you will fight to get your way. Fortunately, you aren't one to hold any grudges. Like most Dragons, you are honest and make your emotions known. Your generosity to others comes from your big heart and you will show it through helping others be a part of your wedding by taking care of a cousin's bridesmaid's dress or looking for small local vendors to support.

THE VIRGO DRAGON
Virgo: August 22 to September 22

A Virgo Dragon is an especially ambitious Visionary Bride. One of your passions in life is learning and constantly improving yourself. Combine these pursuits with your never-say-die work ethic, and you are a force that cannot be stopped. Whether you sign up for the ultimate bridal boot camp to shave off those last few pounds or literally decide to bake and decorate your wedding cake yourself, your fiancé and perhaps some of your friends will be struck with shock and awe. Surely there are easier ways to go about things, but anyone who says that to you does not know you very well. You enjoy the pursuit of knowledge and perfection. Be sure to not take on too many new adventures during the planning process. Your fiancé may actually want to see you during your engagement.

THE LIBRA DRAGON
Libra: September 23 to October 22

The Visionary Bride gets a dose of calm with the influence of Libra. Your Dragon temper is eased by this sun sign, which encourages you to prevent heated discussions from accelerating into arguments. This certainly will make wedding planning easier on your loved ones, especially your fiancé. Your honest nature is one of your most attractive features, but it can stray into naïveté. Since you will be meeting lots of new people, be sure to choose your words carefully, so as to make the best first impression. The truth has the nasty habit of jumping out of your mouth before you have thought about how it can be interpreted. Another word of advice is to not procrastinate. Your Libra leanings may weaken your Dragon will to nail down all the particulars, causing unnecessary heartache.

THE SCORPIO DRAGON

Scorpio: October 23 to November 21

The Visionary Bride already is known for focus and strong willpower. The sign of Scorpio serves as further enhancement of your already strong personality. You exude confidence in your actions as well as your speech. Taking the leadership role will be very natural, especially since you will be communicating your wishes for the perfect wedding day. No one will have to twist your arm to get your true feelings about anything. Your vibrant personality can manifest itself in the highest of highs and the lowest of lows. Since you can be drawn to extremes, you should be especially mindful of how you take care of your health and your pocket book. Don't overindulge at the bar too close to your engagement pictures and don't make big purchases when emotional.

Wedding Synergy: When Dragon Meets Phoenix

As you embark on your planning, check out the Wedding Relationship pairings below to see how your strengths and weaknesses come together during the planning process. These compatibility descriptions are based on year of birth combinations, which is the tip of the iceberg when it comes to each of your charts. As described in Chapter 2 "Reference Dates and Tables on the Chinese Zodiac, East-West Sign Combinations, and Animal Hours," a different animal governs each of the four time components of your birth date and time.

RAT HUSBAND AND DRAGON WIFE

Because you both come from the same Affinity Triangle of Doers, you two work fairly well on projects together. You are both people of action and can respect each other's strengths, trusting each other to do his or her part. In other words, you do not have to be joined at the hip to get every part of the wedding planned. But if there is a person who has the tendency to try to take over the show, it will be the Visionary Bride herself. Your fiancé's sign is no slacker, so be careful with your tone when giving reminders. You can count on him to always get the job done.

OX HUSBAND AND DRAGON WIFE

Yours is an attraction of opposites. The Ox serves as the backbone of this relationship. Where your Dragon heart may encourage you to sometimes take a chance on a new adventure, your fiancé always likes to investigate before pulling the trigger. By now you have discovered and come to appreciate how your differences can bring good balance to your relationship. You may have to strong-arm your man out onto the dance floor, but he likes being pushed into new territory every once in a while. Be careful not to push for too much change too quickly. After all, getting married is a big transition in itself. Oftentimes the Ox has to do things on his own schedule to feel most comfortable.

TIGER HUSBAND AND DRAGON WIFE

Both of your signs have lots of energy that will aid you in being creative with your big day. Much of this stems from your great chemistry. With such strong personalities, it's difficult to say who will lead all the big plans. This obviously can create a few problems. After all, if both of you are brainstorming, who is going to handle the actual *doing*? It might be wise to employ a professional who is good at gathering the details and tying everything up with a nice bow. Having a third party can also alleviate any power struggles that may occur between the two of you. Both the Tiger and the Dragon like to have control, which can create battles when compromise is necessary.

RABBIT HUSBAND AND DRAGON WIFE

Harmony and vision come together with your engagement, resulting in a very happy working relationship for planning for your wedding. The sign of the Dragon is one of strength and energy, which makes you a very positive bride. You will be very ambitious with your goals, and your fiancé will be a great person to bounce ideas off. Your husband-to-be is blessed with the Rabbit's sense of good taste and prudent thought process. He will challenge you in a positive way that helps you two grow as a couple. He will be especially thoughtful about who to invite and how to seat them, so go with his advice.

DRAGON HUSBAND AND DRAGON WIFE

Pairing two Dragons on a work project is like casting two stars in a show and asking them to share top billing. It'll take some work. Both of you are strong individuals who like to lead and love to win. Planning a wedding means balancing the desires of the couple, often keeping family members and other important people in mind. Therefore, you need to have frank discussions/arguments early on to decide who is in charge. Perhaps you want to delegate the responsibilities to a professional wedding planner or agree that the bride is truly queen bee. Making the leader clear from the get-go is imperative to a smooth wedding planning process with two Dragons.

SNAKE HUSBAND AND DRAGON WIFE

As the Visionary Bride, you like to imagine and share your thoughts with your fiancé. He will be a good listener, but may not always engage you in the kind of discussions passionate Visionary Brides like to have. Does he prefer purple or blue? Should you serve cupcakes or do the traditional wedding cake? Don't be surprised if he says "whatever you want" or seems lackluster about his preferences. You two are a good balancing force, but you should be aware of when your inner Dragon wants to engage in lively debate—that might be a good time to meet with a more opinionated friend.

HORSE HUSBAND AND DRAGON WIFE

You and your fiancé hold common ground in a great energy for life. Unlikely to be homebodies, you like to explore uncharted territory together. Well, marriage is the ultimate journey, isn't it? On this trip, understand that your husband-to-be expects you to be taking the lead as navigator. Your passion for your wedding will encourage you to stay organized and keep both of you on track. He will be happy to help and be a companion to you. However, the Horse sign is not known for loving the details, so be realistic about his short attention span.

SHEEP HUSBAND AND DRAGON WIFE

Your husband-to-be is born under one of the kindest, most encouraging personalities. He is most assuredly drawn to your passion for life and will admire how you embrace wedding planning with both arms. But challenges may occur when it comes to how daring your wedding wishes are. Your fiancé will want to indulge his beautiful bride, but too much change all at once can make him paranoid. Understand that marriage is like any adventure, exciting but scary. He may still be easing into all the things that come with it.

MONKEY HUSBAND AND DRAGON WIFE

Your union is one that comes out of the Doers Affinity Triangle. This is a wonderful thing because it means that you both have similar sensibilities when it comes to approaching big projects like wedding planning. Your role as a Visionary Bride enables you to energize all the tasks that need to be accomplished to make your big day a success. He will partner with you in coming up with creative ways to make your wedding special or negotiate challenges out of the way. With this kind of partnership, you feel you can tackle anything. Just make sure you don't get too ambitious for your time or budget.

ROOSTER HUSBAND AND DRAGON WIFE

The sign of the Rooster gave you a fiancé who can match your level of energy and who approaches life with a similar desire for constant improvement. This is in most ways a blessing. Roosters make great budget managers because they have a natural eye for the details. He is not afraid of having you be the lead decision maker, but he will always want to give his two cents about your big day. If he feels that he is not treated like an equal, it will certainly ruffle his feathers. Good communication will help you avoid a lot of rehashing of details.

DOG HUSBAND AND DRAGON WIFE

The pairing of a Dog and a Dragon can be harmonious, but without compromise, it can be a series of highs and lows. You will find that your Dragon tenacity makes it more difficult to give up a battle or two, but try to remember that compromise has to come from both sides. Take the often contentious invite list. He may suggest splitting the number in half, allotting an equal number of guests to each of you, seeing it as a fair and equitable solution. You may negotiate for more because things are not so black and white. Try to approach big decisions diplomatically, and your fiancé will be more inclined to cooperate. If you push too hard, he can unbottle his anger in a way you are not used to.

BOAR HUSBAND AND DRAGON WIFE

Your two signs share a passion for life that when combined can be almost dangerous. The Visionary Bride's wedding wishes can flirt with the overly optimistic at times. The blessing and cautionary advice comes from your fiancé's tendency to indulge your every desire. Of course, you love to get what you want, but his love of spoiling you can get out of hand. Whether it's throwing you off your diet plan or wedding impulse buys here and there, you two can support each other in some expensive decisions. The sign of the Boar loves to indulge in life, so don't look for him to be the brakes in this relationship.

The Dragon's Relationships with Friends and Family

Family and friends are an important part of most weddings. Since we all operate differently in our nonromantic relationships, the pairings of your Chinese zodiac sign will take a slightly different form. Knowing the compatibility of your animal sign with your family and friends is a real asset when planning and setting expectations for responsibilities. As you think about how best to integrate your vast network of friends, review the relationship overviews below. They will help cast light on your friends' and family members' strengths, weaknesses, and working styles.

Δ WITH A RAT

The Dragon has a real friend in a person born under the Rat sign. Because the Dragon and the Rat are part of the same Affinity Triangle, you have a natural connection, which makes work and play very easy for you two. Not only is this person dependable and creative, the Rat will be a good source of support for your wedding endeavors. You can happily chat about your wedding's trials and tribulations while multitasking with a craft project or working off those pesky few pounds.

WITH AN OX

Idealism and realism come together when you pair an Ox with a Dragon. You have a natural ability to lead a project well, and the Ox will carry out your wishes to the best of her ability. If you are still getting to know each other, take this opportunity to start your relationship off on the right foot. The Ox may offer some guidance, always with the desire to make things better, even though your ego can mistake it for pure criticism. Respond with polite honesty if you disagree. Neither of you will back down from a fight, so it's best to be careful when your Dragon temper cannot be kept at bay.

WITH A TIGER

You and the Tiger can become fast friends, or perhaps you already are. Both of you are strong, independent individuals who have sure footing in your ambitions. This friend will be instrumental in helping tame your highly ambitious nature. She is also a good candidate for taking on the duty of communication and negotiation. The sign of the Tiger makes an excellent negotiator. In the end, whether this person's contribution to your wedding was big or small, be sure to give plenty of praise to keep both of you happy.

WITH A RABBIT

While the influence of the Dragon gifts you with great vision and good leadership, it never hurts to hear new ideas and opinions. The Rabbit is an ideal person to ask for a fresh perspective. With her great sense of style and innate sense of etiquette, this person may spark new ideas or steer you away from trouble. Some Rabbits may be too timid for Dragons, but while they prefer to act behind the scenes, they are known to give good advice. This sign tends to be very traditional, so a hand-written thank-you note will be seen as a thoughtful touch of class.

Δ WITH ANOTHER DRAGON

Double the Dragons can mean double the fun . . . or double the trouble. Your mutual signs respond to clear leadership, so be clear about what kind of help you want and be specific, especially if you have never worked on something as intricate and emotional as a wedding. Fortunately, the sign of the Dragon encourages you to be honest with your feelings, so if you are not able to work as a team, you should figure it out early and be able to adjust or respectfully decline this person's help, for the sake of long-term harmony.

WITH A SNAKE

There is an air of mystery to working with a person born under the Snake sign. If this person is close to you, the Snake will be more open and you will have the tools to interpret the Snake's sometimes secretive ways. However, if you are meeting this person as a result of the wedding, do not be put off by the Snake's vague communication style. This person is more contemplative than you are, resulting in a friend who is quiet, but extremely dependable. She will always exercise good caution when confronted with risks and will probably advise you to do the same.

WITH A HORSE

You and the Horse should have a good working relationship. Both of your zodiac signs are known for being good at communicating feelings, which is the key to preventing many of the worst wedding arguments. If you already have an established relationship, think about how competitive this Horse native has been in the past with you. Arguments may spring out of your shared passion for winning. Fortunately, you both do not harbor grudges, and once settled, disagreements should stay in the past.

WITH A SHEEP

The Sheep's supportive nature can be a comforting asset as you go through the ups and downs of a wedding. As the Visionary Bride, your strengths lie in being a strong leader. Sheep natives are not typically known for being strong initiators, so this person will look to you for direction. Be careful not to overload the Sheep native with especially detailed tasks, because this type of work does not come naturally to them and will require more time and effort on your part. Your personality will most likely be stronger than the Sheep's, so use a gentle approach, especially when you see her pull back from activities.

Δ WITH A MONKEY

The Dragon and the Monkey share the same Affinity Triangle of Doers. Therefore, this pairing has the advantage of a complementary perspective to teamwork. The Monkey sign is known for being a creative problem solver. You can benefit listening to the Monkey's tips and tricks, especially if this is a gal who has planned her own wedding. She will have already discovered some hidden gems around town and can apply her negotiation skills to your wedding endeavors.

WITH A ROOSTER

Bringing a Rooster native into wedding planning is almost always a good idea. You will find working with this person to be refreshing because you share a similar liking of getting things done. In addition, you will be impressed with the Rooster sign's eye for detail. Whether it is putting together wedding favors, proofing your invitations, or reviewing the bill, the Rooster is extremely thorough and strives for things to be fair and equal.

× WITH A DOG

When you look at the Chinese zodiac, you will find that the Dragon is directly across from the Dog. This opposite placement is your hint that your two signs need to work harder to get along, especially if you lack a common ascendant to smooth the relationship. The Dog has a strong desire to be honest, but often isn't as sympathetic as other signs to your ego, which can cause some personality clashes. You might want to downplay the kind of help you ask for to preserve good relations between the two of you. There isn't a concern with the work getting done, but with managing your feelings when working with a Dog.

WITH A BOAR

The Visionary Bride will find fun when working with a native of the Boar sign. Dragons and Boars are naturally happy people who like to enjoy the big and small pleasures of life. Communication should flow freely since you are both honest and can shoulder criticism maturely. However, beware of enlisting the Boar's carpe diem attitude when it comes to spending money or blowing off steam downtown. You know that little voice that always tells you, "Go ahead, you're worth it"? It was most likely born in the year of the Boar.

Eleven

BORN IN THE YEAR OF THE SNAKE
Here Comes the Strategist Bride

Lunar Years of the Snake	Elements
January 27, 1941, to February 14, 1942	Metal
February 14, 1953, to February 2, 1954	Water
February 2, 1965, to January 20, 1966	Wood
February 18, 1977, to February 6, 1978	Fire
February 6, 1989, to January 26, 1990	Earth
January 24, 2001, to February 11, 2002	Metal

Strategist Bride Details

Birth Hours: 9 A.M. to 11 A.M.

Western Sign: Taurus

Western Gemstone: Emerald

Symbolic Color: Red

Flower: Gardenia

Season: Summer

Element: Fire

Famous Strategist Brides:

Indira Gandhi, Greta Garbo, Audrey Hepburn, Grace Kelly, Ann-Margret, Jacqueline Kennedy Onassis, Virginia Woolf.

The Dress:

The Strategist Bride favors the classics. She is drawn to the beauty of the best fabrics, imagining them flowing behind her as she makes her entrance. Her exquisite taste naturally extends to jewelry. Of course, she'll prefer to wear the very best. She'll save up, borrow, or rent her dream look.

The Snake: The Sixth Bride of the Chinese Zodiac

As the sixth sign of the zodiac, the Snake is a deep and introspective soul. She is a part of what we refer to as the Thinkers group. There are four groups: the Doers, the Thinkers, the Protectors, and the Catalysts. The groups are made up of the three animals that have a natural affinity to one another, referred to as a Triangle

of Affinity. Each set of three animals has a social connection—a kind of chemistry that is connected to each zodiac sign.

The Thinkers group is made up of the Ox, the Snake, and the Rooster. No surprise, people with these birth signs or ascendants are your most natural friends and working partners. In fact, it's likely your fiancé has strong ties to this group as well. As their team name suggests, these ladies are never ones to procrastinate. They are deep thinkers and planners who enjoy mapping out tasks, putting them on the calendar, and crossing off each one. One of their great strengths is that they do things from start to finish. They not only create a vision, but also put it in place. Those born in the year of the Snake have the mantra "I plan." She is the bride voted most likely to keep her wedding details a secret for a grand entrance. Here comes the Strategist Bride.

The Strategist Bride—Born in the Year of the Snake

What happens when the most mysterious woman of the Chinese zodiac decides to get married? You get sophistication, elegance, and a few closely guarded surprises. As the Strategist Bride, you are confident in making your own decisions. By and large you don't make a habit of soliciting other people's opinions and you do not like people trying to impose their advice on you. Whether you have a lot of knowledge about weddings or you are starting from ground zero, instinct will be your wedding compass. You like to do things your way, and your gut feelings are typically right on the money.

One of the most famous Strategist Brides is the one and only Grace Kelly, Princess of Monaco. Since the Strategist Bride is a symbol of class and femininity, it's not uncommon for her to waltz into the bridal shop and tell her consultant that she wants a fairy-tale look. The Snake is the ultimate representative of the female. Refined and picture perfect, the Snake knows how to keep up the appearance of confidence that also casts a spell of mystery. The Snake sign actually has a reputation for producing some of the most attractive people. How do they do it? It's not that everyone wins the genetic lottery. As your wedding moniker suggests, you know how to create the best strategy for you. The most beautiful things have an almost magnetic attraction to you, and you'll be able to spot the investment pieces easily (much to the disappointment of your fiancé at times). Your keen sense of style also comes from an enviable amount of patience. Just as the Snake so coolly can wait and surround her prey, the Strategist Bride knows what she wants and will wait for the perfect opportunity to strike.

As a member of the Thinkers group, you are, no surprise, very thoughtful. Not one to be rushed, you are known for liking your alone time. Whether with a good book, favorite playlist, or a journal, when you are contemplating a big decision, you collect your thoughts and reconnect with your instincts. With such a sharp mind, most aspects of wedding planning will be easy for you. Your sense of style will dictate a high level of finish. You'll identify what you want very quickly and will rarely if ever change your mind once you have set something in motion. As a result, your wedding plans will materialize quickly. The Snake woman is incredibly observant and, therefore, a fast learner. Think back to the most recent wedding you've been to, for example. Whether you were the maid of honor or a plus-one, you caught all the successes and pitfalls of the event. Was the caterer a dream, while the centerpieces were a scream? You'll note down all the little details in your wedding book, and take those lessons to refine your own plans. That's just one of those clever tricks that the Strategist Bride is known for.

Although your tastes are refined, you are extremely practical. Having good taste doesn't mean that you have to break the bank every time. The Strategist Bride does her best to use money as a tool, rather than being controlled by her finances. Perhaps you've set your sights on a Vera Wang gown or a cinematic wedding on Lake Como. Perhaps you'll rent the gown or pool together frequent flyer miles to save on travel to your Italian dreamscape. Either way, you don't like taking no for an answer, so it's a good thing you are not afraid of putting in the legwork to make your plans materialize. You are not one to compromise your dreams, so you will get creative, and it would be wise for any naysayers to get out of your way. Your fiancé may throw his hands up into the air when hearing of your next ambitious task. But he won't be surprised when you prove him wrong because you've done it many times before. You like the thrill of a good challenge, the bigger the better. However, woe be the day you don't get what you want. You're not the most graceful loser and you're known for holding your grudges to the grave.

The sign of the Snake is an enigma indeed, especially when it comes to the art of communication. You have a wicked sense of humor and can be quite the femme fatale. At your core, you are a skilled negotiator. You are a master of getting what you want, and you believe one of the keys to success is to keep a few details to yourself, just in case you go into another round of discussions. This is a fine adversarial strategy, but it often affects your regular day-to-day communication. Your competitive nature can close you off from people who have the best of intentions. While you are a great networker, not to mention flirt, think about how these are relationships that usually just scratch the surface. Perhaps, you take comfort in knowing these interactions are often fleeting. Now that you are a bride, you are meeting people who are going to be a part of your relationship as a couple. Your challenge will be to open yourself up and share more. While you take great pains to keep up appearances, you can still be elegant in asking people for help and even venting about the stress of putting the whole wedding together.

East Meets West: When Moon Signs Meet Sun Signs

Many people don't realize that each animal of the Chinese zodiac has a solar calendar connection. In our interpretation of Chinese horoscopes, the lunar calendar links into the solar calendar through the month and season, where the Snake's parallel sun sign is Taurus. But every Western sun sign has a different effect on the lunar moon sign.

THE SAGITTARIUS SNAKE

Sagittarius: November 22 to December 21

The influence of Sagittarius calms the occasionally high-strung Strategic Bride. Its little voice encourages you to stop and smell the roses every once in a while. This more casual approach to life has opened you up to more experience in your life, which your love of variety reflects. Whether you travel by plane or through great literature, you appreciate the many definitions of beauty. You may be drawn to the idea of including a fusion of style and cultures in your wedding, integrating new foods and maybe even foreign traditions into your nuptials. With the Strategist Bride's designer eye, you can weave together a diverse collection of things into a cohesive theme. The sign of the Snake will always steer you toward a more refined look. Like your Snake sisters, you are ambitious and drawn to the most exciting challenges. However, you must temper the temptation to procrastinate that Sagittarius brings.

THE CAPRICORN SNAKE

Capricorn: December 22 to January 20

The combination of Capricorn and the sign of the Snake makes you an especially private person. You possess a quiet confidence in yourself. While some brides may like one thing today and another tomorrow, you sign your contracts in indelible ink. When you've made a decision, you stick with it. In fact, you've probably been like this since you were a child, making a small group of friends that you will stick to for life. It takes a long time for someone to win your trust. So you are especially cautious when meeting new people. You may cringe at the number of people you have to interact with at all the customary wedding gatherings, both from your fiancé's side and from your own. You shun small talk and may even have the desire to duck away at times for the comfort of solitary confinement. Be open with your fiancé about when you are feeling antisocial. First impressions are so important and so is your peace of mind. He'll be understanding about party overload and may secretly feel the same.

THE AQUARIUS SNAKE

Aquarius: January 21 to February 19

The Aquarius sun sign shines a positive outlook on the buttoned-up Strategist Bride. Being born in the year of the Snake, you are a Thinker, finding enjoyment in the process of introspection. While other Strategist Brides may keep their thoughts to themselves, the Aquarius Snake likes to share her opinions with others. In fact, the idea of bottling it up may drive you insane. With that in mind, it'll be very important to speak frankly with your fiancé about any topic that may awaken your nasty jealous streak. Let's face it: you don't have the poker face that most Snake natives have. If your fiancé wants to invite an ex-girlfriend to the wedding, and you just don't trust her, speak your feelings, calmly and rationally. If you suspect that your life-of-the-party best man is going to throw a bachelor party in especially poor taste, you can certainly express your disapproval. Don't try to pretend that nothing bothers you, when it does. After all, people typically cater to the wishes of the bride.

THE PISCES SNAKE
Pisces: February 20 to March 20

The presence of Pisces makes you more approachable than the typical Snake fatale. With a generous nature and positive outlook, you will look at your wedding with great emotion. Tears of joy may spring forth from the mere sight of your family and friends together in one room. You'll present yourself and your fiancé with the best of manners and do your best to make everyone comfortable. However, you're never completely at ease. Both Pisces and the Snake sign are unsettlingly observant. You see both the good and the bad, and with a memory like a steel trap, you don't have the benefit of pretending to forget the details. Your fiancé may have to console you many times during the course of your engagement. A friend's broken promise or a poorly chosen wedding gift can rub you the wrong way. You may have to toughen up your thin skin for the many personalities you will be dealing with. Remember that most people do not put the same care as you into their actions.

THE ARIES SNAKE
Aries: March 21 to April 19

Strategy and execution are the result when Aries merges with the sign of the Snake. The Strategist Bride's instincts help you create clear wedding plans, and Aries gives you a voice to lead. You have no problem delegating your wishes to people you trust and can be very critical if it does not meet your high standards. But be careful with your words. Just like your razor-sharp wit, your words of criticism can rub a gentler soul the wrong way, especially those you are just getting to know. Anyone who knows you understands that you can take what you dish out. You are a very independent person and pride yourself on your ability to take the lead. However, even though you're all business most of the time, Aries encourages you to go out some nights and blow off some steam.

THE TAURUS SNAKE

Taurus: April 20 to May 20

The signs of Taurus and Snake are good complements for each other. The Strategist Bride has strong instincts and creates plans that are thoughtful and elegant. The contributions of Taurus help settle the chaos that can sometimes exist beneath the seemingly perfect surface. When things are not going well, a Snake has a tendency to hide the imperfections and worry that someone may find out that you don't have it all together. The sign of Taurus may help you out of some of these predicaments with the aid of thorough discipline. Taurus Snakes are less likely to worry than other Snakes because when you have taken the time to check and recheck your work, you can calm down, knowing that you have done all that you can. After all, mistakes are a fact of life. Taurus Snakes don't second-guess themselves because they understand that even the best plans encounter a snag or two.

THE GEMINI SNAKE

Gemini: May 21 to June 21

The Gemini twins are known for being creative because they have an intimate connection to their imaginations. Their influence in the Strategist Bride may lie deep beneath the surface, where more of the Snake's tantalizing secrets also dwell. You may show different sides of your personality based on the occasion and environment, but you always exhibit poise and tact. The Gemini Snake combination makes you more openly social than other Snakes. You have the ability to connect with new people, sometimes even finding social gatherings energizing. No surprise, you are known to be more daring than some other Strategist Brides. Who knows what adventures you've been on and want for the future? It's anyone's guess because you do like to keep secrets to yourself. However, it'd be wise to stay cautious in the months leading up to your wedding. This includes limiting risks both social and financial.

THE CANCERIAN SNAKE

Cancer: June 22 to July 21

The only thing that the Cancerian Snake has to fear is fear itself—specifically, the fear of failure. When Cancer cohabitates with Snake, the result is very complex.

On one hand, both sides are unfailingly ambitious. You see your wedding as the chance to be creative, even daring. But, while most Snakes are confident decision makers, Cancerian Snakes can suffer bouts of self-doubt. Can I pull it off? What if it doesn't work? These questions spin around under your cool and collected expression and can even rob you of sleep. Fortunately, you're more open to expressing your feelings than other Snakes. You enjoy the comforts of your loving fiancé, friends, and family. Do not be afraid to lean on others and, most importantly, ask for help. Every bride has minor freakouts. That's why God invented bridesmaids.

THE LEO SNAKE

Leo: July 22 to August 21

The Strategist Bride is the picture-perfect bride, not because she doesn't make mistakes, but because she knows to put her best foot forward. The sign of Leo has a lot in common with the Snake. Both are highly intelligent and do not like to show their weaknesses. You're at your best when all cylinders are running. You've just discovered the best photographer in town. You've lost another five pounds. Everything's coming up roses. Unlike other brides of your sign, you'll gush to your fiancé and mom about your big successes, hoping for more positive reinforcement. You don't think there's anything wrong with commiserating with your loved ones, and that's a good thing. Weddings are an emotional ride and support is needed. However, you must guard your selfish tendencies and compromise more often than you'd like.

THE VIRGO SNAKE

Virgo: August 22 to September 22

The Virgo Snake strives for perfection. You like making your lists and will not cross anything off until it is done to your satisfaction. The Snake sign feeds on getting things done, and Virgo likes to go after the details. With both signs keen observers of the world, you can be your own toughest critic when it comes to your own wedding. Be careful not to be too hard on yourself because you are probably the only one who can identify all the imperfections. Remember that perception is reality, and Strategist Brides are skilled at setting the scene. In order to stay sane and keep the peace with your fiancé and other loved ones, you should err on the side of practicality. You know how to be efficient and what makes sense. Once you focus on these two things, you'll learn to stop sweating the more trivial details.

THE LIBRA SNAKE
Libra: September 23 to October 22

Where the Snake can be a bit of a loner, Libra brings a love of teams to the table, which is an asset for wedding planning. Your bridal instincts are still classic and traditional at heart. You have the patience to nail down all the details and work with a diverse group of people. By and large, because of your birth year, you are a person who makes decisions by instinct. However, Libra is known for changing her mind too often. Unlike the typical Snake sign, Librans not only open themselves up to other people's opinions, but even go asking for them. The collection of advice can be confusing and can shake your confidence. So be secure in your exquisite taste and deflect the negativity of any naysayers. At heart, you have a sunny, positive attitude, with a delightful sense of humor. Your friends will be a great source of support, especially on the occasional rainy day.

THE SCORPIO SNAKE
Scorpio: October 23 to November 21

The Strategist Bride can be a force of nature. When you meet a challenge, you want to beat it. Scorpio has a similar work ethic. With the influence of both of these signs, you are even more ambitious than the typical Strategist Bride, if you can believe it. You'll approach wedding planning with the kind of passion that some people reserve only for war or sport. Most of your big decisions will be made with your killer instinct. When you come across something that you are unsure about, you aren't afraid to do the research before signing on the dotted line. Your biggest challenges will be getting past any old grudges. You have a long memory and perhaps some old wounds, so tasks like putting together the guest list or seating chart may physically pain you, when it comes to people you would rather not see at your wedding. Compromise may taste like medicine, but even the most unpleasant guests usually have a gift in hand.

Wedding Synergy: When Dragon Meets Phoenix

As you embark on your planning, check out the Wedding Relationship pairings below to see how your strengths and weaknesses come together during the planning process. These compatibility descriptions are based on year of birth combinations, which is the tip of the iceberg when it comes to each of your charts. As described in Chapter 2 "Reference Dates and Tables on the Chinese Zodiac, East-West Sign Combinations, and Animal Hours," a different animal governs each component of your birth date and time.

RAT HUSBAND AND SNAKE WIFE

Partners born in the year of the Rat offer support and good planning skills. More tuned in than other husbands-to-be, your fiancé can be depended on to be a good communicator with friends and family. He doesn't need your hand holding to book the DJ or organize his friends to get their tuxedos. Whether you want him to have this much independence is up to you though. You'll find that he is more open to compromises than you are. Your cautious nature may encourage you to do everything together.

OX HUSBAND AND SNAKE WIFE

Your fiancé doesn't know how you always get your way, but you do. The Strategist Bride's ladylike ways get him every time, and he will do his best to indulge your wishes. You are drawn to the luxury and elegance of weddings. As a couple, you two share a respect for quality. The location, the food, the dress—both the Ox and Snake know that the difference between good quality and bad can be felt and touched. However, an Ox is a stickler for living within his means, so he will ask you to temper your tastes to fit your budget. When push comes to shove, your husband may value a deal in place of beauty more highly than you do.

TIGER HUSBAND AND SNAKE WIFE

A male Tiger and a female Snake can be a spicy dish to enjoy. His outgoing nature will result in generous expenditures that can start to concern you. You like to get spoiled and get a little jealous when you see that he sometimes treats others the same way. You will have to have frank discussions on how to handle your families and guests equally because your views are different. He may also get impatient when you do not make decisions quickly, but you can avoid these kinds of arguments by not asking for his opinion until you are absolutely ready to make a decision.

RABBIT HUSBAND AND SNAKE WIFE

The Rabbit fiancé is a real gentleman. He is drawn to music, art, and literature, much like you. He will partner with you on many details about the wedding and give good advice on style as well as on points of etiquette. In exchange, you will have to take the lead and push many small projects forward. Rabbits are not known for having the same laserlike focus of a Snake, and he will expect you to keep him on task, even if he grumbles a bit. Challenges may come from not voicing your complaints or concerns to each other. You drop hints that go unnoticed and he may hold his tongue to avoid rocking the boat. Best to get things out in the open and avoid any last-minute stress or drag-out fights.

DRAGON HUSBAND AND SNAKE WIFE

You and your fiancé have a well-balanced combination, if you can appreciate each other's strengths. Since you are born in the year of the Snake, you have a knack for keeping lots of balls in the air. You can keep track of the wedding budget, arrange lots of appointments, and continue doing the rest of your life's activities. Meanwhile, your ambitious fiancé will come up with grand ideas and present interesting or even off-the-wall ideas for your big day. You prefer subtlety, but a Dragon likes to make an entrance. Hear him out. Dragons are especially creative and can inject some excitement into any party.

SNAKE HUSBAND AND SNAKE WIFE

Two Snakes are very compatible. You have probably already seen through the course of your relationship that you and your fiancé share the same ambitious nature. With this drive to succeed, you two understand that just because you are going to be married you do not have to be joined at the hip. Therefore, wedding planning should be largely smooth sailing as long as you each take responsibility for keeping your partner in the know about important details. While you two may have a sixth sense about each other, that doesn't necessarily extend to your future in-laws.

HORSE HUSBAND AND SNAKE WIFE

Your two signs are very different, but we're probably telling you something you already know. You're more traditionally type A and not the biggest fan of change. He is spontaneous and embraces change wholeheartedly. At the heart of finding harmony in your wedding planning and into your marriage, you both will have to put any selfishness aside and work together. Both of your signs are very independent, and you will go through the growing pains of compromise. For the Strategist Bride personality specifically, you must challenge yourself to be more open with any bruised feelings. Dropping hints will only fall on the Horse's deaf ears, so be direct.

SHEEP HUSBAND AND SNAKE WIFE

As a couple, you two bond in appreciating the luxuries of life. So you will enjoy going around to your favorite stores, signing up for your wedding registry. With your shared love for beautiful things, you'll not be shy in asking for contributions to your new, fashionable dwelling. While you and your fiancé will agree on many of the details of the wedding, dividing up who does what may frustrate you. The sign of the Sheep is known for procrastinating. You'll need to drive the wedding planning and may need to remind him constantly to do his end of the organizing.

MONKEY HUSBAND AND SNAKE WIFE

The Monkey and the Snake are two of the most charming signs in the Chinese zodiac, so it must have been a fun courtship. You both have lofty goals and the smarts to carry them out. Planning the wedding shouldn't present many issues because you both know how to get your work done. Your fiancé may wait until the last minute to tackle his chores, but he will definitely complete them. The big challenge will be calming fits of jealousy. Exes, bachelor/bachelorette parties, or infamous past acquaintances can start many fights, especially if it seems like you're keeping secrets from each other.

ROOSTER HUSBAND AND SNAKE WIFE

A good marriage combination involves balancing two different personalities. The scales find equal weight with the Rooster sign as a husband and the Snake as a wife. Since you both are from the Thinkers Affinity Triangle, you see eye to eye on decision making. You've found a good confidant during the trials and tribulations of wedding planning. At heart, your fiancé is an optimist who feeds on accomplishment. When things go wrong, he will cheer up and try his best to fix it. You bring an exquisite sense of taste and impeccable manners to the relationship, which he will notice and largely support.

DOG HUSBAND AND SNAKE WIFE

Your fiancé's birth year ensures that his approach to life is very cut and dried. He goes with his gut and is largely practical, which means that while he is logical, it will be difficult to change his mind. With that said, the lady Snake's reputation is for getting what she wants, even if it is occasionally at someone else's expense. With your two signs, compromise is a challenge. You'll find that arguments may stem from the question of what is fair. Finances could be a major sticking point. You are too cautious to overspend, but don't expect your fiancé not to go line by line and see where you may have "borrowed" from one area to pay for a fancier wedding dress.

BOAR HUSBAND AND SNAKE WIFE

The Boar and the Snake combination isn't typically the most natural, but this doesn't necessarily dictate an unhappy relationship. You can help ensure a happy engagement by being more open to your romantic and well-meaning fiancé. Snake women like to listen to their own instincts and shun the advice of others. Be mindful of shutting out your husband-to-be. All he wants to do is be a stronger participant in planning the wedding. Integrate him into more conversations and shopping trips, and he will feel like he is a bigger part of the big day.

The Snake's Relationships with Friends and Family

Family and friends are an important part of most weddings. Since we all operate differently in our nonromantic relationships, the pairings of your Chinese zodiac sign will take a slightly different form. Knowing the compatibility of your animal sign with your family and friends is a real asset when planning and setting expectations for responsibilities. As you think about how best to integrate your vast network of friends, review the relationship overviews below. They will help cast light on your friends' and family members' strengths, weaknesses, and working styles.

WITH A RAT

The Rat is an asset to any team. However, the Rat sign's working style differs a lot from your own. You share strong organizational skills and a good work ethic. However, the Rat is a fan of brainstorming and getting other people's opinions. This person also shares opinions freely as well. You, on the other hand, internalize your thinking and share only when you have made up your mind. If you don't know this person very well, you may find the Rat's outspoken nature kind of irritating. Ideally, if you would like to integrate this person into the wedding, pick a task that the Rat can work on independently, just in case you don't work well together.

Δ WITH AN OX

Whether you've known this person a long time or you are just starting your relationship together, the Ox will quickly earn your respect on work ethic alone. The Ox shares your no-nonsense attitude to getting the job done. In turn, the Ox will appreciate your clear direction. Like you, the Ox isn't a fan of people who change their minds too often. Be sure to recognize this friend or family member with a small gift or thank-you note, no matter how small her gift of time. The Ox sign may never complain aloud, but she can be quite thin-skinned when she feels she's been shortchanged.

WITH A TIGER

Those born in the year of the Tiger are likely to be more talkative than those of the Snake persuasion. You might better understand the Tiger's emotional ways when you learn that Tigers are member of the Protectors Affinity Triangle—a group that acts heavily on instinct. While your friend may be an instinctual thinker like you, the Tiger does not take that same moment of pause to plan everything out, which means you might want to avoid asking this person to take on highly detailed tasks. However, the Tiger is a natural entertainer. Perhaps she can show some out-of-town guests around or liven up a table of strangers.

WITH A RABBIT

You and the Rabbit share a natural sense of style and respect for decorum, which will make working together very nice. A Rabbit likes to have her personal space, so she'll be especially mindful of giving the same courtesy to the bride. She'll listen to the kind of help you need and do her best to be helpful. The only challenges that could present themselves will occur if any jealousy or competition exists between the two of you. The Rabbit sign makes this person very sensitive, so recent misfortune in love could dampen her spirits and inclination to be generous with her time and patience.

WITH A DRAGON

Pairing a Dragon with a Snake is a great combination. As the Strategist Bride, you come from the trio of Thinkers. Your friend the Dragon comes from the branch known as the Doers. With you setting the planning and firmly in place as the bride (aka leader), the roles are clear, and the Dragon does not have a problem following well-organized plans. As a Doer, the Dragon completes tasks and has good judgment to deal with setbacks. This person is a big fan of being recognized for contributions, so remember to include some words of gratitude into a toast or a public introduction.

Δ WITH ANOTHER SNAKE

Two Snakes work well together. You'll find a mutual respect for high standards and good manners, and perhaps a friendship too. Working together, you'll be comforted by how you walk through life at the same pace. You are both Thinkers, so you do not like to rush and will appreciate another person who is as thorough as you are in making plans. Communication will be natural between the two of you because you share the same care in choosing words. However, if you two have any past grievances that have not been put to rest, you might want to keep your distance during wedding planning. Grudges can be poison to your working relationship.

WITH A HORSE

The Horse's love of life and unbridled energy can be very helpful to the Strategist Bride, if placed on the right tasks. The Horse is a member of the Protectors group, which means that this person has a high code of ethics. You can entrust this person to be honest with valuable items because the Horse will feel an innate sense of responsibility. While you may not have as much in common with the Horse as you do with the Ox or the Rooster, you will find the Horse to have a very sunny disposition and you can get along quite nicely. Just remember that Horse signs are known for sometimes suffering for attention deficit disorder, so choose your favors accordingly.

WITH A SHEEP

With a big heart and a desire to please, people born in the year of the Sheep are very helpful. You are a responsible organizer, painstakingly creating plans as well as contingency plans. While the Sheep doesn't have the same eye for detail, she is still a great asset to a bride. She has high emotional intelligence and likes to be a comfort to people. You are not as open with your feelings, so having a Sheep on your team can be helpful, especially for a different perspective. Your friend can be instrumental in creating important social connections, especially breaking the ice with strangers.

WITH A MONKEY

Fast friends or competitors, a Monkey with a Snake can be a mixed bag. The two of you have a lot in common. You are both clever, are master strategists, and love playing games. The best way to manage a person born in the year of the Monkey is to be very precise with your wishes and allow this person to work independently. Like the Snake sign, Monkeys do not like to be micromanaged. In fact, doing so may inspire some unwanted mischief or shortcuts that you will not appreciate.

Ultimately, if you already have established trust with this person, there will be few bumps in the road. If not, be confident in delegating your wishes to the Monkey.

Δ WITH A ROOSTER

Much like the Ox, a Rooster will be a pleasure to work with. You all share a place in the Thinkers Affinity Triangle, which means that you have similar working styles. As the Strategist Bride, you're very decisive and careful to plan for every situation. The Rooster also has a critical eye, especially for the details. Your friend may even be able to catch some details that have missed your fine-tooth comb. Fancy that. Even though you're not inclined to ask for second opinions, you'll feel a sense of comfort in knowing you have a person to go to, just in case.

WITH A DOG

People born in the year of the Dog possess some great skills that many people don't often appreciate. They can be great leaders in objectivity and fairness. As the Strategist Bride, you can depend on the Dog sign for tasks big and small, but what may be the most valuable is the Dog's perspective. Brides can often be selfish or oblivious to how their actions are seen by people, so it never hurts to seek good counsel. You might want to get this person's opinion for how your actions can be interpreted by your most sensitive friends or family members. Perhaps it's how you word a thank-you note or how to seat a person. You'll find the Dog has a skill for being diplomatic in a way you aren't.

× WITH A BOAR

A Boar has a way of bringing sunshine into the room. With a jovial spirit, this person can be larger than life at times. The Boar and the Snake are in natural opposition and well exhibited in a stark contract in personalities. However, during the wedding planning process, this person may be the most helpful in showing you how to enjoy life and the adventure ahead. Strategist Brides can be worriers, poring over their plans, never satisfied until they are absolutely perfect. A Boar sign enjoys blessings as they come, and will encourage you to do the same. This person will help make sure that you don't become one of those brides who are all work and no play, even if you are slow to embrace the change.

Twelve

BORN IN THE YEAR OF THE HORSE
Here Comes the Adventurer Bride

Lunar Years of the Horse	Elements
February 15, 1942, to February 4, 1943	Water
February 3, 1954, to February 23, 1955	Wood
January 21, 1966, to February 8, 1967	Fire
February 7, 1978, to January 27, 1979	Earth
January 27, 1990, to February 14, 1991	Metal
February 12, 2002, to January 31, 2003	Water

Adventurer Bride Details

Birth Hours: 11 A.M. to 1 P.M.

Western Sign: Gemini

Western Gemstone: Pearl or Moonstone

Symbolic Color: Red

Flower: Sunflower

Season: Summer

Element: Fire

Famous Adventurer Brides:

Chris Evert, Ella Fitzgerald, Aretha Franklin, Rita Hayworth, Cindy McCain, Rene Russo, Barbra Streisand, Raquel Welch.

The Dress:

High drama and glamour will be the theme for your bridal gown. You are a fan of color, sparkle, and bold graphics. Perhaps you will choose a bright-colored sash or adorn your dress with crystals. You like getting people's attention, so you favor daring cuts, from plunging necklines to backless dresses.

The Horse Sign: The Seventh Bride of the Chinese Zodiac

As the seventh sign of the zodiac, the Horse is a passionate explorer of life. She is a part of what we refer to as the Protectors group. There are four groups: the Doers, the Thinkers, the Protectors, and the Catalysts. The groups are made up of the three animals that have a natural affinity to one another, referred to as a Triangle

of Affinity. Each set of three animals has a social connection—a kind of chemistry that is connected to each zodiac sign.

The Protectors group is made up of the Tiger, the Horse, and the Dog. No surprise, people with these birth signs or ascendants are your most natural friends and working partners. In fact, it's likely your fiancé has strong ties to this group as well. As their team name suggests, these ladies are loyal friends and champions of causes. Those born in the year of the Horse have the mantra "I act." She is the bride voted most likely to have a destination wedding. Here comes the Adventurer Bride.

The Adventurer Bride—Born in the Year of the Horse

People born in the year of the Horse have an innate sex appeal that comes from the confidence with which they travel through life. The Adventurer Bride moves swiftly and with great optimism. Naturally, looking at the sunny side makes you an attractive person with a wide network of friends. You are drawn to dramatic looks and will want to make an entrance at your wedding.

You are blessed with sharp senses and are able to handle money, despite not being a fan of meticulous planning. You have a knack for strong negotiations, with your gift of persuasion and ability to take rejection. Your philosophy is: "It doesn't hurt to ask," which is key to getting on the inside track of a wedding. The Adventurer Bride is a strong believer in following her instincts; you are very decisive when you truly want something, though you can be swayed into changing your mind.

As a member of the Protectors group, you are a passionate person who doesn't like to abstain from opinion. You love deeply and are naturally perceptive. When you want to get to know somebody, you tune in and make friends easily. In fact, you know the art of flirtation very well and are skilled at turning your sex appeal on and off. However, you can be abrupt and quite stubborn, and like your decision making, your emotions can also be impulsive. Your moods can run the gamut. Happy, sad, and often impatient, you can be selfish with your emotions and oblivious to what is going on around you. As a result, you often become easily distracted and can forget your manners. While your closest friends and family know this is just how you are, be careful to make the most of your first impressions, especially with VIPs such as your future in-laws. If you're not up for socializing, sometimes it's better to reschedule than to let someone mistake your bad mood for dislike. To better smooth your moods, you'll want to channel your inner athlete to manage your stress throughout the planning process. Many Horses are naturally athletic. Workouts are an ideal way for you to blow off steam and express all your pent-up energy. A good run can clear your head.

Adventurer Brides have an interesting relationship with money. Not one to be ruled by money, you use it as a tool of independence. Material things do not motivate you as much as life experiences. You are drawn to trips and events more than homes and 401(k)s. The interesting thing is that while you may save up a lot of money, it is difficult for you to commit to long-term investments. You prefer to have your money easily accessible, the better to have fun and be spontaneous. As a result, you frequently pick up the tab and loan people money. However, while you are generous with your money, you can be quite stingy with your time. There are plenty of obligations that will bore your free spirit, but make the most of them and consider the feelings of your fiancé and your new in-laws. The wedding planning road is long, a mixture of walks and sprints. While compromise is difficult for you, you and your husband-to-be will have to have frank discussions about money and family obligation. You will want to preserve your individual personality through free time and nights out with your girlfriends. Is your fiancé ultra-traditional, someone who has dinner with his parents every Sunday? He's probably assuming that you'll be a part of his routine. You may balk at the idea of being tied down to a weekly date, but try to keep in mind that these kinds of things are not only signs of acceptance, but part of joining a new family.

The Adventurer Bride's independent nature is one of your most attractive aspects. Variety is the spice of life, and it's the only thing that can capture your attention. You don't like to waste people's time, and you certainly don't like dwelling on anything that is no use to you. You'll organize your wedding in much the same fashion, making it action-packed, with as little downtime as possible. Your guests will appreciate your choice in quicker ceremonies and longer receptions. When choosing attendants, the Adventurer Bride should choose people who think and act quickly. You appreciate people who speak quickly and succinctly, much like you. Nature is very appealing to the freedom-loving Adventurer Bride. Perhaps you will get married in the beautiful outdoors in a far off destination and get a jumpstart on your honeymoon.

East Meets West: When Moon Signs Meet Sun Signs

Many people don't realize that each animal of the Chinese zodiac has a solar calendar connection. In our interpretation of Chinese horoscopes, the lunar calendar links into the solar calendar through the month and season, where the Horse's parallel sun sign is Gemini. But every Western sun sign has a different effect on the lunar moon sign.

THE SAGITTARIUS HORSE
Sagittarius: November 22 to December 21

Wedding planning is like a marathon for which a Sagittarius Horse will need to train. Fortunately, it will be an exercise in harnessing your energy. You like to stay busy and have been known to bite off more than you can chew. That can easily happen with wedding planning. Whether thumbing through magazines or reading about other brides' adventures and projects on the Web, you say, "I can do that." Your optimism is fantastic, not to mention very attractive, but you must pace yourself by finishing a project before you go off looking for a new one. Otherwise there will be an imbalance that can affect your typically cheery demeanor. You do not have the patience to take on meticulous tasks all by your lonesome, and too much work can actually affect your sleep and cause undue stress. Partner up with friends to share the workload, and schedule athletic activities to help channel your nervous energy.

THE CAPRICORN HORSE
Capricorn: December 22 to January 20

The influence of Capricorn brings balance to the Adventurer Bride. Like your sisters born in the year of the Horse, you aren't one to stay still. You relax by getting things accomplished; whether it's going out for a jog or watching television while multitasking on the Internet, the Adventurer Bride always has a full agenda. Capricorn is a blessing for a Horse sign's wedding planning because it encourages endurance to the Adventurer Bride, who typically favors sprints. The trick to a better bridal experience is good initial planning. Coincidentally, Capricorn is a good planner, which benefits you in spades. The Adventurer Bride excels in executing plans, and Capricorn helps by drawing them up. You will have a strong sense of what to prioritize and what to spend the most time on. As a result, you have an eye for the details that other Horse signs do not.

THE AQUARIUS HORSE

Aquarius: January 21 to February 19

Your favorite part of the wedding planning may actually be the honeymoon getaway. As you have probably picked up on, the Adventurer Bride loves to explore. Will it be sun-drenched beaches or maybe visiting the Seven Wonders of the World? You and your fiancé may look at your wedding budget and think about fattening up the travel budget more than any other item. This makes perfect sense to you. The Adventurer Bride's logic is both romantic and practical. You love to spend time with your fiancé, keep your finances in check, and have your freedom to roam as you please. Therefore, whether you do indulge in a destination wedding or a grand honeymoon, you'll try to minimize any unnecessary fuss over wedding details. No elaborate centerpieces or meticulous party favors for you. You favor focusing your time and money on bigger impact items, like a spectacular location, a memorable dinner, or maybe a guilty pleasure like upgrading your wedding gown.

THE PISCES HORSE

Pisces: February 20 to March 20

Pisces has a calming effect on the typically workaholic Adventurer Bride. The Horse sign is keenly observant, picking up on the feel of the room. When tuned in, you can sense when people around you feel anxious or whether you've won their support. Pisces amplifies this skill and adds an equally handy one for a bride, which is patience. Brides born in the year of the Horse have a need for speed. Sometimes you'd rather cross everything off your to-do list than spend time and go over the details. Fortunately, the Pisces Horse sets a more realistic pace for wedding planning. You're more inclined to dig into the details. Also, you use your instincts to think about remembering and honoring others on your wedding day. This extra step adds a deeper layer to your wedding planning that others will appreciate. Be sure to pack an extra handkerchief, because Pisces brides are known for patting back tears of joy.

THE ARIES HORSE
Aries: March 21 to April 19

People born in the year of the Horse like to live their lives at a rapid pace, and Aries adds a little extra fuel. With your inquisitive nature, you'll enjoy your wedding exploration trips, packing them to the brim with lots of appointments for new ideas and projects. The Adventurer Bride in you likes to keep busy, and Aries encourages you to act on your instincts with confidence. While your intuition is typically very sharp, it would be wise to pause for a moment and get a second opinion before making any big commitments. Your communication skills are excellent and you will find it easy to ask for help and give clear direction to your vendor. However, not everyone will work at the same record-breaking speed that you do, so exercise patience, especially with new people in your life. Your passionate nature also extends to a fiery temper.

THE TAURUS HORSE
Taurus: April 20 to May 20

Most Adventurer Brides like to jump feet first into projects, but Taurus is known for looking before she leaps. The combination of Taurus and the Horse sign results in a more even tempo than the usual sprint that the Horse native favors. While you are still inclined to skip the planning and get to the doing, you're less headstrong about charging forward, especially when other people offer you sound advice. You favor relying on your own instincts, but there isn't any harm in reaching out to friends or thumbing through a few magazines to find out what they did and, most importantly, what they would've avoided. When it comes to weddings, if you've thought of it, some bride has probably done it before. You can benefit from other brides' past experiences, rather than unnecessarily marching bravely into the unknown.

THE GEMINI HORSE

Gemini: May 21 to June 21

The presence of the Gemini twins is like having two extra opinions in the room. On the plus side, you get the benefit of a vibrant imagination and a higher sensitivity to the feelings of others. This results in better connections with new friends and family and sharpens your reflexes to the changing world around you. You're very intelligent and capable of accomplishing a great deal of work, once you plan out exactly what you want and fully commit to the idea. By and large, Horses are practical, but like to guarantee their freedom by always keeping the door slightly ajar. So, without clear deadlines, you'll enjoy vacillating between venues, colors, or dresses until the last minute. You can literally fall in love with one thing one minute and forget about it the next. Fortunately, once you see the price and time that wedding changes require, your practical nature will come back into focus.

THE CANCERIAN HORSE

Cancer: June 22 to July 21

Adventurer Brides are natural charmers, finding it easy to make new friends and start up conversations. When you add Cancer's influence into the mix, you get an added gift of refinement. You're very mindful of manners and have the makings of an eloquent speaker. Whether things are going extremely well or you have a total disaster on your hands, you'll manage to keep a serene look on your face. How does the Cancerian Horse accomplish such a feat? Well, one of your biggest secrets is picking your battles wisely. Many Horses unfortunately take on too many projects and don't like taking them to completion, but you circumvent the last-minute stress by avoiding the mess in the first place. It's a good way to manage yourself because your moods can be rather erratic. Adventurer Brides should always cultivate calm when they can.

THE LEO HORSE

Leo: July 22 to August 21

Both the Horse and the Lion have big hearts and stage presence. This packs quite the punch in one bride. Many brides may find the idea of getting married daunting, even intimidating, but not you. At your core, you're ambitious and optimistic about life. Your positive outlook will energize you in your wedding pursuits. You'll enjoy exploring your options, both independently and with your loving fiancé. After all, the more the merrier when it comes to adventure. When you've made up your grand plan for the wedding, the Lion's leadership and the Horse's communication skills will be a winning combination. However, you'll need to keep your schedule in check, as you enjoy squeezing as much into a day as possible and can burn the candle from both ends. Trust in your leadership, keep your directions clear and succinct, and have the confidence to walk away and trust the job will get done.

THE VIRGO HORSE

Virgo: August 22 to September 22

Both Virgo and the Horse favor practical plans. The fastest road to any destination is the most direct. But, where the Horse enjoys speed to make time for freedom, Virgo likes it for stability. The Horse sign values her time more than money or power, so it isn't a surprise that Adventurer Brides like to pick and choose what they want to spend time on. Some may see the Horse rush through a chore and misjudge her ability to focus. The Horse needs to be captivated to stay attentive. The Virgo Horse finds her focus by the challenge of producing something flawless. You'll always look for ways to improve the situation, but don't be too hard on yourself. Virgo is her own worst enemy. Prioritize projects and trust your planner, fiancé, and the rest of your supporting cast to help you.

THE LIBRA HORSE

Libra: September 23 to October 22

Adventurer Brides usually prefer to work alone, but the Libra Horse sees wedding planning as more of a team sport. You'll be more inclined to have in-depth conversations with your fiancé and seek the ideas of others. Librans try their best to ensure fairness and equality, and this is a great perspective to have when planning a wedding. The big day lays the foundation for your relationship with your in-laws and connects your life to your fiancé's. You have a great sense of humor and know how to communicate with a diverse group of people. Naturally, the gift of gab will result in some great deals, when you put on the hat of negotiator. In fact, it may take some people by surprise because you can find making big decisions challenging. However, once you have made up your mind, you don't have a problem finding or even making the opportunity to obtain what you want.

THE SCORPIO HORSE
Scorpio: October 23 to November 21

Adventurer Brides are known for being quite sexy thanks to a winning combination of independence and confidence. If you can believe it, the sign of Scorpio makes you an even spicier dish to behold. Scorpio Horses have lots of energy and act with lots of passion. With a quieter exterior, the combination places a veil of mystery over the Adventurer Bride. This results in the highest of highs and the lowest of lows. While these mood swings may be more internalized than what other Horses experience, they rumble below the surface. Scorpio has the blessing and curse of becoming borderline obsessive on projects. Scorpio Horses avoid simple, repetitive projects like the plague. No, you set your sights on complicated projects, where it'll be difficult for you to abandon the fight. Where other Horses may lose interest, you can be quite stubborn and insist on seeing it through to the end. Your fiancé and friends would be wise to keep their distance on these occasions.

Wedding Synergy: When Dragon Meets Phoenix

As you embark on your planning, check out the Wedding Relationship pairings below to see how your strengths and weaknesses come together during the planning process. These compatibility descriptions are based on year of birth combinations, which is the tip of the iceberg when it comes to each of your charts. As described in Chapter 2 "Reference Dates and Tables on the Chinese Zodiac, East-West Sign Combinations, and Animal Hours," a different animal governs each component of your birth date and time.

RAT HUSBAND AND HORSE WIFE

The combination of Rat and Horse needs a healthy dose of compromise to reduce a bumpy wedding planning experience. As the Adventurer Bride, you focus on the big picture, and even though you're becoming a wife, you still cherish your independence as an individual. Your fiancé's birth year encourages him to focus on the details and share his opinions about how the wedding should be. His tips and tricks are given with the best of intentions, so try not to take it personally. The Rat is a good and thorough planner, so many of his comments will be beneficial to the wedding.

OX HUSBAND AND HORSE WIFE

Your fiancé is from the Thinkers Affinity Triangle, which makes him a hard worker who is a fan of a quiet home life. On the other hand, you prefer to be out and about, instead of cooped up at home. You two must find balance by integrating your work styles and lives throughout the engagement. It's likely that in your fiancé's mind, you're already married, and he may expect you to start acting more like a "wife." This doesn't have to be defined as Suzy Homemaker. Your husband-to-be can feel that you and he are acting more like a couple by having more discussions and outings together. While he may decline sometimes, he will respect your efforts and feel you're seeing him more as a partner.

TIGER HUSBAND AND HORSE WIFE

In your couple, you've definitely found a kindred spirit. Both the Tiger and Horse belong to the Catalysts group and have a natural balance for working together. You both respect the need for personal space, but are very passionate in your life together. Wedding planning is a happy but emotional time, and you two won't have a problem communicating the pros and cons. You'll find your fiancé can fly off the handle here and there, but you possess the ability to calm him down and focus him on what needs to be done.

RABBIT HUSBAND AND HORSE WIFE

The Horse and the Rabbit journey through life at different speeds, and finding a common tempo will be the key to wedding planning bliss. Your fiancé makes decisions more slowly and more deliberately than you're inclined to. It can frustrate you when, even though you know he's already found his favorite, he'll insist on seeing every other option to know what's out there. You may find it a waste of time, but summon your patience for at least the bigger decisions. The Horse sign tends to choose by instinct, so a second opinion doesn't do any harm.

DRAGON HUSBAND AND HORSE WIFE

The two of you find common ground in cultivating a life filled with constant activity. He's attracted to your independent spirit and no-nonsense attitude about making decisions, and you appreciate his strength and devotion to you. Now that you're merging your lives officially, you'll face growing pains, especially if you've compounded wedding planning by moving in together. Both of you are big-picture people and get frustrated by executing small details. For better peace at home, you must try to keep organized both in mind and with belongings. Your fiancé will support hiring a planner and delegating more projects.

SNAKE HUSBAND AND HORSE WIFE

The Snake and the Horse don't have the most natural husband and wife matchup. However, this shows that you've found an attraction and must continue to appreciate how your differences can make you a good team. At the heart of it, the Snake is a long-term thinker and the Horse is a short-term one. Your fiancé thinks about all the what-ifs, while you go with your gut. You can temper potential arguments by splitting up some of the smaller wedding tasks and discussing the big topics such as date, location, and guest lists in more detail. The Horse sign tends to have a short attention span, so plan frequent small discussions, rather than pulling an all-nighter.

HORSE HUSBAND AND HORSE WIFE

Finding a kindred spirit born under the same sign is very special. You both are independent people who know how to take the initiative in your own lives. Now that you've made everything official, you each have found a partner in crime. You can roll up your sleeves and start planning the party. The benefit of two horses on a team is, of course, double the horsepower. You'll have fun racing around and ticking off all your to-do's. However, your lightning speed needs to be harnessed by a good planner. Whether that's you or a hired professional, someone will need to keep an eye on the details and make sure all the pieces fit.

SHEEP HUSBAND AND HORSE WIFE

The personality differences of the Sheep and Horse signs have the potential for a balanced marriage and productive wedding planning. You're most satisfied when you're busy with lots of variety, and putting a wedding together certainly gives you the opportunity to create as much work as you have the appetite for. Your fiancé expresses his excitement for the wedding in a quieter way. He's romantic and generous, but selfish when it comes to spending time with you. While you're more than capable of planning independently, do your best to integrate him into the process and be sure to plan some date nights to keep your love life in harmony.

MONKEY HUSBAND AND HORSE WIFE

Pairing a Monkey and a Horse can work out splendidly if one person steps up to lead the charge and see it through to completion. You're both motivated by competition and a strong dose of ambition. Working together or independently, you each make practical decisions and aren't shy about executing plans. However, you and your fiancé both prefer quick chores versus long projects. The trick will be breaking up the wedding planning to be more manageable or enlisting the help of a professional coordinator to tie up the loose ends.

ROOSTER HUSBAND AND HORSE WIFE

You and your fiancé must have quite the high level of attraction, because typically Roosters and Horses mix like oil and water. As the Adventurer Bride, you enjoy life's surprises, embracing change easily. You're also known for rocking the boat yourself. Your fiancé lives on the other end of the spectrum. He does his best to create consistency and enjoys delving into the details, much deeper than most animals go. Your different strengths can be an asset if you work more cooperatively on projects and grow a thicker skin to handle the Rooster's constant criticism.

DOG HUSBAND AND HORSE WIFE

Marriages that form out of common Affinity Triangle relationships are very strong. You are both Protectors and work well together because you each appreciate the other's strengths. In addition to your optimistic nature and energetic personality, you've got the gift of good timing. You're also practical and rely on your instincts. Your fiancé is clever and possesses fair judgment, even in sticky situations like seating charts and tipping appropriately. With your combined skills and strong communication, you can accomplish a lot with fewer arguments than most couples during the wedding planning process.

BOAR HUSBAND AND HORSE WIFE

Romance probably sprang out of friendship with the two of you. Your two signs have lots of things in common. Optimism, resourcefulness, and carefree spirits are your link. However, when you're having fun together, your responsibilities literally melt away. From procrastination to being loose with your budget, things can quickly get out of hand. As the Adventurer Bride, you'll have to be the one to keep a close eye on your spending. It wouldn't hurt to earmark any monetary wedding gifts for your joint savings, just in case the open bar is too free-flowing.

The Horse's Relationships with Friends and Family

Family and friends are an important part of most weddings. Since we all operate differently in our nonromantic relationships, the pairings of your Chinese zodiac sign will take a slightly different form. Knowing the compatibility of your animal sign with your family and friends is a real asset when planning and setting expectations for responsibilities. As you think about how best to integrate your vast network of friends, review the relationship overviews below. They will help cast light on your friends' and family members' strengths, weaknesses, and working styles.

× WITH A RAT

Fundamentally, the Rat and Horse live life with different priorities. The Adventurer Bride's approach is efficient and speedy, while the Rat sign favors planning and exercises big moves with caution. With the best intentions in mind, she makes suggestions to improve on your ideas. This advice rarely sits well with you because once you've made up your mind, you don't like to be slowed down by dissenters. It may be best to use your wedding planner or a mutual friend as a buffer between the two of you. However, depending on this person's position in your life—mother,

mother-in-law, or fiancé's friend, you may have to exercise more patience than comes naturally. If this person is willing, you may want to enlist her to help with meticulous tasks—an area Rat signs excel in and Horses avoid.

WITH AN OX

While the Adventurer Bride is a skilled negotiator, you'll find people born in the year of the Ox more difficult opponents. For wedding planning bliss, your best bet may be to circumvent heavy discussion with this person. Ask your Ox friend to help with specific tasks that you and your fiancé have already chosen. The Ox respects the rules of the wedding game and always comes through. If this person has closer ties, expect unsolicited advice and some occasional criticism.

△ WITH A TIGER

Tiger natives are great friends to the Adventurer Bride. Whether you're new or old friends, you'll find communication flows freely because you both come from the Protectors Affinity Triangle. Every bride needs a person she can speak with casually who shares similar views, and you'll find that in a Tiger friend. In addition to the role of confidante, the Tiger native can aid you in tasks with great speed. Like you, she can be depended on to do things independently, which can be a load off your back.

WITH A RABBIT

The Adventurer Bride is an independent woman who marches to life at her own beat. Rabbit natives may challenge you because they tap into their instincts very differently than Horses. Your Rabbit friend or future family member tries to establish harmony by looking to other people for cues. If you're stressed, she'll ask what's wrong; if you look disappointed, she may think it's her fault. Keep this in mind when you interact with a Rabbit. Choose your words wisely because Rabbits have long memories. Be gentle with criticism and gush with praise.

WITH A DRAGON

You'll find lots of common ground with people born in the year of the Dragon—and some challenges too. Both of you are open communicators, which is a great

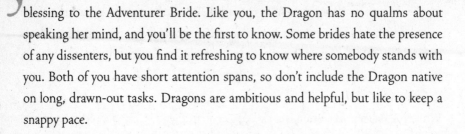

blessing to the Adventurer Bride. Like you, the Dragon has no qualms about speaking her mind, and you'll be the first to know. Some brides hate the presence of any dissenters, but you find it refreshing to know where somebody stands with you. Both of you have short attention spans, so don't include the Dragon native on long, drawn-out tasks. Dragons are ambitious and helpful, but like to keep a snappy pace.

WITH A SNAKE

As the Adventurer Bride, you're the outgoing social butterfly and pride yourself on being able to break the ice with anyone. Hate to break it to you, but people born in the year of the Snake can put up quite the wall to new people. Don't take it personally. It takes a while to earn the trust of this person. But, with regard to the wedding, Snakes are some of the best guests and big day helpers. Snake natives have a refined sense of style and great respect for etiquette. You can depend on this person to carry out your wishes without complaint or criticism. Even better, the Snake is great at keeping secrets.

Δ WITH ANOTHER HORSE

People born in the year of the Horse like to make the most of their day. You like to do things quickly or cut your losses. This philosophy extends past activities and into relationships with you. Both you and your fellow Horse native will settle into a comfortable working relationship. If your heads butt, you'll part ways with few hurt feelings because sometimes things work, sometimes they don't. Nevertheless, the Horse can tackle the most challenging tasks, as long as they're interesting and not repetitive. Don't even think about asking her to create two hundred Jordan almond favors or fold a thousand cranes—would you want to do the same for her?

WITH A SHEEP

If you have chosen a person born in the year of the Sheep to be a part of your wedding, it'd be wise to send lots of reminders because Sheep are procrastinators. It seems like deadlines don't really apply because the Sheep always has a strange stroke of luck. Someone always keeps the shop open a few minutes' late to take those bridesmaid dress measurements or adds that plus-one way after the

RSVP—that's just how it goes for the Sheep. While if someone else tried to pull these shenanigans, you'd blow your top, you somehow feel the need to watch over this person. Be prepared to shepherd her through wedding necessities, and even budget for a personal loan, in case her finances are in transition.

WITH A MONKEY

An Adventurer Bride can work well with a Monkey, as long as there is open communication. You'll appreciate this person's quick thinking and resourceful ideas. If you send this person out for a task and a challenge presents itself, the Monkey will develop a workaround on the spot. Since both of you are good improvisers, you don't come to blows over petty issues. In fact, if tension does come up, you'll naturally part ways and not hold a grudge. The Horse and the Monkey are too practical to harbor sore feelings over small quarrels.

WITH A ROOSTER

Working closely with a Rooster may slow down the Adventurer Bride's lively rhythm. Rooster natives are perfectionists. They live by plans and don't deal well with change. It's best to limit advice seeking with this person, unless you're looking for someone to go over your plans with a fine-tooth comb. Proofing your wedding invitation is an ideal task, while asking her opinion on a rough prototype of a centerpiece may lead to frustration. The Rooster cannot conceptualize well when flaws are in the plans. Since you're a woman who relies on her instincts, move forward without the Rooster's two cents, if you can help it, or implore the assistance of a go-between to keep the peace.

Δ WITH A DOG

The year of the Dog produces some of the best bridesmaids. Dog natives are great listeners and incredibly loyal. The Adventurer Bride will find it easy to chat or have intense discussions with Dog signs. Whether you are already friends or developing a closer relationship, you can bond through your wedding journey. Bad first impressions with in-laws and other wedding setbacks can be worked out over a cup of tea. Your friend's advice will reflect her more cautious nature, which can temper your impulsive ways.

WITH A BOAR

A person born in the year of the Boar sports a sunny disposition and a don't-rain-on-my-parade attitude, much like you. The Adventurer Bride can be frank with a Boar sign and not worry about any hard feelings. The Boar native is a blast to hang out with. Your spontaneous ways can combine with some adventurous results and surely a great story or two. However, you'll have to set the limits on almost everything. With the Boar, the sky's the limit, and nobody wants a maxed-out credit card or hangover too close to a wedding.

Thirteen

BORN IN THE YEAR OF THE SHEEP
Here Comes the Peacemaker Bride

Lunar Years of the Sheep	Elements
February 5, 1943, to January 24, 1944	Water
January 24, 1955, to February 11, 1956	Wood
February 9, 1967, to January 29, 1968	Fire
January 28, 1979, to February 15, 1980	Earth
February 15, 1991, to February 3, 1992	Metal
February 1, 2003, to January 21, 2004	Water

Peacemaker Bride Details

Birth Hours: 1 P.M. to 3 P.M.

Western Sign: Cancer

Western Gemstone: Ruby

Symbolic Color: Red

Flower: Lotus

Season: Summer

Element: Fire

Famous Peacemaker Brides:
Christina Aguilera, Anne Bancroft, Catherine Deneuve,
Nicole Kidman, Billie Jean King, Barbara Walters.

The Dress:

You have the soul of a connoisseur who loves to indulge in the top fashions and finest workmanship. Quite simply, you enjoy being a bride and will choose luxurious designs with an intricate touch. Lace, ruffles, and all the trimmings, you'll search out a dress that attracts attention and will want to splurge on accessories of the same top quality.

The Sheep Sign: The Eighth Bride of the Chinese Zodiac

The eighth sign, the Sheep is most compassionate member of the Chinese zodiac. She is a part of what we refer to as the Catalysts group. There are four groups: the Doers, the Thinkers, the Protectors, and the Catalysts. The groups are made up of the three animals that have a natural affinity to one another, referred to as a

Triangle of Affinity. Each set of three animals has a social connection—a kind of chemistry that is connected to each zodiac sign.

The Catalysts group is made up of the Rabbit, the Sheep, and the Boar. No surprise, people with these birth signs or ascendants are your most natural friends and working partners. In fact, it's likely your fiancé has strong ties to this group as well. The Catalysts Affinity Triangle is made up of women who are skilled communicators and patrons of the arts. Those born in the year of the Sheep have the Vmantra "I love." She is the bride voted most likely to have the biggest wedding. Here comes the Peacemaker Bride.

The Peacemaker Bride—Born in the Year of the Sheep

Women born in the year of the Sheep are some of the most feminine in the Chinese zodiac. You're a woman in every sense of the word, from the inside out. The Peacemaker Bride enjoys putting together the perfect outfit and meticulously creating the coordinating hairdo. You're also a well of emotion. You are a true romantic at heart, and your wedding is a dream come true. Whether you'd like to admit it or not, you're the kind of girl who doodled your future married name in the margins at school, thinking about the day it would be your time to walk down the aisle. With that in mind, your maid of honor should prepare to hand you a handkerchief at the appropriate time on your big day because your emotions will get the best of you.

As delicate as your emotions can be, no one should count you out when it comes to toughness. When you have truly set your mind to something, you can attack as well as any of the other animals in the Chinese zodiac. It's simply a matter of commitment, and oftentimes that is the only thing standing in the way of getting what you want. There are lots of voices going on in your head that contribute to bouts of indecision. You're a constant worrier about all the what-ifs in life and look for the reassurance of close friends and family. You'd frankly be lost without them. Criticism cuts especially deep with you because it's almost as if all your worst fears have come to life, and loved ones would be wise to shield you from this unpleasantness close to the wedding. Stress can get the best of you, leaving you withdrawn and unhappy. On your wedding day, there will be something that goes wrong. It happens to every bride. The best attendants anticipate and deflect drama, only bringing matters of the utmost importance to the attention of the bride. By the end of your wedding planning, your fiancé and friends will not make the mistake of raining on your parade with a small issue.

When someone is referred to as emotional, it can often be seen as a bad thing, but the Sheep sign's strong set of emotions is as much a strength as it is a weakness. You're an intuitive soul who feels deeply. The benefit is that you are not oblivious to the feelings of others and take their body language and subtle hints as opportunities to bring people closer together. We don't call you the Peacemaker Bride for nothing. For example, you can anticipate when a friend feels left out because she's not one of your bridesmaids, so you instinctively invite her to read one of your favorite sonnets, or you invite your mother-in-law shopping, just so she feels like a bigger part of the wedding. These may seem like small gestures to you, but it's the little things that make people reflect on how lucky they are to call you friend and family.

If you're not a believer in karma, you should sit back and reflect on your life and take account of all your many blessings. You're generous with your time and money and are fully committed to responsibilities of love and friendship. Thanks to these qualities, the Sheep sign seems to have generated a lot of goodwill through the generations because many born in this year have the benefit of being cared for throughout their lives. Are you under the protective and watchful eye of your fiancé, who takes every opportunity to spoil you just to see you smile? Perhaps you're a daddy's girl, whose father is so thrilled to see his baby girl get married that he has literally taken out a second mortgage on the house just to make sure that she gets all her wedding day wishes. It's strange but true that Peacemaker Brides are often the ones who have the biggest budgets when getting married, on account of a generous benefactor in their lives.

The Peacemaker Bride generally assembles a large wedding because there are so many people in her life, and she favors a spouse who also shares a love of family and friendship. A shameless romantic, you'll be filled with joy on your wedding day and eagerly look forward to building a new home with your Prince Charming. You're a natural homebody and secretly love the idea of staying in more on weekends, enjoying your new title of Mrs.

East Meets West: When Moon Signs Meet Sun Signs

Many people don't realize that each animal of the Chinese zodiac has a solar calendar connection. In our interpretation of Chinese horoscopes, the lunar calendar links into the solar calendar through the month and season, where the Sheep's parallel sun sign is Cancer. But every Western sun sign has a different effect on the lunar moon sign.

THE SAGITTARIUS SHEEP

Sagittarius: November 22 to December 21

The combination of Sagittarius and the Sheep sign produces a confident and stylish bride. While you're still not the biggest fan of details, you have a thicker skin when it comes to constructive criticism. This is because you're less emotional with the influence of Sagittarius. Most sheep prefer to avoid the unpleasantness of giving bad news, but you view one of your roles as peacemaker as being honest about your feelings. This is a great asset to have because every bride is faced with balancing the wishes/obligations of family and friends with her own. Your outspoken personality will help prevent complicated situations from growing into wedding headaches.

THE CAPRICORN SHEEP

Capricorn: December 22 to January 20

Capricorn's influence gives the Peacemaker Bride a compass for decision making. Where your sister Sheep may waver, you can choose a direction without second-guessing yourself. This confidence extends to the greater vision of your wedding. The Capricorn Sheep is proactive in conceiving the look, feel, and overall plan of her big day. The Sheep sign's quiet determination is prominent in this sun-moon combination. You're not one to let a few setbacks discourage you either. Whether it's losing the last ten pounds or dealing with the broken promise of a friend, you don't wallow for long because you've got your eyes on the prize.

THE AQUARIUS SHEEP

Aquarius: January 21 to February 19

Both the Aquarius and Sheep signs are high on the emotional intelligence meter. Aquarius is especially deep and contributes an inquisitive nature to the Peacemaker Bride. Motivated by a genuine desire to make other people happy, you do your best to get to know people, in hopes of learning what makes them tick. Your efforts are not lost on others. It makes you a very thoughtful bride, which does your parents proud and ingratiates you to in-laws. The Aquarius Sheep is drawn to new and creative things. You enjoy the unconventional and are more prone to taking risks than other Peacemaker Brides. You can also be a little too spontaneous—make sure you budget realistically for the wedding.

THE PISCES SHEEP

Pisces: February 20 to March 20

Sheep ladies are natural entertainers, knowing how to break the ice and work the room. Even though you can be very social, the Pisces influence encourages you to retreat into yourself. You find peace in solitude, and with all the hustle and bustle from engagement to big day, it's no wonder. Moments of silence recharge you, so that you can face the stress that comes from being a bride. The Pisces Sheep can become a little self-absorbed with her bride-to-be status, but your generous nature smooths the way with most people. You're a romantic at heart who will take special care in preparing the perfect toast and crowd-pleasing slideshow. Some of your friends may be surprised at how specific your standards can be, but when you want things a certain way, you always find your focus.

THE ARIES SHEEP

Aries: March 21 to April 19

The Peacemaker Bride gains a loud voice with the influence of Aries. While you still have the patience of the Sheep sign, the Ram produces a forceful leader. You'll see your wedding as a challenge to be met with clear direction and example setting, which to you means living by your high standards. You can be less compromising than other Peacemaker Brides, which will be better tolerated by your friends and family than by your fiancé. There's a history of you getting your own way in the relationship, so you'll have to open up a few more things to negotiation than you would prefer.

THE TAURUS SHEEP
Taurus: April 20 to May 20

This Peacemaker Bride is a woman who knows what she wants. Where other Sheep natives have trouble making up their minds, Taurus always guides you in a logical direction. The Taurus Sheep is a realistic bride with a taste for luxury. You understand that your dream wedding can be achieved through hard work and aren't afraid to roll up your sleeves to make it happen. Gym time, extra hours at work, perhaps calling in a favor or two are all challenges you're willing to take on. Your fiancé and loved ones will appreciate your open mind to new ideas of how to improve. However, you do like to maintain control and hate to have plans change without your consent.

THE GEMINI SHEEP
Gemini: May 21 to June 21

The Peacemaker Bride gets two helpers for the price of one with the Gemini twins. With the gift of innovative thinking as well as a good sense of humor, the Gemini Sheep encounters less stress than others of her sign. You'll still have challenges when making up your mind, but not be as discouraged when things don't go your way. Lots of people will share advice with you, whether you like it or not, but this flurry of ideas actually inspires your sense of action rather than confusing it. You'll try to be practical in your approach, but you do have an appetite for trying as many things as possible. In fact, your fiancé may have a hard time keeping up with all your creative energy.

THE CANCERIAN SHEEP
Cancer: June 22 to July 21

The Cancerian Sheep is the ultimate humanitarian and ideal loved one. You regularly take on sacrifices to help others and see your wedding as a chance to include all the VIPs in your life. Cancer's influence results in a thinner skin than other Peacemaker Brides. You'll look to your fiancé and close friends and family to calm you down when you get near your breaking point. It'll be difficult for you to keep your feelings inside, but that is part of your charm. Your sign combination loves children. You'll delight in your godchildren or nieces and nephews as flower girls or ring bearers. It wouldn't be surprising if you're already thinking about babies of your own.

THE LEO SHEEP
Leo: July 22 to August 21

It's difficult to find a challenge that Leos don't want to take on. Confidence radiates from the Leo sign, and its regal qualities combine well with the Peacemaker Bride. Your caring, protective nature is enhanced by Leo's sense of action and independence. You'll be able to step back from emotional situations and make difficult decisions more easily than other Sheep natives. Can't choose your old college roommate as a bridesmaid? You'll be able to give her the news in a gracious way and offer up another way to include her in the wedding. Your optimistic perspective makes you a bride who can deal with the ups and downs of planning a wedding.

THE VIRGO SHEEP
Virgo: August 22 to September 22

Where the Sheep is easygoing and enjoys regular splurges, Virgo exists on the other side of the spectrum. More controlled and prone to denying her true wants, Virgo serves as a good balance. The Virgo Sheep results in a healthy work-hard, play-hard combination. You're just as sweet as your sister Peacemaker Brides, but more self-disciplined. You'll need less coaching (and reminding) to stop procrastinating and do the legwork for the projects you've been avoiding. A good deal of the motivation will come from your loving commitment to your fiancé, friends, and family. You're your own worst critic and will work tirelessly to perfect the projects closest to your heart.

THE LIBRA SHEEP
Libra: September 23 to October 22

Your sense of taste is quite refined and you gravitate to the most luxurious looks. Know this and move forward with greater confidence in your decisions. The Libra

Sheep battles with making up her mind, and even once she chooses a direction, has the nasty habit of looking back as well. Your fiancé and friends can be a great support in maintaining your hard-won choices. Since Sheep natives are greatly influenced by their environment, it's best to help shape situations to your tastes before you walk into a decision. If you walk into a wedding dress store and say, "Show me a bit of everything," you'll become overwhelmed by new ideas you never thought of. Identify what you like through magazines and Web sites, so you can give vendors a direction and focus yourself.

THE SCORPIO SHEEP
Scorpio: October 23 to November 21

Scorpio's influence is positive on the already stylish Peacemaker Bride. You're still an emotional bride. You love deeply, you voice your frustrations, but you're not so pessimistic that you throw in the towel at the first roadblock. Your confidence pushes you forward, even when the going gets rough. One of your greatest strengths is your gift of communication. Your wedding party will appreciate your clarity when wedding details are flying back and forth. You're also a class act when listening to other people's advice. Whether you take it or ignore it, you hear people's suggestions gracefully. Ultimately, you'll listen to your heart and move forward.

Wedding Synergy: When Dragon Meets Phoenix

As you embark on your planning, check out the Wedding Relationship pairings below to see how your strengths and weaknesses come together during the planning process. These compatibility descriptions are based on year of birth combinations, which is the tip of the iceberg when it comes to each of your charts. As described in Chapter 2 "Reference Dates and Tables on the Chinese Zodiac, East-West Sign Combinations, and Animal Hours," a different animal governs each component of your birth date and time.

RAT HUSBAND AND SHEEP WIFE

Money management will be the most haggled over topic in the Rat Husband–Sheep Wife household. As the Peacemaker Bride, you have a more short-term focus. You like to satisfy your bridal indulgences to the max. Your loving fiancé comes from a saver sign. Rat natives are hardworking hoarders, so you two may have conflicts over wedding spending. If you're fortunate enough to have your parents footing the wedding bill, naturally there will be fewer arguments. But your fiancé will still push for the good discounts as a matter of sport. You can ease the wedding planning road by consulting him on the budget and earn brownie points by suggesting a savings account for any cash wedding gifts.

OX HUSBAND AND SHEEP WIFE

Though the Sheep and the Ox are in natural opposition, the Peacemaker Bride can find domestic harmony with the dependable Ox man. The key to marital harmony will be embracing your signs' differences and finding the right balance. He's serious, and you're more creative. When setting out on a car trip, he'll bring the GPS and detailed notes, while you will encourage him to just drive and see where the day takes you. Your more reserved fiancé appreciates your eye for style and your caring ways. Teaming up on wedding details can result in a good exercise in checks and balances, if done correctly. Where you can be indecisive, he makes quick and intelligent judgments. He's also a real stickler for spending within your means, so while he may indulge you in a splurge or two, he's always aware of the total accounting. At the end of the day, your fiancé is fair-minded. He'll be there to carry his weight, but if you put too much on his plate, he has no problem pushing back, even if you are the bride.

TIGER HUSBAND AND SHEEP WIFE

You and your fiancé are both highly social animals, and when paired up make a popular couple. But the Tiger likes his alone time more than you do. While he's obviously very happy about your wedding, he'll want to be a part of only the big decisions. Don't take it personally, but he only has patience for so many things. You can avoid a lot of argument by taking the initiative with the nitty-gritty. Of course, keep him in the loop with regular updates, but more frequent discussions won't inspire lots of conversation. In fact, a brush-off or short reply may bruise your thin skin.

RABBIT HUSBAND AND SHEEP WIFE

Pairing these two signs from the Catalysts Affinity Triangle produces a loving couple not afraid of public displays of affection. You each try your best to tune into the other's feelings. Being born in the year of the Rabbit makes your fiancé more patient than most husbands-to-be. He'll be a great listener when you need to vent or bounce ideas off someone. The Peacemaker Bride often wavers between ideas because she overthinks problems. Your Rabbit mate not only has excellent taste, but can give you direction when you need it, so keep him well tied into the process.

DRAGON HUSBAND AND SHEEP WIFE

Your two signs exemplify the coupling of masculine and feminine zodiac signs. The Dragon is a strong and fearless personality. He enjoys tackling big challenges and almost prefers to meet these battles alone. Meanwhile, your strength is more undercover, shown to the world through your emotional intelligence. Your combination can be harmonious, but you'll have to manage your communication styles. Keep lovers' quarrels to a minimum. He's not inclined to dive into any details about the wedding that don't concern him. When he hears a problem, he'll want to fix it for you, so if you're venting about a temperamental bridesmaid or the flighty florist, you might want to call a friend. You're only going to get sympathy from your fiancé in moments of true panic or injustice.

SNAKE HUSBAND AND SHEEP WIFE

The Snake and Sheep natives possess different decision making behaviors. While the Peacemaker Bride thinks out loud and asks for other people's opinions, the Snake sign acts alone and with little discussion. Even if he strongly disagrees with a situation, he weighs the trouble of making his voice heard. Often, he will chose silence—the path of least resistance—to keep the peace. Instead of looking to others, try to get your fiancé's true feelings out of his mental vault. Don't get discouraged, but try to avoid being a nag as well. If you focus discussions toward making a decision, he'll be more receptive. If it's just a discussion about feelings, you'll get little more than a "whatever you think is best."

HORSE HUSBAND AND SHEEP WIFE

The Peacemaker Bride is a product of her environment. Fortunately, you've paired yourself with an optimist by marrying a Horse native. His energy can push you forward during hard times. On the other side, he is drawn to your caring personality and loves all the attention you give him. Horses are happy to work with others as long as they get some time to be by themselves. If you can balance couple time with personal time, your wedding planning can go quite smoothly. Your fiancé is a good problem solver and rarely gets stressed. In fact, his good sense of humor will help keep wedding planning and social situations light.

SHEEP HUSBAND AND SHEEP WIFE

A marriage of two sheep will produce a comfortable and luxurious home life. You both enjoy the good life. Registering for stylish gifts and cake tastings are all fun activities for Sheep signs. As Peacemakers, you're deep feelers, trying to keep everyone happy. Shouldering this kind of responsibility can be stressful with so many close friends and family involved. As the bride, you'll have to take the lead making the difficult decisions. In your effort to please everyone, you'll both try to avoid the tough issues, such as omitting someone from the guest list. However, if you don't face them head-on, you're making a difficult conversation only more awkward.

MONKEY HUSBAND AND SHEEP WIFE

The Peacemaker Bride has the great fortune of being very lucky and perhaps a bit spoiled as a result. People like to take care of you and come to your aid when problems arise. Meanwhile, the Monkey sign is a very practical person and enjoys being selective of whom and what to lavish his attention on. Perhaps the Monkey's habit of playing hard to get is what sparked the attraction, but will be a thorn in your side during the wedding planning process. A monkey is clever and has lots of creative ideas, so you'll be tempted to share your problems with him. However, be selective with what you ask for from your fiancé. Your emotional nature can mean that you see a disaster when in fact it's really a small bump in the road, which you realize only after you've had a chance to cool down. Your husband-to-be will be more engaged if there are fewer dramatic problems and more challenges to tackle.

ROOSTER HUSBAND AND SHEEP WIFE

The working relationship of a Rooster sign and Sheep native can be a struggle without compromise and patient communication. Between the two of you, the Peacemaker Bride is the more sensitive. You don't take criticism well, while your fiancé is the analytical mind of the zodiac. The Rooster can be a tad myopic to the Peacemaker Bride. He's a natural planner, enjoys the details, and deals with stress calmly, while you are struggling with these very things. The ways to harmonious planning will be a combined effort. You can get a lot of brownie points by asking for help early, before any problems arise. Your fiancé hates to wait to the last minute. If he creates the plan, he's more inclined to follow it to completion.

DOG HUSBAND AND SHEEP WIFE

There are natural challenges to this relationship. Do not be discouraged by this— every marriage has internal conflicts, but attraction inspires the compromise necessary to make it work. At heart, the Dog is a Protector who defends fairness. You're a person who makes choices with her heart. Therefore, you can see how emotional decisions aren't always fair to someone who favors equality. You'll need to communicate openly and patiently. The big thing will be curbing any favoritism. Will you pay for the bridesmaid's dress for his younger sister because she's a poor college student, but not for his sister-in-law because she made you pay for yours in her wedding? These are the discussions to be had. You won't want him to feel slighted or have your feelings hurt. It's best, though, to appeal to his logic, rather than fight with emotion.

BOAR HUSBAND AND SHEEP WIFE

The Boar and the Sheep are both members of the Catalysts Affinity Triangle. This provides a strong foundation for romance and friendship. The Peacemaker Bride has her fair share of ups and downs planning a wedding. Stress doesn't sit well with you, but fortunately, your fiancé is a great source of support. His fun-loving nature can lighten any tense situation and help you refocus on the big picture. Both of you share a deep love for each other and do what you can to make each other happy. You can do great things when given a safety net. Your fiancé is happy to catch you in return for lots of love and affection.

The Sheep's Relationships with Friends and Family

Family and friends are an important part of most weddings. Since we all operate differently in our nonromantic relationships, the pairings of your Chinese zodiac sign will take a slightly different form. Knowing the compatibility of your animal sign with your family and friends is a real asset when planning and setting expectations for responsibilities. As you think about how best to integrate your vast network of friends, review the relationship overviews below. They will help cast light on your friends' and family members' strengths, weaknesses, and working styles.

WITH A RAT

The Rat sign has a reputation for getting things done. Your friend's organized personality and natural discipline can be quite the guiding force. Wedding coordinator, maid/matron of honor, or even personal trainer are all easy roles for her to play. While you're capable of doing all these things, you're reluctant to start and finish projects, for fear of failure or paralysis from stress itself. Your friend will be a motivating force who won't pull any punches. Even though you're not a fan of criticism, it can be a blessing to hear another perspective. The Rat sign will do her best to be kind while coaching you forward.

✕ WITH AN OX

The Peacemaker Bride will find challenges working with the Ox, as they're at opposite sides of the Chinese zodiac. If you two don't share a common ascendant, it can be difficult to see eye to eye. The Ox native prefers to go things alone and maintain her rigid standards. You'll find she's trustworthy and straightforward, but doesn't have patience for lots of change. With her personality in mind, choose her role and adjust your expectations accordingly. If she's a bridesmaid, involve her after decisions have been finalized. If you've asked her to take on any role that requires preparation, such as a reader or vocalist, do not wait until the last minute to give her all the details.

WITH A TIGER

Your friend born in the year of the Tiger comes from the Protectors group. This means that, like you, she listens to her intuition to make decisions and feels deeply about important people in her life. The Peacemaker Bride works well with Tiger natives because you possess the right amount of patience to communicate with passionate people. In turn, your friend can be depended on to carry out any wedding tasks. She's also a great friend to talk to, whether it's brainstorming or venting. However, be careful with sharing any secrets. Tigers aren't known for discretion and can unintentionally say the wrong thing at the wrong time.

Δ WITH A RABBIT

The Rabbit and Sheep signs have quite a bit in common. You both possess an eye for style and an appreciation for all life's luxuries. Therefore, you'll enjoy talking about the wedding because they bring together so many delightful things to the two of you. Your friend possesses great intuitive skills and a good eye for body language. She'll be able to take a hint when you need to be left alone or a kind ear to talk about wedding stress with. One of her most valuable skills to the Peacemaker Bride may ironically be on the topic of diplomacy. The Rabbit negotiates the best deals and can deliver bad news with great care. Listen to her coaching on how to deal with problems head-on, rather than wishing they'd sort themselves out.

WITH A DRAGON

Your friend or family member is a part of the zodiac trio known as the Doers. Dragons are strong personalities, who have a big appetite for accomplishment. Whether you've known each other for years or met as a result of the wedding, you'll be inspired by this person's energy. In fact, her leadership abilities can easily take over, depending on how much free rein you give. This may be a blessing if you're a fan of the Dragon's taste and decision making. If not, it's best to limit help to well-structured projects or use a diplomatic go-between.

WITH A SNAKE

Even though your personalities can differ dramatically, you share similar tastes. The Snake sign may be a challenge to get to know, as you've experienced or are quickly finding out. This person tries to keep the peace by holding her tongue, so don't look for sympathy or words of encouragement unless you've established a close friendship. The Snake has exquisite taste and impeccable manners, so keep that in mind if you need someone to assist in a design element. Just make sure it's a project she can work on independently, so that she can focus on her work.

WITH A HORSE

Old friend or new, the Peacemaker Bride can achieve a great deal with a Horse on her team. The Horse native works best on urgent projects, finding it exciting to tackle challenges and, better yet, save the day. Ambitious and agile, this person enjoys racking up accomplishments. She will be short on patience, and once her promises have been met, her presence will be scarce. Rest assured though that the Horse honors her responsibilities. After the wedding, don't be hurt if your friendship doesn't progress. Take solace in the fact that you live life at different speeds.

Δ WITH ANOTHER SHEEP

Working with your common sign ensures smoother communication than usual. Your animal is known for an easygoing nature and kind disposition. Together you'll indulge in all the wedding pleasantries. From flowers to party favors, you two can spend hours on what catches your fantasy. Time flies when you're having fun, and between the two of you, you'll have to step up as the leader. After all, it is your wedding. Otherwise you may dwell too long on some tasks while ignoring others that are more important, but perhaps less glamorous. Sheep like to procrastinate, and wedding planning is no fun when left to the last minute.

WITH A MONKEY

Whether you've just met or grown up together, you'll be impressed by this person's intelligence. Monkey signs can get a lot done in a short amount of time and can find a solution where there is seemingly none. You'll be thankful to have her around during an emergency, when your emotions can cause bridal paralysis. Fortunately, Monkeys can be depended on to embrace any challenge. This person is also very observant and can easily turn her critical eye to your work. So when you ask for her opinion, beware, she'll motivate you to work faster and smarter.

If you're asking for any favors, be sure to be punctual, though, because Monkeys don't like waiting around.

WITH A ROOSTER

Your relaxed ways and the Rooster's carefully crafted plans may not mix. The Rooster native is a master planner and all-around perfectionist. You're a reluctant leader, even though you're very capable. Depending on your relationship, this person may be more or less tolerant of your requests. You're used to special treatment from your fiancé, but don't expect it from this person. Roosters enjoy finding flaws because they enjoy fixing them. If possible, since you're not a fan of criticism (no matter how constructive), it's best to limit her presence during decision making or work through an intermediary.

WITH A DOG

The Dog native can be a great asset to your wedding planning. You'll find that she can keep her cool amid chaos. It's a lucky thing she's around because stress can take its toll on the Peacemaker Bride. Every girl needs a calm voice to give guidance every once in a while. The Dog sign takes on that responsibility well. Your friend or family member feels a sense of duty in making sure you're in good shape for the wedding. Be sure to acknowledge this person and all of her valuable contributions because this sign has a long memory for disrespect. You can be confident that your charming way of thanking others will be much appreciated.

Δ WITH A BOAR

The Peacemaker Bride and the sign of the Boar have a high degree of compatibility. You're both very giving in friendships. Long conversations come easily, and this person is a fantastic listener. The Boar sign's philosophy is carpe diem, and she'll encourage you to do whatever makes you happy. So hold on to your purse strings, because your friend knows how to run up a bill. Overall you've got a great friend here, but not an accountant.

Fourteen

BORN IN THE YEAR OF THE MONKEY
Here Comes the Innovator Bride

Lunar Years of the Monkey	Elements
January 25, 1944, to February 12, 1945	Wood
February 12, 1956, to January 30, 1957	Fire
January 30, 1968, to February 16, 1969	Earth
February 16, 1980, to February 4, 1981	Metal
February 4, 1992, to January 22, 1993	Water
January 22, 2004, to February 8, 2005	Wood

Innovator Bride Details

Birth Hours: 3 P.M. to 5 P.M.

Western Sign: Leo

Western Gemstone: Peridot or Sardonyx

Symbolic Color: White

Flower: Hydrangea

Season: Autumn

Element: Metal

Famous Innovator Brides:
Christy Turlington Burns, Kim Cattrall, Joan Crawford,
Bette Davis, Bo Derek, Debbie Reynolds, Eleanor Roosevelt,
Diana Ross, Elizabeth Taylor.

The Dress:

You like the latest fashions, especially those with a clean and tailored look. Always an individual, you'll want a dress that's different. You're comfortable spending a high amount on your dress or adding ornamentation to a good foundation dress. You're a good critic who can identify a bargain and tailor it to your needs as a bride.

The Monkey Sign: The Ninth Bride of the Chinese Zodiac

As the ninth sign of the zodiac, the Monkey is famously clever. She is a part of what we refer to as the Doers group. There are four groups: the Doers, the Thinkers, the Protectors, and the Catalysts. The groups are made up of the three animals that have a natural affinity to one another, referred to as a Triangle of Affinity. Each set of three animals has a social connection—a kind of chemistry that is connected to each zodiac sign.

The Doers group is made up of the Rat, the Monkey, and the Dragon. No surprise, people with these birth signs or ascendants are your most natural friends and working partners. In fact, it's likely your fiancé has strong ties to this group as well. As their team name suggests, these ladies don't like to stand still—they are the ones who make things happen. Those born in the year of the Monkey have the mantra "I think." She is the bride voted most likely to commit most of her wedding details to memory. Here comes the Innovator Bride.

The Innovator Bride—Born in the Year of the Monkey

The Innovator Bride is a dynamic overachiever. She is famous for her ambition, intelligence, and creative personality, and her wedding will be another accomplishment to add to her wall of achievement. Your outgoing personality is your lucky charm to getting into the good graces of in-laws and vendors and makes you a charismatic bride to say the least. It's your ability to create fabulous ideas out of thin air that will make your wedding a magical day and one that none of your guests will soon forget.

Less personable animals find it difficult to be thrust into the role of being a bride. All of a sudden you are the center of attention, everyone wants to meet you, and you're expected to call the shots. This isn't a problem at all for the Innovator Bride because she's a big fan of getting attention, and why shouldn't she be? You're full of good ideas and a natural leader. The Monkey native is a social chameleon, cleverly adjusting her personality to the audience and type of occasion. You're a master at choosing the right words and have a laser-accurate memory when it comes to details. While you are crafting seating charts and writing out invitations, you'll literally absorb all the names of your guests with frightening accuracy. One shouldn't compete with you in the areas of trivia or past events. Your fiancé will undoubtedly be impressed by how much you learn during your time of wedding planning.

Monkeys have the reputation for being master strategists. They can think far ahead and aren't thrown by changes in plan. Monkey natives see all sorts of possibilities in change because they're quite fond of bending the rules on a regular basis. With such a mind for games and puzzles, the Innovator Bride is one of the fiercest competitors in the Chinese zodiac, and frankly isn't the most gracious winner or loser. You simply love to be number one and you're not above competing with another bride for the best photographer in town or the last box of stationery. You'll treat your budget with similar fervor. You don't like to waste money because to pay too much is to lose in one of the easiest games to play.

With your gift of gab, it's easy for you to describe what you want to your fiancé and anyone else involved with the wedding. However, you aren't the best listener when the topic of compromise or criticism is coming back at you. It's not that you can't take heat, but you're very selective about what you want to listen to. You'll simply tune out when someone is pushing back on one of your brilliant ideas. At the first sound of no, you'll start thinking of what your next course of action is before your poor opponent has even finished his or her thought. As wedding planning is a long process and the prelude to your marriage, you'll have to subdue your sense of competition and choose your battles, especially when working with your fiancé and his family. Some battles are not worth winning, and compromise is a necessity to wedding harmony, which is a tough lesson for some Innovator Brides to accept.

With all your talents and attention, you run the risk of becoming a selfish bride. You can actually be so competitive that it dampens some of your appeal, especially for those most involved in your wedding. As a member of the Doers group, you're blessed and cursed with the obsession for getting things done—the more, the faster, the better. Your creative personality looks for shortcuts, but remains so optimistic that you convince yourself that none of the negative consequences of taking the easy way could possibly affect you. Even after a project is done, it's never completely out of your mind. Everything seems to be filed under "room for improvement." You have no problem throwing an almost completed project in the trash for a new, never before seen strategy. The thrill of the challenge and the bragging rights are just too much to be resisted. Monkeys love experiments just to see what's going to happen. All this is fine if you were to be working on all aspects of your wedding individually, but don't forget that the money you're spending could be seen as joint funds and that not all your attendants will be as jazzed about redoing past work.

On your wedding day, put some of your plans aside and embrace your ability to improvise. You're actually best when you don't have a script. With your talent for observation, you can quickly assess what your audience needs. The Innovator Bride can make them laugh or cry. But on this day, choose to speak from the heart, rather than simply entertain. Wedding guests are there to share in a rite of passage in your and your fiancé's life and are the biggest fans of authenticity. Your natural charisma simply cannot be suppressed, so let out your feeling of love and gratitude for everyone to hear.

East Meets West: When Moon Signs Meet Sun Signs

Many people don't realize that each animal of the Chinese zodiac has a solar calendar connection. In our interpretation of Chinese horoscopes, the lunar calendar links into the solar calendar through the month and season, where the Monkey's parallel sun sign is Leo. But every Western sun sign has a different effect on the lunar moon sign.

THE SAGITTARIUS MONKEY
Sagittarius: November 22 to December 21
The Sagittarius Monkey knows how to have fun and get her work done all at the same time. The Innovator Bride is a master at creation, but following the path is harder than envisioning the finish line. In comes Sagittarius, who provides a compass to the planning process. With straightforward plans and direct communication style, this sign will be particular about wedding plans because things should be done at a high standard. Some people close to you may be surprised at your sophisticated level of organization and taste, but take it as a compliment. No matter how stressed you feel on the inside, you try to not pass it on to others.

THE CAPRICORN MONKEY
Capricorn: December 22 to January 20
With Capricorn's influence, you're a calmer Innovator Bride than your sister Monkeys. The Monkey sign gives you creativity and quick wit. Capricorn encourages you to be more consistent and not wait until the last minute. You like to face chal-

lenges in small bites. Rather than a crash course diet, you'll start scaling back a little bit of dessert or a cocktail here and there, right after the ring makes everything official. You'll favor being more cautious about your wedding plans, but that extroverted Monkey could show itself on the dance floor or in a dazzling speech to your guests.

THE AQUARIUS MONKEY
Aquarius: January 21 to February 19

The Aquarius Monkey is certainly an original. You'll only listen to your heart, your fiancé, and few other close members of your inner circle when planning your wedding. You're very open-minded and like to explore every option, but ultimately you'll go with what you think is best. Funny how you'll always come back to your first pick, but you enjoy the journey of exploring everything that's possible. Your wedding will reflect ultramodern tastes because you like to stay up on the trends and embrace change. Not one to be challenged, you'll use your debate skills as a weapon and fight for your right to make decisions.

THE PISCES MONKEY
Pisces: February 20 to March 20

You're a natural charmer. The Monkey sign excels at getting on people's good side, and Pisces people are emotionally intelligent. Your sweet smile is a cunning disguise for a master strategist who knows when and with whom to share her true opinions. You're very observant and conscientious when it comes to your wedding. You'll go after a deal as hard as the next bride, but will choose to do your research and perhaps do a bit of stealth work beforehand by consulting friends, published rankings, and online reviews. Your diligence combined with your intellect will result in a well-planned and meaningful wedding.

THE ARIES MONKEY
Aries: March 21 to April 19

The Innovator Bride knows how to entertain, which gives you a great foundation for a wedding. The Aries Monkey is a particularly good orator. You won't shy away from the microphone, and you'll find that the words for thoughtful thank-you cards come as easily as the gifts came through the doors. You're a lady in every sense of the word, honoring social graces to the best of your ability. It's rare for anyone to see you lose your cool because you almost never do. You should be cautious about rethinking wedding plans after they have been set in motion. While being the bride means that you have the right to call the shots, beware of changing your mind too often and rearranging other people's lives in process. Being a tad selfish is tolerated and somewhat expected for brides, but too far down the line, it can be a big imposition.

THE TAURUS MONKEY
Taurus: April 20 to May 20

Taurus favors a more consistent pace than the native Monkey, who tends to start and stop at the pace of her active mind. The result of this combination will be an even-tempered bride with a lively imagination at work underneath. Like your sister Monkeys, you're a fan of orchestrating great deals, but won't be tempted to pull any tricks on the opposition. You're more likely to negotiate until a person simply realizes that you won't quit and just gives in. This straightforward approach is a breath of fresh air because you know what you want and aren't shy about asking for it.

THE GEMINI MONKEY
Gemini: May 21 to June 21

With focus and formidable mental muscle, you're the kind of Innovator Bride who doesn't ask for a lot of help because you may not need it. In your daily life, you enjoy tackling life's challenges with clever shortcuts. That's the Monkey brain for you, always trying to take things apart, figure out how they work, and improve on them in the end. You've probably been studying other friends' weddings for years, collecting ideas and waiting to unveil your own masterpiece. With your wedding strategy in place, it'll be hard for anyone to sway your decisions, even your fiancé. Stand firm, but work on letting people believe you're listening.

THE CANCERIAN MONKEY

Cancer: June 22 to July 21

Known as a fan of luxurious goods and clever investments, you've raised the bar high for your wedding. Anyone who knows you recognizes that you have a talent for seeking out the best, but it's not pure materialism for the sake of supporting the economy. You believe in buying for the long term and the power of first impressions. Naturally, you'll turn special attention to your wedding dress (or dresses). Your public has come to wish you well and you certainly can't disappoint. You'll be drawn to high-glamour dresses, and you'll find no shame in renting or in adding your own embellishment, one Swarovski crystal at a time.

THE LEO MONKEY

Leo: July 22 to August 21

A Monkey and a Lion come together to create a perfect bride-in-chief. The Leo sign is a natural leader who is fair and clear-minded. The Innovator Bride is fast on her feet and has a delightful sense of humor. Your flair for mischief is subdued by Leo's regal discipline, but that doesn't mean you won't enjoy some delicious gossip here and there. You're an open book who naively assumes everyone else is as ready to share her life story as you are. You may need to guard your inquisitive nature to help prevent any unintentional discomfort when meeting new people, not to mention future in-laws.

THE VIRGO MONKEY

Virgo: August 22 to September 22

The Innovator Bride's brain is always running. It never stops, and so your options continue to multiply. Perhaps that's why the Virgo Monkey can get overwhelmed and waver in important decisions. Fortunately, you're not so stubborn that you're unwilling to reveal this weakness around your fiancé and loved ones. They'll help set you straight by listening to you talk through your likes and dislikes. Once your wedding theme, location, and all the big items are sorted out, you'll be off and running. The Virgo Monkey excels at getting things done according to the schedule.

THE LIBRA MONKEY

Libra: September 23 to October 22

This Innovator Bride believes in strength in numbers. You embrace the idea that a wedding is more than the bride and will bring together a diverse group of people for your big day. Your loved ones and in-laws love your approach, but you'll have to deal with more unsolicited advice than usual when you choose to be this open. Be prepared for the onslaught. Your Monkey intellect will serve you well by putting everyone's strengths and personalities to good use, and your gift of gab can smooth the way for more peace than you can imagine.

THE SCORPIO MONKEY

Scorpio: October 23 to November 21

The Scorpio Monkey is a popular bride who knows how to keep lots of balls in the air. Calling vendors, maintaining your Web site with every last detail, bridal boot camp—you name it, you've got it covered. With well-thought-out plans, you're clever about which topics need your attention. Your bright ideas can get you out of any jam. If you reflect on your wedding, though, your self-sufficient work ethic can create some problems. You may shut out others or become especially rigid to criticism or broken promises. Try to avoid any wedding drama by being honest with yourself about your friends' capabilities, because someone who crosses you may not be prepared for the Scorpion's sting.

Wedding Synergy: When Dragon Meets Phoenix

As you embark on your planning, check out the Wedding Relationship pairings below to see how your strengths and weaknesses come together during the planning process. These compatibility descriptions are based on year of birth combinations, which is the tip of the iceberg when it comes to each of your charts. As described in Chapter 2 "Reference Dates and Tables on the Chinese Zodiac, East-West Sign Combinations, and Animal Hours," a different animal governs each component of your birth date and time.

RAT HUSBAND AND MONKEY WIFE

You find bliss with the Rat sign because you are joined by an optimistic attitude toward life. Growing together as a couple involves having similar priorities. In your case, productivity and achievement are the foundation of your daily lives. Whether working together or separately, you approach your wedding practically. You enjoy looking at the big picture and finding all the opportunities to make the most of all the details. The two of you will employ the powers of negotiation and networking to find the best deals and invest in items that can be used at your wedding and in your new home.

OX HUSBAND AND MONKEY WIFE

Like many husbands-to-be, the Ox is a fan of simplicity. He doesn't like how complex, not to mention expensive and stressful, weddings can be. As the Innovator Bride, you'll have to remind him that your choices only look pricey; your taste is exquisite, but your methods are savvy. He'll admire your creativity in getting what you want and meeting the budget that you agreed on. You'll find that he's also not as open to many impositions on his time. While he will indulge in your bridal fantasies, be mindful of involving him in too many unplanned tasks. He doesn't like the fuss of assembling invitations and finds it difficult to write his own vows.

TIGER HUSBAND AND MONKEY WIFE

As Affinity Triangles connect, the Monkey Doers club and the Tiger Protectors group don't typically mix well, but attraction is sometimes too tempting. The Innovator Bride and Tiger sign have a lot in common, which can attract and repel. Both you and your fiancé like attention. Since weddings are the biggest stage of all, be sure to give the groom his time to ham it up to the guests. While the bride is typically fawned over as the center of attention, your Tiger husband will want a piece of the limelight. Tiger signs are a proud bunch and like to brag and boast about their accomplishments, with weddings as a prime candidate. You'll also have to own the budget because your fiancé's generosity can get the best of him.

RABBIT HUSBAND AND MONKEY WIFE

There is a deep attraction between the Rabbit and the Monkey. Both of you are masters at reading people, so it will be in your power to choose and defuse arguments as they come up in wedding planning. As the Innovator Bride, your drive to accomplish great things may make you impatient and aggressive. You'll have to tame your temper with your fiancé, who can be reclusive and seek alone time when stress gets the best of him. Share the responsibilities, grant him total autonomy on his tasks, and promise to not make tweaks when they're complete. He'll see your trust as a sign of respect and enjoy taking a more active part in the wedding.

DRAGON HUSBAND AND MONKEY WIFE

An Affinity Triangle marriage like yours boasts a strong foundation. Like Monkey signs, Dragons have ambitious natures and the energy to make their dreams come true. You'll team up well as you know how to tap into each other's strengths. You'll need to channel your husband's energy, so that it is used most effectively. Your charming ways of asking and saying thanks will ensure he leaps to the challenge. At the wedding, your guests will enjoy watching your natural chemistry. Whether it's dancing, heartfelt vows, or a witty toast, you're both entertainers who rise to the challenge.

SNAKE HUSBAND AND MONKEY WIFE

The Innovator Bride enjoys seeking out challenges. Perhaps your greatest challenge will be planning your wedding with your fiancé born in the year of the Snake. Monkeys and Snakes are both bright individuals, but the Snake's solitary ways may be a roadblock for your wedding planning. Keep communication lines open and resist passive-aggressive tactics. Getting opinions out of your fiancé may feel like pulling teeth, but you're clever enough to come up with the best method. Watch his body language and draw clues from items that he buys himself. When in doubt, employ a good friend or future sibling-in-law for a final consult.

HORSE HUSBAND AND MONKEY WIFE

Pairing up a Horse and a Monkey can produce many advantages, as long as you truly become a team that talks to each other. Both your signs are practical and optimistic, which certainly helps make discussions easier. It's your spontaneity that can lead to arguments. Whether it's picking up a good deal with a vendor before talking to your soon-to-be-spouse or adding a few people to the guest list—you need to keep each other in the loop. You both vehemently dislike redoing the same piece of work and will not enjoy having to adjust your seating chart when a plus-one has been overlooked.

SHEEP HUSBAND AND MONKEY WIFE

Romantic and affectionate, the Sheep likes to exist at a slower pace than the Innovator Bride. Most times, you'll find his relaxed attitude a blessing, other times you may feel he's not pulling his weight. The Sheep has a difficult time self-motivating for long, detailed projects, so you will have to inspire his will. Remember that compliments open more ears than criticism, especially with the Sheep sign. If you support him, you'll be amazed at how much he'll accomplish.

MONKEY HUSBAND AND MONKEY WIFE

Monkey business can be both fun and profitable. You and your fiancé have creative minds that love a good challenge. What better special assignment than your own wedding? From location to honeymoon, you'll enjoy creating the vision of the big day and crossing items off your to-do list. However, be prepared for unexpected problems—drama with relatives or misunderstandings. You and your fiancé need to give helpful hints to each other and use your keen powers of observation to anticipate problems rather than deal with them when they're full-blown. You'll have to resist pointing fingers at each other when stuff does hit the fan because fault-finding never solves the core problem.

ROOSTER HUSBAND AND MONKEY WIFE

Roosters and Monkeys don't typically mix, but when romance casts its spell, they can build a great partnership. In fact, wedding planning can benefit from both of your strengths. As the Innovator Bride, you're clever and an A student at doing your homework for the best deals in town. Your fiancé is a very detailed taskmaster. He'll be a great Webmaster, taking care to keep everything up-to-date and giving the best directions to a difficult-to-find ceremony or reception. However, he may bruise your ego on occasion with his constant bits of constructive criticism, so you may have to grow a thicker skin or you'll just have to avoid sensitive topics.

DOG HUSBAND AND MONKEY WIFE

You've found a man who is generous with his heart. The Dog sign's love grows out of respect, which was sparked by your charming and intelligent manner. Your wedding disagreements may arise from how you use your wedding budget. While you're wise with your money, your fiancé may not agree with too many bridal indulgences. He may push back on the idea of multiple dresses, unless it's of cultural importance or for a practical reason (such as a shorter style for all-night dancing). In his eyes, extra money should be used to spend on accommodations for out-of-town guests or for your first home down payment, so budget for a splurge fund early in the process to better prepare for the costs of discovering a new must-have item or to fund some unanticipated creative project.

BOAR HUSBAND AND MONKEY WIFE

The Innovator Bride may be a social animal, but she's skeptical of others (probably because she's known for being such a competitive personality). Therefore, this attraction may be built on the Boar's refreshing honesty. And he's definitely the type of person whom you cannot change easily. Your fiancé tells it like it is and trusts you'll give him the same fair treatment, so curb the games because they won't get you anywhere. Your tastes are prone to be lavish, but his spending may be the part that's too rich for your collective budget. Designer dresses may be expensive, but an open bar adds up!

The Monkey's Relationships with Friends and Family

Family and friends are an important part of most weddings. Since we all operate differently in our nonromantic relationships, the pairings of your Chinese zodiac sign will take a slightly different form. Knowing the compatibility of your animal sign with your family and friends is a real asset when planning and setting expectations for responsibilities. As you think about how best to integrate your vast network of friends, review the relationship overviews below. They will help cast light on your friends' and family members' strengths, weaknesses, and working styles.

Δ WITH A RAT

As a fellow Doer, you're fast friends with the Rat because your strengths are complementary. The Innovator Bride conjures up many a grand scheme when planning her wedding vision. While there are plenty of naysayers out there, the Rat is always a positive source of support. With a we-can-do-it attitude, she'll roll up her sleeves to take on a crazy DIY task or fitness challenge, so you won't go it alone.

WITH AN OX

The Ox sign is a no-nonsense, extremely consistent person, which can be a real asset to the Innovator Bride. The trick will be to tailor activities to match the Ox's strength and avoid ones that clash with the Monkey sign. Work with the Ox on detailed tasks, which require patience and care, and save your vague, creative projects for people who are on a similar wavelength. Your sister Doers the Rat and Dragon are great candidates for brainstorming. The Ox is a master at executing the details.

× WITH A TIGER

The Innovator Bride finds the most challenges with the Tiger sign. The fact is that you are both competitive and unfortunately terrible losers. If there's a hint of jealousy between you two, it's wise to work with common friends or family and limit interaction to keep things peaceful. You should also take care with your words. Even your sarcasm, albeit funny, can rub this person the wrong way. The Tiger's known for being emotional and hard to predict, another reason to test the waters before deciding to involve this person very intimately with your wedding.

WITH A RABBIT

The Monkey and Rabbit signs both believe in keeping up appearances, so even if friendship doesn't come easily, there's no cause for alarm. The Innovator Bride can look to the Rabbit for a second opinion on style, since this sign is known for her elegance. However, difficult or time-intensive tasks (unless you've established a strong commitment) aren't the best match. While always polite, she'll frequently turn down high involvement. Don't be offended, though; it's much better for someone to push back at the beginning than to commit and let you down at the last minute.

Δ WITH A DRAGON

The Dragon sign is another close ally of the Innovator Bride. With your ties through the Affinity Triangle, your work styles blend well together. Driven and highly ambitious, your Dragon friend or family member feeds off challenges. More importantly, she'll be supportive of your creative missions as well. After all, the Doers group practically invented the process of thinking outside the box. She's ideal to have as a bridesmaid and will be helpful with projects and emotional support.

WITH A SNAKE

The Innovator Bride can't break through the mysterious exterior of the Snake sign. Don't feel discouraged, because you're not alone: Snakes are solitary people who build trust slowly. They hold on to their opinions as well-guarded secrets. If you and this person are just getting to know each other, invite her to all pre-wedding social events and start breaking the ice early. However, unless you or your fiancé has strong ties, don't expect a lot of willingness to take on public roles at your wedding.

WITH A HORSE

By and large, the Innovator Bride works well with the Horse sign. This person is quite sharp and gets things done quickly. However, both of you can divert your attention and lose focus easily. This can test the patience of both of you. Feel free to call this person out because she won't pull any punches with you. Neither of you hold grudges, which allows you to have good, honest communication. If you two don't seem to find your groove in working together, there'll be no hard feelings if you decide to include other people in the mix and limit this person's involvement to get the job done.

WITH A SHEEP

The Innovator Bride knows how to make the Sheep shine on any project. The Sheep sign is a caring and genuine person. She'll be quick to offer help and actually follow through on her promises. As the Innovator Bride, you'll have to be a part-time cheerleader for the Sheep if she's one of your attendants or part of the general wedding entourage. This friend or family member excels with praise, particularly if you've asked her to be a part of the talent portion of the ceremony or reception. She'll be a nervous wreck, so recruit others to build up her confidence on the big day.

Δ WITH ANOTHER MONKEY

Working with a fellow Monkey sign can be a blessing or a curse—twice the creativity, but twice the ego. Keep communication flowing and be honest with yourself about whether you really trust this person. If there's jealousy or a past of irrational competition, cut your losses and limit your interaction. You'll argue over petty issues, and while neither of you holds grudges long, you don't need the additional stress with all your other responsibilities.

WITH A ROOSTER

The Innovator Bride can round out her team with a Rooster sign, if she's willing to be flexible with some adjustments. The Rooster is a perfectionist—a hard worker, a stickler for details, and also quite the negotiator. The Innovator Bride may not always be able to stomach the Rooster's honesty. Test the waters and see how you react to this person's style of criticism and plan accordingly. Let's just say that if she has a lot of opinions while flipping through a wedding magazine, it's only going to be amplified if you go shopping in real life.

WITH A DOG

You won't experience any drama with the Dog sign as long as you're a good leader. The Dog sign is a team player and will always pull her own weight on a team project. However, don't be tempted to give her more to do just because she's cleared her plate of responsibilities and others have dragged their feet. If you must, make sure you ask politely, as she'll be sore at the inequality. Also, she's not a fan of tall tales or lies, white or otherwise. These things lose her trust easily because the Dog sign is most likely to come to the rescue only in matters of crisis. She'll be the first to volunteer to help a person who has fallen ill or experienced a traumatic life situation, such as a death or divorce.

WITH A BOAR

As the party animal of the zodiac, the Boar is a popular gal. She seems to know everybody, and you'll be wise to tap into her network for advice and possible discounts. The eternal optimist, the Boar sign can cheer the Innovator Bride on even the most frustrating day. The Boar native is incredibly selfless when it comes to people she cares about. She'll literally move mountains when you're in trouble and stand on her head just to make you laugh.

Fifteen

BORN IN THE YEAR OF THE HEN
Here Comes the Perfectionist Bride

Lunar Years of the Hen	Elements
January 26, 1933, to February 13, 1934	Water
February 13, 1945, to February 1, 1946	Wood
January 31, 1957, to February 17, 1958	Fire
February 17, 1969, to February 5, 1970	Earth
February 5, 1981, to January 24, 1982	Metal
January 23, 1993, to February 9, 1994	Water

Perfectionist Bride Details

Birth Hours: 5 P.M. to 7 P.M.

Western Sign: Virgo

Western Gemstone: Sapphire

Symbolic Color: White

Flower: Carnation

Season: Autumn

Element: Metal

Famous Perfectionist Brides:

Cate Blanchett, Gloria Estefan, Angie Everhart,
Katharine Hepburn, Deborah Kerr, Frances McDormand,
Gwen Stefani, Renée Zellweger.

The Dress:

The Perfectionist Bride is drawn to classic dresses with simple lines. An elegant dress will be the ideal foundation for your penchant for dramatic accessories. Whether borrowed or bought, exotic or family heirloom, you enjoy adding your own personal flair.

The Hen Sign: The Tenth Bride of the Chinese Zodiac

As the tenth sign of the zodiac, the Hen is one of the most objective animals. She is a part of what we refer to as the Thinkers group. There are four groups: the Doers, the Thinkers, the Protectors, and the Catalysts. The groups are made up of the three animals that have a natural affinity to one another, referred to as a Triangle

of Affinity. Each set of three animals has a social connection—a kind of chemistry that is connected to each zodiac sign.

The Thinkers group is made up of the Ox, the Snake, and the Rooster. No surprise, people with these birth signs or ascendants are your most natural friends and working partners. In fact, it's likely your fiancé has strong ties to this group as well. As their team name suggests, these ladies are never ones to procrastinate. They are deep thinkers and planners who enjoy mapping out tasks, putting them on the calendar, and crossing off each one. One of their great strengths is that they do things from start to finish. They not only create a vision, but also put it in place. Those born in the year of the Hen have the mantra "I improve." She is the bride voted most likely to have everything come in on budget. Here comes the Perfectionist Bride.

The Perfectionist Bride—Born in the Year of the Hen

Ah, perfection. Is it possible? As a bride born in the year of the Rooster, you believe that the pursuit of perfection is never-ending, but that it's always worth aiming for the stars. You have one of the strongest work ethics in the Chinese zodiac. You feel passionate about difficult assignments and love to get into all the details. You'll enjoy many of the small tasks that other brides may not see the pleasure in, making sure that your invitations are arranged and set perfectly, finding just the right type of wedding favors, and arranging every bouquet of flowers so that they photograph well at every angle. It's all part of a day's work for the Perfectionist Bride, and everyone will appreciate the results. You'll have to resist the urge to continue mulling over the details while you're walking down the aisle. When the music starts, it is officially the time to relax and enjoy the fruits of your labor.

The Rooster sign has a scientific mind, precise and full of stamina. Like a lovable mad scientist, you lock away yourself to experiment and refine your greatest inventions before unveiling them to the masses. You'll always be pleased with the results, but some frankly will not always get it. The Perfectionist Bride has a reputation for being a little bit eccentric, which will delight most wedding guests, especially those who have sat through the same run-of-the-mill wedding over and over again. Whether it's an offbeat song to walk down the aisle or a creative assortment of all your favorite desserts and snacks for the reception hall, it's fantastic to see a celebration that has lots of personal details. A Hen also has the confidence to take fashion risks. With your taste for the unusual, you might want to bounce all your ideas off your fiancé before putting everything in motion. He or his family may be more conservative than you are and ask you to compromise on a few items.

While you are prone to liking some unusual or misunderstood tastes and fashions, at heart, you're quite traditional. You'll most likely go with a classic ceremony and reception, but add personal touches here and there, so that it reflects your signature. You can actually be very conservative when it comes to a lot of details. This may read as strange to people who do not know you. You may forgo wearing white at your wedding, but absolutely hate the idea of having exposed arms in a church. All this seems perfectly logical to you, but be aware that some people will need more explanation.

As your tastes are particular, your leadership style is very specific. You have a very clear vision for what you want and will not accept something that does not reflect it. No one can ever say that you're guilty of sitting on the fence. You'll also never hold back your honesty. People who cannot stomach criticism should not take the most active roles in your wedding without developing some thicker skin. This is your wedding, and you will not pull any punches. You'll micromanage until you are satisfied. Unfortunately, sometimes the VIP role of bride-to-be can get a little too intoxicating for you. You're quick to pull rank when faced with opposition. Hens can be loud or quiet, but when they're unhappy, everyone gets the message.

Your offbeat humor and showstopping personality makes you a fun and unforgettable bride. Your wedding will be organized and rich with personal details and symbolism. With your ability to bring lots of pieces together, you'll manage people and aspects of the wedding with great ease. You won't be hesitant to involve friends in different time zones and won't shy away from planning a wedding overseas. All it will take is a little bit of work, and for people who have the same work ethic, you're a natural leader.

East Meets West: When Moon Signs Meet Sun Signs

Many people don't realize that each animal of the Chinese zodiac has a solar calendar connection. In our interpretation of Chinese horoscopes, the lunar calendar links into the solar calendar through the month and season, where the Rooster's parallel sun sign is Virgo. But every Western sun sign has a different effect on the lunar moon sign.

THE SAGITTARIUS HEN
Sagittarius: November 22 to December 21

While Roosters are known for pinching pennies, that doesn't mean that they don't have the capacity to be generous. Your sign combination is definitely an example of a big-hearted Hen. You're most likely to sacrifice to help the ones you love during your wedding. Whether it's covering the travel expense of a family member or dear friend or going the extra mile to find your mother the right accessories for your wedding, you extend your standard for excellence to those you care most about. On the project management front, your discipline comes with lots of energy that fuels your missions. Once you've set your mind on something, you won't stop until it's complete. You're terrible at hiding your emotions, so when it's on, it can be quite intimidating for the opponent.

THE CAPRICORN HEN
Capricorn: December 22 to January 20

You're a cool and collected Perfectionist Bride. You take stress in stride because you have confidence in your capability to get everything done with your impressive set of skills. Not one to procrastinate, you actually like creating a new schedule and sticking to it. Perhaps you'll start an early morning weight-training class to sculpt the perfect arms for your dress. You won't complain because you'll see the results of sticking to your routine. Your biggest wedding challenge is dealing with control issues. You excel at organizing your own life, but you quickly learn that weddings become more about all the people and things that occur on the periphery. In other words, not everything will turn out as you plan. You'll find it frustrating, but you'll learn to become more flexible because it's not possible to bring everyone into line, though you will certainly try.

THE AQUARIUS HEN
Aquarius: January 21 to February 19

It's hard to imagine adding wedding planning to your already busy life, but you enjoy having a full plate. Never one to sit still, you enjoy learning about many of the things that come from organizing a wedding. From reading about cultural traditions to seeing all the new fashions, it's another fun adventure for you. Sometimes it seems like you enjoy learning all the rules just to be able to break a few. You'll be drawn to dramatic colors or high-drama styles. Aquarius Roosters favor dresses that really make an entrance—plunging backs and intricate detailing could all be possibilities. You'll take pleasure in challenging conventions, but you're careful to take into consideration the feelings of others. If you know your fiancé likes you to be a bit more modest, you'll tone down some of the fanfare in the name of love.

THE PISCES HEN
Pisces: February 20 to March 20

The Pisces influence helps calm the busy ways of the Hen and results in a nice balance of work and play. As the Perfectionist Bride, you know that you do your best work when your mind is at its sharpest. So listen to your inner Pisces: take your breaks seriously and resist the temptation to multitask. As a Hen, you can always be depended on to be honest. Fortunately, the Pisces Hen is a refined speaker who wraps her gifts of criticism with pretty paper. It's all a part of your natural flair for public relations. Any kind of medicine can be swallowed with the right amount of sugar. All this diplomacy can be a lot of work, but it helps ensure a more peaceful wedding experience.

THE ARIES HEN
Aries: March 21 to April 19

She was the best of brides and she was the worst of brides—all in one. Aries gives the gift of leadership and the Rooster sign contributes confidence that borders on megalomania. You'll excel at giving direction to everyone helping make your wedding happen, but you'll have to guard against your love of doing things at a breakneck pace. If your bridesmaids are not born to signs as proactive as yours, they could call you a slave driver. However, if your friends are all type A's too, they'll finish one project and ask for more, please. This is why it's so important to carefully select who'll be a part of Team Wedding. At the end of the day, you're a great leader with a positive attitude. You do your best to be fair and objective like your sister Hens and always leave the door open for people to be honest about how you're doing.

THE TAURUS HEN
Taurus: April 20 to May 20

Both Taurus and the Hen are hardworking signs. As the Perfectionist Bride, you love complicated challenges, and your wedding has to be your most favorite project of all. Motivated by goals, you don't have a problem putting your dreams in line with reality. As you flip through this book and bridal magazines, you identify what you want and think about how you can add it into your budget. Skipping your morning latte and bringing your lunch to work are all perfectly reasonable ways for you to stretch a dollar. You don't see cutting out these things as sacrifices but rather as strategies to your end goal. Your financial discipline also extends to your style of communication. As opposed to other Hens who can sometimes be too honest for their own good, you choose a subtler route, which is more palatable for sensitive friends and acquaintances.

THE GEMINI HEN
Gemini: May 21 to June 21

The presence of Gemini helps you look at the world in a glass-half-full kind of way, which is a great asset in the unpredictable world of wedding planning. Your sun sign and moon sign work together to balance out your type A personality with your imaginative, artsy side. Like your sister Hens you prefer to speak as directly as possible. Your lively personality and great sense of humor will help you deliver the difficult messages that are too often the responsibility of the bride. Whether it's turning down a friend's offer to "style" your wedding or declining the well-intentioned but painful musical ambitions of a family friend, you'll be able to say no with no hard feelings in the long term. Hopefully your fiancé and maid of honor have a similar skill for constructive criticism because you often take feedback too defensively.

THE CANCERIAN HEN
Cancer: June 22 to July 21

The Perfectionist Bride is an overachiever with a pleasant disposition. While most Hens prefer to think out aloud, the Cancerian Hen is more cautious in airing her true opinions. It's like you observe the old adage of "measure twice, cut once" except with the art of choosing words, and this will help you make more friends than enemies on your road to the wedding. You're a very social person and prefer working with others, as opposed to independently. Your motivation comes from a love of mentoring others; younger, older, no matter—you love to share knowledge. It'll be hard for you not to offer your wedding planning services to others after you've discovered so many tricks of the trade for your own wedding. Just remember to not be too aggressive with your assistance to more independent types. Sometimes unwanted help is as unpopular as unsolicited criticism.

THE LEO HEN
Leo: July 22 to August 21

Here's a Perfectionist Bride who doesn't have a hard time getting noticed. With the Hen's attention to detail and the Leo's regal personality, your leadership ability showed itself well before the wedding planning began. You're a natural problem solver, and are most at ease when you've got plenty to do. In fact, you've got the type of energy that feeds on finding more to do, the more high-profile the better. Happily for you, when it comes to weddings, everything takes center stage. Your strong personality can be quite polarizing, so select your wedding helpers carefully. Not everyone is up to the challenge of meeting your high standards or skilled at dealing with you when plans fall apart.

THE VIRGO HEN
Virgo: August 22 to September 22

A wedding is yet another area in which the Virgo Rooster can become an expert. This Perfectionist Bride is a meticulous person who likes to learn about a subject in the most thorough manner. Like a good student, you'll absorb the names of your entire guest list just by writing them out by hand. You're already an expert on your fiancé, so now is the time to get to know his family and friends and integrate some of those special details into the wedding. As far as your family's details, you probably had those planned well before you even got engaged. As a Hen, you gravitate to fashions that can be offbeat and different, and it's only amplified with the individualistic sign of Virgo. With such specific tastes, you can be quite particular about how everything should come together, so be kind with your criticism when you find errors.

THE LIBRA HEN
Libra: September 23 to October 22

Here comes a Perfectionist Bride who finds the time to enjoy the pleasures of being treated like a VIP. Libra helps the workaholic Hen schedule moments of relaxation and stress-free celebration with her fiancé and friends. After all, the wedding isn't the only day for partying. The Libra Hen is a member of the Thinkers Affinity Triangle, so you aren't the spontaneous type. You like to read up, ask for opinions, and consider all your options. However, Librans can find it difficult to pull the trigger on big decisions, and increasing the number of options won't make the process any easier. Employ the assistance of your fiancé, maid of honor, or mother to help you feel confident about difficult choices. One simple way to make decisions is to establish a theme first and mercilessly cut out any options that do not complement the look.

THE SCORPIO HEN
Scorpio: October 23 to November 21

The combination of Scorpio and Hen creates a no-nonsense kind of bride with an extreme set of emotions. Your leadership skills are very well formed. While other brides may shy away from delegation, you assign tasks with great ease, and give direction that is clear and concise. People new to working with you may find your style a blessing or a curse, depending on whether they meet your high standards. Call it a sign of love, but your expectations increase for those closest to you because you show your devotion with a tireless work ethic. And when people let you down, the Scorpio in you remembers and harbors the bad memory.

Wedding Synergy: When Dragon Meets Phoenix

As you embark on your planning, check out the Wedding Relationship pairings below to see how your strengths and weaknesses come together during the planning process. These compatibility descriptions are based on year of birth combinations, which is the tip of the iceberg when it comes to each of your charts. As described in Chapter 2 "Reference Dates and Tables on the Chinese Zodiac, East-West Sign Combinations, and Animal Hours," a different animal governs each of your birth date and time.

RAT HUSBAND AND HEN WIFE

Love and attraction will bring about the patience that's necessary for you to build a good wedding plan and a happy home life. Your fiancé is a practical animal. He's not afraid of rolling up his sleeves and getting a lot of work done for the wedding. He'll be happy designing and updating the wedding Web site or researching travel deals for the honeymoon. Just be sure to give him his space to make his mark on a project before you start helping him. You can avoid lots of arguments by not doing everything together because the Rat sign likes to enjoy some personal achievement.

OX HUSBAND AND HEN WIFE

The two of you have a strong intellectual connection built on similar philosophies of life. You'll see your wedding as a joint effort and will start planning early. As a couple, you're unified in honoring and respecting your families at the event. Your commitment to hard work will be reflected in your actions in a variety of ways, like a balanced budget and planning for the future. Whether it's playing down the wedding to save up for that first house down payment or preferring to make rather than buy many of your wedding items, you'll both be on the same page.

TIGER HUSBAND AND HEN WIFE

The Tiger and the Rooster don't work well together, unless you accept your difference in working styles. The Perfectionist Bride likes to contemplate all the details of her wedding, taking the time to do research and window-shop. Your fiancé is a spontaneous romantic who's more inclined to elope than plan a big, traditional wedding. Fortunately, you won't have to pry too hard to get at his true feelings about wedding duties because Tigers are pretty vocal spouses. You'll have to make some compromises and expand the budget to make him feel more included in the wedding. It'll be even better if you give him the decision-making power for an especially visible part of the big day, so he too gets some bragging rights.

RABBIT HUSBAND AND HEN WIFE

The Rabbit and the Rooster are at opposite sides of the Chinese zodiac, which indicates that only true love can overcome your differences. Complementary ascendants are also a big help. You're a sharpshooter who doesn't play games. Your attention to detail can be a blessing—or a bother if you forget to carefully choose words with your sensitive fiancé. Rabbits are lovers of beauty and harmony, so harsh words can put them in a foul mood. You'll have your ups and downs in wedding planning, but the biggest thing the Perfectionist Bride can do to minimize stress is to keep your criticism and arguments private. Your fiancé hates to make a scene, and doing so will only extend an argument.

DRAGON HUSBAND AND HEN WIFE

Your fiancé is a member of the Doers Affinity Triangle. He's most happy when he's accomplishing something. So make use of that energy! He learns by doing, unlike you, who prefers the tried-and-true path to unexplored territory. It would work best to divide and conquer with your wedding tasks or employ the help of your maid of honor in taking on the activities that you'll want to review and perfect. Your fiancé doesn't have the ego or the patience to have you correct him too often, so it's best to reduce any opportunity for argument.

SNAKE HUSBAND AND HEN WIFE

This wedding combination is an ideal match of beauty and brains. Your fiancé doesn't have a problem having you take the lead on most of the wedding plans. He appreciates your organizational skill and detail-oriented nature. Between the two of you, you're the more communicative and outgoing, while he's content to keep most of his thoughts to himself. He'll be happy to help you where he can. Note that Snakes are known for killer style and investment skills.

HORSE HUSBAND AND HEN WIFE

Your fiancé is a kindhearted and dependable guy, who's known for putting a big priority on his freedom. Horse natives like to run at their own speed and don't take too kindly to taking on new regimens. While he's happy to soon be married, he'll want to always keep his own identity intact. Don't be hurt if he wants to hang out with his friends more often. It's his way of transitioning into marriage. He'll support wedding plans and will follow through, but avoid too much at a time because his attention span can be very short.

SHEEP HUSBAND AND HEN WIFE

The Sheep and Rooster couple can plan a successful wedding with the Perfectionist Bride at the helm. Your fiancé is sweet and generous with support, but not prone to being the most organized. Therein lies the idea of completing each other. You're not only good at putting complicated projects like weddings together, but you actually enjoy the process, unlike your husband-to-be. He does excel, though, at being a great host, and people gravitate toward his fun-loving nature. You should employ his natural charm in tricky negotiations where you may be having difficulty.

MONKEY HUSBAND AND HEN WIFE

Your couple is a match of two clever animals who will have to learn when to work together and when to get out of each other's way. Getting married has all sorts of activities that you both enjoy, from endless toasts to zapping your favorite things into a wedding registry. However, it's the details where the most arguments happen for couples, especially with a Rooster in the house. You'll get frustrated with you fiancé's pursuit of shortcuts, and he'll wonder why you always make things so complicated. The two of you will find success in splitting tasks. You may also warm to his quicker approaches as your to-do list grows and time starts to run out.

ROOSTER HUSBAND AND HEN WIFE

This can be a great match with lively discussion and open communication. As you have probably picked up on by now, your sign is unfailingly honest. It's a blessing and a curse when interacting with other signs, but it may be the key to a long and happy marriage for the two of you. Since you don't like to bottle up your feelings or keep secrets, everything will get out in the open as it comes, which will smooth the road for wedding planning. However, all this talk means you'll come to decisions slower. Start discussions early and keep them private initially. Bringing in other people before you have an agreement doesn't make a lot of sense.

DOG HUSBAND AND HEN WIFE

As a Perfectionist Bride, your wedding dream is that everything goes off according to your meticulous plan, while your fiancé is quick to tell you that life can be unpredictable. Murphy's Law certainly applies to weddings. In other words, relax. But there's that little voice in your head telling you that you can achieve the unachievable. So, of course, it doesn't hurt to create some contingency plans together, in the name of thoroughness, right? Split it down the middle and agree on deadlines where when the project is final, you put it to bed. Rest assured when you ask your fiancé for an opinion, he will always gives you the truth.

BOAR HUSBAND AND HEN WIFE

Your fiancé has a jovial personality that is a welcome part of any wedding. Boar grooms are a pleasure for guests and families alike because they're natural showmen and hosts. You'll shine as the master strategist behind the wedding, by giving structure to all the intricacies of the big day. He'll be good at taking your lead and following through on whatever tasks are needed. Fortunately, he doesn't mind being corrected, but he does give with his heart rather than mind. You might want to volunteer to be in charge of the finances for the wedding and beyond.

The Hen's Relationships with Friends and Family

Family and friends are an important part of most weddings. Since we all operate differently in our nonromantic relationships, the pairings of your Chinese zodiac sign will take a slightly different form. Knowing the compatibility of your animal sign with your family and friends is a real asset when planning and setting expectations for responsibilities. As you think about how best to integrate your vast network of friends, review the relationship overviews below. They will help cast light on your friends' and family members' strengths, weaknesses, and working styles.

WITH A RAT

The Perfectionist Bride meets the Initiator Bride. You two have common ground in being responsible with money and putting family first. Common birth hour ascendants can help bridge the gap in communication between the two of you. You are a Thinker while your friend or family member is a Doer. She'd prefer to jump in and get cracking, while you'd rather evaluate and discuss. If you can build the patience to listen to each other, your time together will be much more enjoyable.

Δ WITH AN OX

Working with an Ox sign is a pleasure for the Rooster native. Coming from the Thinkers Affinity Triangle, you operate on the same wavelength. You share priorities and you both value time and money as equally precious. Whether you've known each other all your lives or have recently been brought together through the wedding, you have all the making of a lifetime bond. You both have the discipline to tackle any task and not be intimidated by the scale or timeline.

WITH A TIGER

Combining a Tiger with a Rooster can be the best or worst of relationships. Frankly, it depends on the unpredictable Tiger. As a Perfectionist, you like to be objective in evaluation, and whether you like or dislike someone doesn't matter. If there's something to be improved, you tell it like it is. Your Tiger teammate is ruled by emotion and lacks your discipline for impartiality. However, Tigers are known for their entertaining personalities and so are you. If you two can laugh together, you can find a way to work together. If conversations prove difficult, working on a high-stress wedding can be a terrible way to build goodwill.

× WITH A RABBIT

Without a common ascendant, you will probably have some difficulty working closely with people of this sign. The Rabbit comes from the Catalysts Affinity Triangle, a trio that is skilled in working with people due to a high emotional IQ. The negative of this ability is that Rabbits are very thin-skinned to criticism from others. Meanwhile, your feedback to any problem is given to everyone the same— friend or stranger. If you can couple every criticism with a compliment, the Rabbit may warm to working closely with you. Otherwise, you could have a person who may harbor resentment by looking for subtext that doesn't exist.

WITH A DRAGON

The Perfectionist Bride will find some good challenges from the Dragon sign. You'll be enchanted by the Dragon's energy for life and strong personality. In fact, you're each attracted to the other's confidence and shoot-from-the-hip manner of speaking. While the Dragon is more of an emotional animal than you, with your preference for looking at the facts, you'll find his or her perspective interesting and take it to heart. You're open to working with the Dragon because you can have heated discussions without any hard feelings afterward. Neither of you sees criticism as a personal attack.

Δ WITH A SNAKE

Many signs find it hard to read the Snake sign, but for Roosters it's second nature. Even though you're inclined to be more talkative than the quiet Snake, your brains work at a similar speed, coming from the Thinkers Affinity Triangle. You'll appreciate that this person is a great listener. Brides hate to be interrupted, especially Perfectionist Brides. The Snake sign has tremendous respect for order and will give you your time to expound on your wedding wishes. In fact, she will rarely find fault except to steer you away from a mistake. Your friendship is very strong and will endure for many years to come.

WITH A HORSE

It's funny how two people can be saying the exact same thing, but find a way to disagree about it. Unfortunately, that's how the Horse and Rooster signs interact when it comes to something like planning a wedding. As the Perfectionist Bride you're a natural planner and favor observing traditions and etiquette. The native Horse sign specializes in rocking the boat. Her spontaneous ways may enchant others, but can leave Perfectionist Brides pulling out their hair. Horses can be late and tend to have very short attention spans. However, the Horse is not a flake, so if you or a common friend can communicate your priorities well, this person can fall into line to keep the peace. However, if you're vague, the Horse will reprioritize as she wishes and you could be frustrated.

WITH A SHEEP

The Sheep is the second member of the Catalysts Affinity Triangle—the group of emotionally intelligent people who don't mix well with Thinkers like you. Your task when working with this sign will be how to integrate the Sheep into your neatly organized wedding arrangements. (We can imagine your wedding plan now, all nicely put together in a spreadsheet or carefully tabbed binder.) The Sheep doesn't have the same knack for creating a game plan, so know that you will need to hold her hand to get things done the way you want them. If asking for help on something subjective, such as decorations or food, temper your criticism with appreciation. The Sheep can interpret your constructive suggestions as being ungrateful.

WITH A MONKEY

Monkey signs like to accomplish things quickly and often in clever ways. Perfectionist Brides like to do things by the book. Therein lies the big clue of achieving the most harmonious working relationship with this person—employing a hands-off approach. Most people don't like being micromanaged, but the Monkey sign really hates it. In fact, Monkeys can literally walk off the job when interrupted too many times. If you're specific about what kind of help you need from a Monkey and give her the independence to accomplish the job, you will be pleased with the end result.

Δ WITH ANOTHER HEN

Working with a Rooster twin can be quite intense. Two hens will have more difficulty working together than a balanced male and female pair of Roosters. Women born in the year of the Rooster can get a lot of work done on a wedding, but the time to do anything can literally be doubled with the amount of discussion. Perfectionist Brides like to be thorough and can overdo a task, analyzing, reanalyzing, and starting all over again until it is absolutely right. When integrating another Rooster into your wedding plan, be prepared to delegate clear tasks. You don't want to get caught up in a debate when you need to run off to handle something only the bride can do.

WITH A DOG

A person born in the year of the Dog is very helpful to a wedding. With a cool head and a realistic point of view, this person likes to solve problems rather than to overcomplicate situations. As the Perfectionist Bride, you'll find the Dog's practical approach refreshing. Like you, this person tries to be objective. The Rooster is motivated by getting the numbers to balance, while the Dog aspires to have everything be fair. You can put the Dog in charge of planning the bachelorette party or any small fête where a responsible person needs to divide things fairly.

WITH A BOAR

The Boar is the third member of the Catalysts Affinity Triangle, which can present some challenges to the Perfectionist Bride, primarily caused by a difference in work styles. Charming and good at bringing harmony to a situation, she can be a real asset to your wedding. A Boar native can warm up any dance floor and encourage people to get out of their shells. Aside from her knack for public relations, she can be a tireless worker. However, you must resist your micromanaging skills and give this person her space. Her methods are most likely not as elegant as yours, so you'll have to mind your tongue and don your poker face when things get messy.

Sixteen

BORN IN THE YEAR OF THE DOG
Here Comes the Guardian Bride

Lunar Years of the Dog	Elements
February 14, 1934, to February 3, 1935	Wood
February 2, 1946, to January 21, 1947	Fire
February 18, 1958, to February 7, 1959	Earth
February 6, 1970, to January 26, 1971	Metal
January 25, 1982, to February 12, 1983	Water
February 10, 1994, to January 30, 1995	Wood

Guardian Bride Details

Birth Hours: 7 P.M. to 9 P.M.

Western Sign: Virgo

Western Gemstone: Opal or Tourmaline

Symbolic Color: White

Flower: Lavender

Season: Autumn

Element: Metal

Famous Guardian Brides:

Brigitte Bardot, Candice Bergen, Sophia Loren, Cher, Zsa Zsa Gabor, Ava Gardner, Judy Garland, Liza Minnelli.

The Dress:

The Guardian Bride favors a less-is-more look. You prefer dresses that are classic, with an uncomplicated structure. Your greatest accessory will be a flowing hairstyle.

The Dog Sign: The Eleventh Bride of the Chinese Zodiac

As the eleventh sign of the zodiac, the Dog has a warm personality that wins her lots of popularity. She is a part of what we refer to as the Protectors group. There are four groups: the Doers, the Thinkers, the Protectors, and the Catalysts. The groups are made up of the three animals that have a natural affinity to one another, referred to as a Triangle of Affinity. Each set of three animals has a social connection—a kind of chemistry that is connected to each zodiac sign.

The Protectors group is made up of the Tiger, the Horse, and the Dog. No surprise, people with these birth signs or ascendants are your most natural friends and working partners. In fact, it's likely your fiancé has strong ties to this group as well. As their team name suggests, these ladies are loyal friends and champions of causes. Those born in the year of the Dog have the mantra "I watch." She is the bride voted most likely to divide responsibilities equally. Here comes the Guardian Bride.

The Guardian Bride—Born in the Year of the Dog

Women born in the year of the Dog are team players and big believers in hard work and equality. You treat people the same at a wedding, whether you are there as a bridesmaid or center stage as the bride. This will be a surprise to anyone who has had the uncomfortable situation of dealing with an irrational bride; you're a welcome change. As a Guardian Bride, you try to exercise logic and objectivity in how you make decisions and evaluate situations. You give criticism with a focus on getting the work done, rarely making your comments personal. This approach is received well by most people, except for the most oversensitive types. Your level head makes you the friend your loved ones call for advice. Friends listen to you because you are skilled at mixing in some humor with your message of tough love.

The Guardian Bride is one of the most dependable women in the Chinese zodiac. You do not make promises that you don't intend to keep, and when circumstances get in the way, you don't make excuses and you still try to do everything in your power to make it happen. You can hear the sighs of relief from all your attendants and vendors when they realize that you will not be subject to flaky bride syndrome. However, with such high ideals, you naturally possess a high standard for the people in your life. Your set of high morals is actually the filter by which you undoubtedly chose your select group of friends and agreed to marry your fiancé. While many women make the mistake of giving people too many chances in life, Guardian Brides have a one-strike-and-you're-out policy. Your trust is your gift and when someone lets you down, you'll never forget it. Friendship can be rebuilt, but they'll never have the same intimate relationship with you—and don't even mention infidelity. Fortunately, these situations are rare because the Dog sign is an excellent judge of character.

The sign of the Dog has the reputation for being one of the most likable. Warm, funny, and outgoing, you find friends wherever you go. People enjoy being around you and seek your advice because you are very rational and honest in your recommendations. Now just because lots of people like you, it doesn't mean that you necessarily reciprocate the feeling. You just do a better job at being silent about it. Most mothers advise their children that if you don't have anything nice to say to someone, it's best to keep it to yourself. Guardian Brides took this message to heart a long time ago, but still, sometimes your facial expressions can give you away. You really dislike lying and find it difficult spending time with people you dislike. In the interest of the equality that you hold so dear, you'll have to summon your inner actress when you're in the presence of people you dislike, especially if they fall under the category of future in-laws or fiancé's friends.

The Guardian Bride takes pleasure in a wedding as a formal union with her soul mate. You're more focused on the symbolic details of the wedding, rather than the material splendor. Therefore, you're not as interested in buying an expensive wedding gown or spending money on lavish decorations unless they are particularly meaningful to you or your future spouse. You're no-nonsense when it comes to fashion in your daily life. Of course, you like things to look nice, but you prefer classic styles and cuts that are straightforward and not too complicated, much like you. The Guardian Bride often takes the role of silent protector in her daily life, preferring to be a part of the supporting cast rather than the star. The idea of being the center of attention as a bride can be a bit daunting, and taking hours of pictures can be tiring for the practical Dog sign. However, it is the right thing to do and your families are salivating over the idea of distributing pictures, so you grin and bear it.

Your big day will be a traditional celebration, filled with heartfelt speeches and affectionate hugs. Smiles will come easy to your bridesmaids, a group of lifelong friends who will appreciate that their stint as wedding planning support was organized and rational.

East Meets West: When Moon Signs Meet Sun Signs

Many people don't realize that each animal of the Chinese zodiac has a solar calendar connection. In our interpretation of Chinese horoscopes, the lunar calendar links into the solar calendar through the month and season, where the Dog's parallel sun sign is Libra. But every Western sun sign has a different effect on the lunar moon sign.

THE SAGITTARIUS DOG

Sagittarius: November 22 to December 21

This East meets West combination produces a balanced Guardian Bride who is realistic about the ups and downs that are part of a wedding. One of the most valuable tools in your wedding tool kit is one that is often undervalued—the gift of likability. Your method of communication is casual, but thoughtful. And your ability to keep a secret is a mark of your attention to manners. However, Sagittarius does make you careless on occasion. You never know whose feelings can get hurt in the course of the wedding, so if you've forgotten to do something or rubbed someone the wrong way, be sure to inquire about any sour faces. While you're open and honest, some may not be as forthcoming with their feelings.

THE CAPRICORN DOG

Capricorn: December 22 to January 20

Trust doesn't come easily to your sun sign or your moon sign. Dog signs employ a wait-and-see strategy to see whether a person can be brought into their inner circle. You're especially guarded, but once someone is close to you, there's almost no limit to your generosity. Your good deeds are well-known, and your biggest fans are eager to show you the same royal treatment now that you're the bride. As the Guardian Bride, your standards are unshakable and you'll fight till the sun comes up for what you want. Hopefully, your fiancé and you have ironed out any details about religion and children before you've gotten this far because you're unlikely to compromise on these important life issues.

THE AQUARIUS DOG

Aquarius: January 21 to February 19

The combined influence of Aquarius and the Dog sign creates a logical bride who doesn't take herself too seriously. You're open-minded and adventurous. With that said, weddings aren't exactly the time where people like to get too adventurous, and this is a prime area for discontent with your fiancé or family members. Depending on your husband-to-be's personality, he may or may not be game for getting married at an offbeat location or walking down the aisle to anything other than "Here Comes the Bride." Most likely, you'll both be happy by mixing some established traditions with your whimsical sense of humor.

THE PISCES DOG

Pisces: February 20 to March 20

For a Guardian Bride, trust is a gift you give to few people, and your wedding is so precious to you that you actually build an additional wall around yourself for protection. Pisces people are emotionally intelligent, which can be a blessing and a curse. You pick up on every frequency and can occasionally get so wrapped up in your reactions that it throws off your whole day. Well, times like these are why brides have fiancés, mothers, and maids of honor. Your defense mechanism will be to rely on your inner circle for guidance and sanity checks when your intuition is on overload.

THE ARIES DOG

Aries: March 21 to April 19

You have all the makings of the best kind of leader, with the guidance of the objective Dog and energetic Aries. You've always tried to look beyond material objects to see the bigger picture. You'll pursue wedding objectives that are close to your heart and personal beliefs. Honoring a loved one who left your life too soon is a special mission for you. Whether you choose to make it public or private, you'll take comfort in integrating his or her memory into your big day. You're also likely to ask family and friends to support a charitable cause in lieu of gifts. The wedding favor budget is another popular candidate for your philanthropic approach.

THE TAURUS DOG

Taurus: April 20 to May 20

A traditional wedding template will be the starting point for your planning. The practical Guardian Bride likes to go with the tried-and-true methods, rather than breaking rules for the fun of it. That doesn't mean that there won't be some adjustments made. If there's an opportunity make your fiancé or your families happy by blending traditions or making some changes, you're happy to do so. Considering other people's families is a big part of being a thoughtful hostess, which most Guardian Brides are. You also favor settling into schedules, so if you have plans to trim down before your wedding, getting into a good routine will be most effective, whether it's a class you can schedule or making a fitness calendar of your own.

THE GEMINI DOG

Gemini: May 21 to June 21

The Gemini Guardian Bride is the proverbial multitasker. While other brides may view having a full plate of chores as intimidating, you rise to the challenge. Workaholic? You prefer to be called productive. Bridal planning brings out your practical side, as well as your creativity. After your engagement, you're quick to gather as much information together as possible, so that you can be realistic about what you can and can't do. Once the plan is set, you're quick to get a lot done. The Dog sign is very self-reliant, so be cognizant of how others may feel if you whip through your bridal tasks without other people's buy-in. Your fiancé may want to have more input about the wedding cake than you thought, or perhaps your mother wanted to be a part of your first wedding dress trip. Much of wedding planning can be memories in the making.

THE CANCERIAN DOG

Cancer: June 22 to July 21

Wedding planning will have its ups and down. There'll be laughter and arguments that no one can possibly see coming. While the Dog sign gets along well with most people, when you dislike someone, your face is an open book. You'll have to be careful not to be obvious in playing favorites in planning your wedding. Treating people differently can rub people the wrong way, and you're more likely than your other Guardian Bride sisters to take things personally. You'll rely on your husband-to-be and friends for support during your sulky moments when things go off course. The Cancerian Dog enjoys the presence of pretty things, so you'll take pleasure in picking out flowers and visual touches for your wedding.

THE LEO DOG
Leo: July 22 to August 21
You've got a strong intuitive sense and a set of high standards that your loved ones know quite well. If someone doesn't share your same commitment to love and loyalty, you're not afraid to show them the door. Your fiancé probably knows this fact most of all. So be true to yourself and avoid any disappointments by putting together a group of attendants who will be with you rain or shine. You can certainly add new VIPs to the day, such as a sister-in-law or close friends of your husband-to-be, but be sure to rely more on your friends and family, who know what you like and won't be hurt when you're more honest than kind.

THE VIRGO DOG
Virgo: August 22 to September 22
As a member of the Protectors Affinity Triangle, you take on more responsibilities than the average citizen of Earth. You may stay up at night, troubled by the news report on a grave situation far from home or even a fictional story about an orphaned child. It's your nature to want to take care of people and make the world a better place. As you go through the wedding planning, you'll find that the project extends outside yourself. You'll go crazy if you worry about every detail and every person, so break it into pieces and choose a few causes to champion. Asking for gifts to a charitable cause, choosing environmentally responsible companies to register with, or helping a new small business are all ways for you to feel that your wedding is making a difference.

THE LIBRA DOG
Libra: September 23 to October 22
The Libra Guardian Bride brings together the protective nature of the Dog and Libra's pursuit of fairness. Weddings put a lot of pressure on a bride, with all the

important people in your and your fiancé's life watching (and perhaps secretly judging) your every move. Fortunately, participants and guests alike will find little to complain over. You're a charming and generous hostess, often putting others before yourself. If anything, your attention to making other people happy can be a hindrance to being decisive. Stand firm on the things that make you and your man happy, and don't compromise on too much. The nice thing about weddings is that what makes people happy is seeing the bride happy.

THE SCORPIO DOG

Scorpio: October 23 to November 21

The Dog is a Protector and the Scorpion is infamous for the power of her sting. Put this together and you've got a bride that can pack a punch when she doesn't get what she wants. You're the kind of bride who will work tirelessly toward your goals. Call it willpower or obsession, you'll lose those last ten pounds, write every last thank-you note, and personally review every contract without complaint. People will be in awe of how much you can accomplish. Perhaps your greatest challenge will be finding ways to compromise with your fiancé. Your competitive nature always pushes you forward, but in order for you to maintain wedding harmony, you'll have to push yourself to concede a couple of issues.

Wedding Synergy: When Dragon Meets Phoenix

As you embark on your planning, check out the Wedding Relationship pairings below to see how your strengths and weaknesses come together during the planning process. These compatibility descriptions are based on year of birth combinations, which is the tip of the iceberg when it comes to each of your charts. As described in Chapter 2 "Reference Dates and Tables on the Chinese Zodiac, East-West Sign Combinations, and Animal Hours," a different animal governs each component of your birth date and time.

RAT HUSBAND AND DOG WIFE

Both the sign of the Rat and the sign of the Dog are team players who look to preserve the group rather than fight for their own individual preferences. Well, if every bride and groom listened to everyone else's needs over their own, it would make for a pretty boring wedding. You and your fiancé should speak freely of your wedding wishes to each other and do your best to keep singular items as true to their essence as possible, especially before parents or in-laws start providing advice. The best weddings are those that reflect the couple's personality, so don't sacrifice the things you really want. A few heated discussions are worth the results.

OX HUSBAND AND DOG WIFE

During wedding planning, every couple learns more about each other's strengths and weaknesses, but here's a sneak preview for you two. Your fiancé will be most focused on the bottom line before the wedding plan. "Just the facts, honey." He'll care that the wedding looks good and comes in at what you said it was going to. You're fine with taking the reins on the project, but you'll object to his giving orders, especially if he delivers them in a bossy tone. Since you're happiest when things are divided equally, split duties and set clear guidelines. Your fiancé is no-nonsense in many ways, and he responds to goals and zones out during the long backstory.

TIGER HUSBAND AND DOG WIFE

If you two were in high school today, you'd be voted most popular couple. The Guardian Bride makes friends easily wherever she goes because of an intuitive sense of how people operate. Your fiancé is very animated and could easily be a great public speaker or comedian. You will complement each other well as bride and groom. The challenges you'll face leading up to the wedding will be in temper flare-ups spawned by impatience, most likely from your husband-to-be. Whether it's love or hate, there's no in-between with him, but fortunately, your level head knows how to talk him down so that you can fix problems, rather than make them worse.

RABBIT HUSBAND AND DOG WIFE

Your native signs can nurture each other during times of stress because you prioritize fairness and balance in a relationship. The Guardian Bride in you is drawn to your fiancé's cool-guy style. Rabbits are known for gravitating to the finer things in life and doing their best to make home life a sanctuary. This is music to your ears because you aspire to have a life of balance. With the external forces of putting together a wedding—family, friends, and new faces—your husband-to-be doesn't always deal well with the stress. Any friction can leave him withdrawn, you'll have to take his subtle cues to figure out what's wrong and get him out of the occasional funk.

DRAGON HUSBAND AND DOG WIFE

The Dragon and Dog signs are in opposition in the Chinese zodiac, which explains why disagreements can get so heated. Without common ascendants helping your two signs find common ground, your relationship probably wouldn't have happened because your signs disagree so often. Your fiancé has the Dragon's big male personality. With high standards and an ego to match, he doesn't like anyone finding fault with him. You are a peace lover, but quickly string up the boxing gloves when there's a justifiable war to be waged. You two must strive for an equal division of labor for the most harmony. As the Guardian Bride, you can win points with your fiancé by giving him lots of praise and the limelight, where he really comes alive.

SNAKE HUSBAND AND DOG WIFE

To truly know a person is to understand what moves him. You're motivated by the greater good, whether it's protecting the interests of others or spreading the word on a civic issue. Your fiancé, born in the year of the Snake, is ambitious as well, but prefers clever strategies that benefit him and his family. This can bring up some interesting arguments. Your fiancé will take more aggressive measures to get deals and call in favors. You'll not always agree with his methods, but he'll be effective at garnering the advantageous position. If you're not comfortable with haggling, you may not want to accompany your husband-to-be to the negotiation.

HORSE HUSBAND AND DOG WIFE

The Horse sign is a fellow member of the Protectors group, so it's only natural that you and your fiancé have a strong affinity for each other. Your philosophies are naturally aligned. Whether it's your strong commitment to family, common religion, or a social movement, you see each other as partners in life, beyond just home and hearth. Your fiancé is drawn to your keen wit and knack for bringing people together. You have great respect for his intelligence and passion for action. He's got a short attention span and a spontaneous attitude, however, so you'll have to use your charm to get him to do what he needs to do without waiting until the last minute.

SHEEP HUSBAND AND DOG WIFE

Like your native sign, the Sheep is a popular person. Friendly and highly social, your fiancé is always swimming in invitations to this wedding or that bachelor party. Now that you're well on your way to becoming his wife, you're beginning to see how much the Sheep enjoys being cared for. It's not that your fiancé isn't very capable of taking care of booking a DJ or getting an address list together, it's that he's used to other people taking care of the job. Sheep seem to be blessed with generous caregivers. Now, while you're protective of those you love, you may simply not have enough time to do everything that comes with your many roles. You'll have to summon your fiancé's help through some sweet talk and encouragement. When he understands how important something is, he'll step up to the task, but he'll always try to get out of his chores when he can.

MONKEY HUSBAND AND DOG WIFE

Your fiancé is a member of the Doers club. Famous for ingenuity, the Monkey sign likes to accomplish tasks and enjoys complicated projects that challenge him. Well, a wedding holds many twists and turns that can entice even the playful Monkey to take notice. As the Guardian Bride, you see the world in black and white and can err on believing that there's a right way and a wrong way to do things. Your fiancé likes to challenge conventions and think outside the box. Trust in your husband-to-be's ability to get things done. You can be a stickler for always following the rules, but if you concentrate on the results, and let your fiancé work independently, you'll be amazed at what he can accomplish.

ROOSTER HUSBAND AND DOG WIFE

Your fiancé comes from the Thinkers Affinity Triangle, which means he likes to ponder and then ponder some more. People can find fault with the eccentric

Rooster on many levels, but no one can say he isn't thorough. The Guardian Bride can depend on the Rooster to make sure every "i" is dotted and every "t" is crossed. Your fiancé is objective with criticism to the point where he can be insensitive. As a natural diplomat, you put more care into how you communicate than your husband does. With the Rooster, you almost need to internally preface everything with "Don't take this personally, but . . ." in your own head. Without accepting your fiancé's perfectionist mindset, you'll get into too many arguments caused by hurt feelings.

DOG HUSBAND AND DOG WIFE

Marrying another Dog sign is a harmonious match. You can depend on each other's faithfulness and loyalty because your moral compass is always accurate. With your commitment to equality, you like to view your wedding planning as a democracy. Each member has a set of responsibilities and a vote on the big issues. Because of this, you favor doing things together. Meet with photographers as a pair, walk your reception site hand-in-hand, and go to each other's family's homes to have joint discussions. This method is a good match for the Dog sign because you both dislike being left out of anything, especially something as personal as a wedding.

BOAR HUSBAND AND DOG WIFE

You've fallen in love with a man who is a member of the Catalysts group, a trio known for strong emotions and generosity. One of the biggest benefits of a Boar is open and honest communication. Your fiancé doesn't believe in holding in feelings, which is an admirable way to approach life. He probably blurted out, "I love you" first because in his mind it makes no sense to wait! Planning your wedding involves a lot of detailed work that isn't your fiancé's strong suit. He doesn't have the patience for details and can be lax on serious projects. You'll have to be the taskmaster and push him for what you need, more often than not, but he'll prefer someone managing him to not getting the job done.

The Dog's Relationships with Friends and Family

Family and friends are an important part of most weddings. Since we all operate differently in our nonromantic relationships, the pairings of your Chinese zodiac sign will take a slightly different form. Knowing the compatibility of your animal sign with your family and friends is a real asset when planning and setting expectations for responsibilities. As you think about how best to integrate your vast network of friends, review the relationship overviews below. They will help cast light on your friends' and family members' strengths, weaknesses, and working styles.

WITH A RAT

A Rat can be a wonderful addition to any group of attendants or hired professionals. Much like you, your friend doesn't feel comfortable not pulling her own weight. In fact, if she's planned a wedding herself, she may err on the side of being too helpful. Of course, it's all in the delivery, but Rat natives are very sincere to people they care about. If you two have only recently been brought together because of the wedding, be sure to share your guiding principles in addition to your larger theme. Maybe you'd rather purchase items from small companies instead of large, or integrate organic materials. Better let your friend know early, because her instinct is to go for the best deal.

WITH AN OX

The Ox and Dog signs are cut from similar cloth. You both take pride in your reputation for dependability and fair-mindedness. Whatever job needs to be done, the Ox will not let you down. She'll be a tireless worker. However, she finds it as difficult as you to compromise on issues she's passionate about. If she's an attendant, she'll probably keep her thoughts to herself because you're the bride, after all. Whatever you say goes, unless she's absolutely against something, like a wild weekend in Vegas or a dress she finds too revealing. But if the Ox sign views herself as a higher rank than you, perhaps a future mother-in-law or sister-in-law, you can have a standoff on your hands.

Δ WITH A TIGER

As the Chinese say, you always know when you've got a Tiger in the house. Your friend or family member is an emotionally led person. She's an entertainer who may even flirt with the melodramatic. As the Guardian Bride, you approach wedding planning in a more practical and methodical way than the other bridal signs. The Tiger does not fit neatly into especially organized boxes because spontaneity is her signature. However, she's a fellow Protector, so an appeal to her sense of duty is a powerful motivator. Your friend will support things that make the important people in her life happy. That's not to say there might not be some complaints, potentially public, in store, but she doesn't hold a grudge and neither do you.

WITH A RABBIT

A Rabbit can be a real asset to the Guardian Bride. Your personalities work well together and can set the stage for you to get some great guidance from a highly intuitive sign. Dog natives are slow to give trust because you like to wait and see how relationships go. With weddings, there's frankly not a lot of time to watch the pot simmer. Consider employing your friend to help with reading first impressions— Did the hairstylist really understand what I want? Was it just me, or did that photographer seem flaky? Her gut will point you in a good direction. Not to mention her instincts for fashion are quite refined as well. She may encourage you to try on a wedding dress that you passed by, but you will absolutely look stunning in.

× WITH A DRAGON

With the Guardian Bride, the name of the game is trust. It's one of your most treasured gifts, and you guard it quite closely. People born in the year of the Dragon have to work that much harder with Dog signs because they are at opposite ends of the Chinese zodiac. Your differences in personalities reflect in your communication styles. The Dragon is louder and prone to theatrics, while you're toned down and conversational. Conflicts stem from Dragons preferring the pilot's seat, when you're the bridal leader. You should avoid bringing this person into any situation where there are still decisions to be made, or work through an intermediary to reduce the chance of an argument.

WITH A SNAKE

Your friend or family member comes from the mysterious sign of the Snake. What gave this animal such an intriguing reputation? Well, she'll never tell you, and therein lies the secret—a commitment to discretion. When you need to vent to someone or entrust a special detail that you're going to unveil at the wedding, you can trust a Snake sign. You share a mutual respect for friendship and develop relationships slowly. However, even if you aren't very close friends, Snake natives are too proper to take part in open gossip, so don't worry about her airing your dirty laundry. She'll keep her lips sealed and her thoughts to herself.

Δ WITH A HORSE

It's likely that you and this person are already close friends or well on your way there, because you come from the same Protectors Affinity Triangle. In regard to friendship, career, or social cause, Protectors are instinctual people. It takes a lot of courage to listen to your heart, and that's what makes both of you individuals. The Horse sign will respect how you treat other people and can be helpful in carrying out tasks that other friends may find a hassle. Forgot your shoes in your hotel room? Need someone to drive across town to pick up a last-minute item? A Horse finds tasks like these adventures. Note that this sign has a short attention span, so repetitive tasks like assembling wedding invitations or favors will not be her cup of tea.

WITH A SHEEP

The Sheep sign is known as a Peacemaker thanks to her strong intuitive sense for others' feelings and her reputation for being a loyal friend. You both prioritize your loved ones in your life, which is a great bonding point for working on the wedding together. Your friend can be very helpful to you, but may be hesitant at first, feeling performance anxiety about your wedding and all that's involved. She'll be afraid of making mistakes, so will look to you for confirmation, and while you're at it, a compliment wouldn't be so bad either. Nurture a Sheep native's talents and you will get wonderful results. As the Guardian Bride, you'll appreciate the Sheep's attention to your wishes and coach her well.

WITH A MONKEY

Working with the Monkey can be a bit of a nail biter for some Guardian Brides. Monkey natives are known for being a little too clever, and that can make the hair on your back stand up. Without an established relationship, you'll be hesitant to give this person the reins on important items. You prefer to play by the rules, while the Monkey looks for ways to game the system. She may wait till the last minute for the sport of it, and if there's a hint of jealousy between you two, this route may even give her the bonus of seeing you squirm. But don't worry about giving a Monkey responsibility; friend or acquaintance, her ego will ensure she will always come through because she cannot stand failing.

WITH A ROOSTER

There are all different kinds of Roosters, as is the case with all the animals, but in general, the Rooster's core motivation is seeking out perfection. Call it anal or difficult to please, but just as you may be unwavering on politics or religion, the Rooster's calling is finding errors and fixing them. As the Guardian Bride, you're practical and realistic and may find the Rooster's constant criticism not all that constructive as the timeline shrinks before you. Try to focus on the fact that the Rooster gives criticism to everyone, and probably even more to the people she cares about most. However, you can use it to your advantage and give her the tasks that require the most detailed work. She'll take pride in her work, and you'll be pleased with the results.

Δ WITH ANOTHER DOG

Partnering with another Dog native should work fairly well, as long as you do not have conflicting birth hour ascendants. Guardian Brides are believers in the Golden Rule of weddings: Do unto other brides as you would like to be treated when it's your big day. Dog signs respect the chain of command, so as the bride, your position as numero uno is not going to be questioned. But sparks can fly when there's any question of fair treatment or perceived injustice. As a Protector, your nature is to protect the ones you love, and your fellow Dog sign can interpret this behavior as inequality. If you're working with a potential in-law, you'll need to treat everyone equally, even new members to your clan whom you don't especially like.

WITH A BOAR

The Boar and Dog signs are popular animals and have lots of friends, but their spark comes from appreciating each other's differences. Your friends respect that you treat people as equals, give people the benefit of the doubt, and always stand up for what you believe in. Boar natives are famous for being generous with time and money and for having a carefree, fun attitude. If you don't know this person well, you could misjudge her as too mellow for the important responsibility of being part of a wedding. You'd be missing out on a great addition to your wedding. Boars are incredibly selfless to people they care about and will go to the ends of the earth to make your wedding a success. However, try not to make this person be the bearer of bad news. You've got a stronger stomach for dealing with unhappy situations.

Seventeen

BORN IN THE YEAR OF THE BOAR
Here Comes the Unifier Bride

Lunar Years of the Boar	Elements
February 4, 1935, to January 23, 1936	Wood
January 22, 1947, to February 9, 1948	Fire
February 8, 1959, to January 27, 1960	Earth
January 27, 1971, to February 15, 1972	Metal
February 13, 1983, to February 1, 1984	Water
January 31, 1995, to February 18, 1996	Wood

Unifier Bride Details

Birth Hours: 9 P.M. to 11 P.M.

Western Sign: Scorpio

Western Gemstone: Topaz

Symbolic Color: Blue

Flower: Rose

Season: Winter

Element: Water

Famous Unifier Brides:

Julie Andrews, Lucille Ball, Maria Callas, Hillary Clinton, Glenn Close, Georgia O'Keeffe, Jada Pinkett Smith, Emma Thompson.

The Dress:

Boar natives are prone to extremes. Some women will take pains to flawlessly put themselves together while others throw on something and do not even look in the mirror on the way out. Your dress will be couture or modest and natural, reflecting your daily style. You'll choose whatever you feel most comfortable in and buy what makes you happy, no matter the cost.

The Boar Sign: The Twelfth Bride of the Chinese Zodiac

As the last sign of the zodiac, the Boar is famous for her party-throwing abilities. She is a part of what we refer to as the Catalysts group. There are four groups: the Doers, the Thinkers, the Protectors, and the Catalysts. The groups are made up of the three animals that have a natural affinity to one another, referred to as a Triangle of Affinity. Each set of three animals has a social connection—a kind of chemistry that is connected to each zodiac sign.

The Catalysts group is made up of the Rabbit, the Sheep, and the Boar. No surprise, people with these birth signs or ascendants are your most natural friends and working partners. In fact, it's likely your fiancé has strong ties to this group as well. The Catalysts Affinity Triangle is made up of women who are skilled communicators and patrons of the arts. Those born in the year of the Boar have the mantra "I join." She is the bride voted most likely to have an open bar. Here comes the Unifier Bride.

The Unifier Bride—Born in the Year of the Boar

The Unifier Bride is famous for being a generous host, whose laughter and jovial spirit are second to none. With a mothering nature, you delight in helping others. Your friends and family treasure your selfless nature and are probably thrilled to be able to repay you with the same generous treatment you gave them in the past. Your popularity has brought the blessing of many friends, who will all want to share in your and your fiancé's big day. It'll be just as hard for you to pick attendants as to settle on the final guest list, but you'll do your best to include as many people as possible because you want everyone to be able to share your happiness.

You can practically pick out a Unifier Bride by seeing her walk down the street. The Boar sign is true to who she is. A natural woman, her appeal stems from her confidence in herself. Boar women seem to be able to pull off any look, fancy or casual, just by the ease with which they walk. Your intuitive sense for what you feel comfortable in helps you avoid one of the common pitfalls of picking a wedding dress—buying something that doesn't reflect the bride's true personality. As many bridal shops advise, "Don't let the dress wear you." You instinctively follow this advice by listening to your heart. On your wedding day, the confidence that comes with choosing the right dress lets your radiance shine through.

Listening to your heart is your mantra, but it can encourage some impulsive behavior. As one who finds it difficult to deny what your heart wants, the Unifier Bride has trouble saying no. Your excitement can get the best of you and end up in a shopping bag. There's nothing like some good retail therapy for the Boar sign, and weddings hold many opportunities to splurge. Unifier Brides can often end up with multiple wedding dresses or buying things prematurely, such as for a first house . . . that you don't live in yet. Try to combat the threat of overspending by using a shopping list and by bringing a trusted adviser such as your mother or best friend for a second opinion. By exercising some restraint you can save some money, avoid the nasty task of returning things, and leave some items on your wedding registry for your guests to buy.

Now, as kind and popular as you are, there are some areas where your generous side can get the best of you. You believe so much in looking for the best in people that you're blind to other people's faults. Thankfully you've found your Prince Charming. Your girlfriends can testify to consoling you through many breakups where everyone else could see a guy was bad news long before you did. Your sweet nature likes to look at the glass as half full, but neglects to consider whether the contents are worth saving. Now that you are planning your wedding, embrace your ability to call the shots and don't feel that you have to obey every single obligation. It's your time to make the decisions that make you happy, so it's okay to not reciprocate the bridesmaid invitation to a friend who did you wrong in the past. You absolutely hate to give bad news, but trust in your capability.

Wedding planning is a test of organization and diplomacy, of which you are known more for the latter. Those close to you know that much of your inspiration is for the people you care about most. You can outwork and outlast many people all in the name of love, but can unfortunately neglect yourself in the process. Even worse, your optimistic nature can be your worst enemy, encouraging you to procrastinate by assuring you that you always have more time. Your generosity knows almost no bounds, and it may drive your fiancé and loved ones crazy seeing you bend over backwards to help people, while you should be indulging more in being a bride. On the other hand, your giving approach to life is the reason that so many people give to you.

East Meets West: When Moon Signs Meet Sun Signs

Many people don't realize that each animal of the Chinese zodiac has a solar calendar connection. In our interpretation of Chinese horoscopes, the lunar calendar links into the solar calendar through the month and season, where the Boar's parallel sun sign is Scorpio. But every Western sun sign has a different effect on the lunar moon sign.

THE SAGITTARIUS BOAR

Sagittarius: November 22 to December 21

The Sagittarius Unifier Bride is a pleasure to be around. Your native Boar sign encourages you to always be positive and spread your sunshine when spending time with others. Informal and inviting, you can turn a small gathering into a party that lasts for hours. Naturally, you'll view your wedding as a big wonderful party, and not be one to skimp on the food or the libations. You'll follow the Golden Rule of weddings and think about how you would want to be treated as a guest. However, be thoughtful about picking up too many expenses for attendants who are low on cash. You're always loaning people money. Avoid breaking the bank and uncomfortable moments by getting a sense of what each girl's comfort level is with the bridesmaid budget early into the process. Estimate the total cost of participating in your wedding, from dress type to accessories to the amount of travel each person is taking on. Share the total damage to friends up front and have frank discussions. Full disclosure gives you all the flexibility to plan ahead.

THE CAPRICORN BOAR

Capricorn: December 22 to January 20

The presence of Capricorn makes you a more cautious Unifier Bride than your sister Boars. You feel safe with choosing the traditional route of things, so you'll look to friends who've been recently married for advice. Those closest to you will be your best resource because the Capricorn Boar doesn't build trust as quickly as purer Boar personalities whose kindness can be taken advantage of. It never hurts to be careful and get a second opinion, so this is a nice gift from your East-West combination. You believe in showing people the utmost respect and will go to great pains to make sure that you get to know your new in-laws and fiancé's friends so you can make them comfortable at the wedding.

THE AQUARIUS BOAR
Aquarius: January 21 to February 19

Aquarius is the reason that you are a quieter Unifier Bride. Your sun sign is an intellectual one that encourages you to sit back and think about the mechanics of how things work. As a result, you almost have two different bridal personalities— the outgoing friend whose sense of humor is infectious, and the introspective girl sitting alone and contemplating her life at the moment. Your fiancé shouldn't be concerned if you need to detach yourself every once in a while to de-stress. There's a lot of change going on right now, and you'll need time to let it all sink in.

THE PISCES BOAR
Pisces: February 20 to March 20

Your East-West combination brings together two peaceful signs that are both optimistic. Needless to say, you're a very popular person and treasured friend. You enjoy the act of giving. From volunteering and giving back to the community or going to the aid of a friend or neighbor who needs support, you're seen as a godsend to those around you. With all your past good deeds, you should expect an outpouring of generous gifts and helping hands now that you're getting married. One thing to bear in mind is that the native Boar sign is a nonconfrontational sign and so is Pisces, so you may need to call in some bigger muscles for challenging situations.

THE ARIES BOAR
Aries: March 21 to April 19

You're a Unifier Bride who is as generous and hospitable as your sister Boars, but has a much shorter fuse. With the presence of Aries, you have a more direct way of communicating than other Boar natives and are far less likely to let people slide when they're in the wrong. People who don't know Boars well sometimes make the mistake of thinking that there's no limit to the kindness train, but you'll speak quite plainly about where you draw the line for people outside your inner circle.

You're already busy moving mountains for your fiancé and doing countless favors for friends. The Aries Boar remembers that if you don't say no, when will you find time for yourself?

THE TAURUS BOAR
Taurus: April 20 to May 20

This East-West combination is a well-balanced bride who wins fans for her sweet and charming disposition. Since you are armed with a personality that encourages conversation, it'll be difficult for people to say no to you. There's a reason that the Boar sign comes to depend on the kindness of strangers. Frankly, if it happens to you all the time, you start to get used to it. The Taurus Boar benefits from a sort of halo effect of health and happiness. When life is in balance, your smile is infectious. As any vendor or bridesmaid will say, a happy bride is a joy to be around.

THE GEMINI BOAR
Gemini: May 21 to June 21

The Unifier Bride is aided by the influence of Gemini. This combination of sun sign and moon sign creates a bride who is a skilled and sociable problem solver. While too many choices can overwhelm other brides, the Gemini Boar embraces options. You can easily pick out what dress you want from a sea of samples, being able to quickly identify the diamonds from the glass. The Gemini Boar has all the components of a star athlete too. Wedding training time will be a good opportunity to find a new workout routine or sport to help manage your stress and channel your abundant energy.

THE CANCERIAN BOAR
Cancer: June 22 to July 21

The Cancerian Boar is where homebody meets party hostess. You'll have to find a balance of your two sides during the busyness of planning your wedding to maintain your sanity. Your two signs share the same loyalty and commitment for others, but differ on the topic of criticism. The Unifier Bride will keep up a good face for the benefit of others, but underneath, your Cancerian side can still feel the sting of poorly chosen words. The Cancerian Boar prefers to live a comfortable life and delights in the many luxuries that weddings bring with them. You'll choose the tastiest wedding cakes over the pretty towers that are all fondant and no flavor.

THE LEO BOAR

Leo: July 22 to August 21

The Lion and the Boar are two animals that live life on a large scale, so guests better come to this wedding with an empty stomach and a pair of comfortable dancing shoes. The Leo Unifier Bride sure knows how to throw a party. And with generosity comes the need for someone to keep track of the dollars spent. It's just too easy for you to rationalize the expense. You want to be a generous bride, be a loyal friend, and indulge your dramatic side at your wedding—the grandest of all stages. Hopefully, your fiancé is comfortable with managing the budget and blowing the whistle when you need to tone it down.

THE VIRGO BOAR

Virgo: August 22 to September 22

The Unifier Bride gets all the benefits of Virgo's practical nature. The Boar native can suffer from being too optimistic when making decisions, often saying yes before thinking about any potential downside. The Virgo Boar thankfully hesitates when pulling the trigger, by asking more questions or bringing in a second opinion. You're also savvier in matters of finance than most Boars and will be able to manage a budget and start merging your and your fiancé's financial lives. The numbers will help you curb the Boar's indulgent spending habits and focus your efforts on the big priorities of the wedding.

THE LIBRA BOAR

Libra: September 23 to October 22

Both of your signs are giving to the point of selflessness. Your fiancé, family, and friends will have to be more forceful with lending a hand because you're inclined to take care of things yourself. While you don't want to be a burden, remember and embrace the fact that you're the bride and people *want* to help you. Giving your friends and family projects to do is a great compliment to many. It shows your trust in others and allows people to give the special gift of their time and talents. The best way to help people help you is by being decisive in your actions. Libra can sometimes waver on what's best, so employ the opinions of your best friends and let them execute once you've decided on a plan.

THE SCORPIO BOAR
Scorpio: October 23 to November 21
The Scorpio Unifier Bride steps up as leader more than any other of her Boar sisters. You don't need convincing that when you're the bride, you're entitled to some special VIP treatment. Always charming in delivery, of course, you'll ask sweetly for the help of others and negotiate your needs as well. You won't take no for an answer easily and will ask others to compromise with the full force of diplomatic bridal immunity. You also won't forget the people who let you down when you needed them most. The Scorpio Boar can be downright vengeful when she feels she's been done wrong.

Wedding Synergy: When Dragon Meets Phoenix

As you embark on your planning, check out the Wedding Relationship pairings below to see how your strengths and weaknesses come together during the planning process. These compatibility descriptions are based on year of birth combinations, which is the tip of the iceberg when it comes to each of your charts. As described in Chapter 2 "Reference Dates and Tables on the Chinese Zodiac, East-West Sign Combinations, and Animal Hours," a different animal governs each component of your birth date and time.

RAT HUSBAND AND BOAR WIFE
You both like to fully embrace life through friends, family, and giving back to the community. One of the more difficult tasks for the two of you will be coming up with your invite list—you just know too many people and have a difficult time saying no. You might want to consider throwing multiple engagement parties or some other small fetes, so that all your friends can participate, even if they can't partake of the main event. The Rat and the Boar do their best to make each other

happy and aren't afraid to take part in public displays of affection. Your candid engagement shots will probably turn out best because you are best when natural and unposed.

OX HUSBAND AND BOAR WIFE
The Unifier Bride may quite simply be the perfect match for a man born in the year of the Ox. Men born in the year of the Ox are known for being successful through their total dedication to hard work. Slow and steady wins the race with your future husband. As a result, he can work long hours and may not always be as tuned in to the wedding planning as you'd like. But, while he's not one to gush, he's very happy with how much care you put into the wedding day. Your fiancé's commitment to marriage is deep, but his sign is not as forthcoming with his emotions as you are. If you're writing your own vows, it'll be a challenge for him and he may need your encouragement.

TIGER HUSBAND AND BOAR WIFE
The Tiger and Boar signs make one red-hot combination. Each of you possesses passion for love and life. You're both spontaneous and casual; it wouldn't be surprising if you have a quick engagement or decide to elope and throw a party on your return. As Protectors, Tiger natives are very emotional because they think with their heart before their head. You were probably instantly attracted to your fiancé's energetic personality as well as your shared commitment to your loved ones. Both of you can be self-sacrificing and generous, so much that it could take up a sizable part of your budget. Be sure to communicate to whom you've offered your guest room or couch, so that your friends don't show up to find no room at the inn.

RABBIT HUSBAND AND BOAR WIFE
The Unifier Bride finds a stylish match with a male Rabbit. You're a natural beauty, and he's a lover of beauty, with the refined tastes that come with being a connoisseur of the good life. The Rabbit can be a valued adviser to the Unifier Bride on a few levels, beyond just aesthetics. Since you like to look for the good in everyone, you can sometimes trust some people that you should be avoiding. Be sure to get

a second opinion from your fiancé because Rabbits have a strong intuitive sense. Your husband-to-be is also quite savvy at negotiation and getting the most value out of items. Crafting a well-balanced menu or bar are two good areas to give him free rein over.

DRAGON HUSBAND AND BOAR WIFE

Strength and weakness will come to your partnership based on how you work through your differences. Your husband-to-be is strong-willed and emotional. He also undoubtedly possesses the infamous Dragon ego. You're an emotional giver who doesn't mind supporting your man because you feel the good times are worth the occasional dark times. Well, wedding planning does have its dark times, so be prepared to hash out some long discussion with your fiancé. Unlike some other grooms, he will be very opinionated about what he wants and will not always concede to the bride's wishes. As the Unifier Bride, take a cue from your fiancé and don't be shy about asking for what you need. Be vocal about what you truly want for the wedding. Once Dragons are aware of the goal, they can self-motivate quite expertly.

SNAKE HUSBAND AND BOAR WIFE

The Unifier Bride is an open book to all. You can chat with a stranger, and he or she can walk away feeling like you two have known each other your entire lives. Meanwhile, getting any information out of your Snake fiancé is like pulling teeth, even for someone as close as his bride-to-be. It's obvious to say that communication is the core ingredient in creating wedding harmony. While your fiancé may dislike being questioned for his opinions, remind him that your choices affect his family and all the people you've invited to the wedding. He can be tight-lipped about his true feelings (compliments included), so you'll have to drag the details out of him or enlist the advice of his close friends. Wedding planning might be a good opportunity to bond with your new mother-in-law.

HORSE HUSBAND AND BOAR WIFE

The Unifier Bride is drawn in by the seductive powers of the Horse sign. Your husband's sex appeal comes from the confidence he exudes in life. Horses do what we all wish we had the guts to do. While other animals never seem to find the right time to go on vacation, the Horse is most likely to travel around the world because he likes to exercise his free will. In your wedding planning, you may get frustrated that your fiancé isn't always joined at the hip as you go from appointment to appointment. He'll still be easing into being part of an official couple, balancing his individualistic nature and his new role as husband. To help appeal to your man's sense of adventure, you can employ the tactic of combining wedding chores with exploring a new part of the city or a new restaurant.

SHEEP HUSBAND AND BOAR WIFE

The Catalysts Affinity Triangle brings together kind and affectionate couples, much like you two. The Unifier Bride and the Sheep native keep a loving household. As the best of neighbors, you like to be involved in your community by helping people almost as generously as you support each other. Wedding planning will be an easier time for both of you than for other couples because you understand the importance of compromise. The Unifier Bride isn't the type to throw a fit for any small thing, and your fiancé doesn't like to have you shoulder all the weight of wedding responsibilities. Your only struggle may be to bring your husband-to-be out of his bouts of shyness when meeting the onslaught of extended family and friends.

MONKEY HUSBAND AND BOAR WIFE

As the Unifier Bride, you're an innocent soul who gives freely and frequently reaps the reward of paying it forward. Your fiancé, born in the year of the Monkey, is a master strategist. He's always one step ahead of the competition, and if there's a shortcut, he'll find it and may or may not share his secret. As a married couple, you can really combine forces and conquer on many fronts. Starting with wedding planning, it'd be wise to have your fiancé control the purse strings of the wedding (with a little stashed away for your bridal slush fund, of course). He's got a mind for numbers and is more predisposed to negotiating than you. But don't underestimate your inherent likability, which is a big negotiation point in itself. There's always room for the good cop.

ROOSTER HUSBAND AND BOAR WIFE

Women born in the year of the Boar are known for being nice, but your fiancé should know by now that you're a tough cookie as well. When pushed you will certainly push back, and the most likely time for this is when your Rooster fiancé gives you too much criticism. You and your man share an observant nature and act on your findings in different ways. You're quick to aid people with action, while your guy reacts verbally with advice. This is how the Rooster shows love, but unfortunately, you'll not always be able to stomach the critical review. Choose your battles wisely and manage your timing with getting his opinions. If a project is in its beginning stages, you'd be wise to keep it under wraps until it's ready for viewing.

DOG HUSBAND AND BOAR WIFE

You've found a friend and lover for the long haul with a man born in the year of the Dog. Since he comes from the Protectors Triangle, he's a guy who is of the highest moral fiber. He'll be your biggest supporter and protector because while he loves your sweet and giving nature, he worries about how easily you put your trust in the kindness of strangers. Therefore, he'll be your best guide in choosing the right people to hire and perhaps even the right group of attendants for the wedding. You may have put a girlfriend's past arguments behind you, but your fiancé has a long, detailed memory. He'll want to keep as much stress as possible out of your engagement and out of your wedding day by involving the right people.

BOAR HUSBAND AND BOAR WIFE

Some Chinese believe that pairing two Boars cannot work, but we believe the reality is that this pairing is one that can have the pendulum go from the bad extreme to the good extreme. The Boar native is known for being generous and kind to the point of excess. Both of you are strong and protective of your inner circle. You'll always be tuned in to each other's feelings and try to keep each other happy. However, without one of you as the lead in any given situation, it's easy for you two to exist without direction—enjoying today, while tomorrow fast approaches. As the Unifier Bride, you'll need to step up first and set the course for the wedding because your fiancé will need your direction to get focused.

The Boar's Relationships with Friends and Family

Family and friends are an important part of most weddings. Since we all operate differently in our nonromantic relationships, the pairings of your Chinese zodiac sign will take a slightly different form. Knowing the compatibility of your animal sign with your family and friends is a real asset when planning and setting expectations for responsibilities. As you think about how best to integrate your vast network of friends, review the relationship overviews below. They will help cast light on your friends' and family members' strengths, weaknesses, and working styles.

WITH A RAT

Choosing a person born in the year of the Rat as an attendant is wise. Organized, thoughtful, and committed, these people more than carry their own weight. Like you, your friend or family member is affectionate and protective of those close to her. If you've been a part of this person's wedding before, she'll give you the same VIP treatment both out of appreciation and out of a sense of duty. Rat signs are Doers who feed off accomplishment, not to mention the thrill of the deal. You certainly won't mind when she takes it upon herself to make on-the-spot negotiations and haggle for the best price.

WITH AN OX

There's a role for everyone to play in a wedding, and the Ox is tough enough to shoulder the not-so-fun responsibilities. Whether it's something like collecting the money for the bachelorette party or keeping you on track with your wedding detox diet, Ox signs are confident and caring enough to keep their loved ones in line. The Unifier Bride's optimism can actually hold her back from progress, by encouraging procrastination or prayer for divine intervention. This Ox could be the solution. If this person is new to your life, you'll have to understand that Oxen rarely compromise. Your best bet is to pull rank and appeal to the Ox's sense of responsibility because, after all, you are the bride.

WITH A TIGER

A Tiger can be a partner in crime to the Unifier Bride. Fun and vibrant, this person is someone you've bonded with in the past or present over a glass of wine and a good laugh. You're both known for being social animals and the life of the party. Like you, she's very giving of herself to people she feels close to. Tigers are Protectors, and she'll naturally want to take you under her wing and take some of the weight off your shoulders, as you're busy with all your other wedding responsibilities. She can also be a great heavy hitter in a negotiation. Where you shy away from confrontation, this person can really go to bat.

Δ WITH A RABBIT

The Unifier Bride will find a good working relationship with a person born in the year of the Rabbit. Whether you've been close for years or have been brought together as a result of the wedding, you'll find that communication flows fairly easily. Rabbit signs take it upon themselves to uphold good manners or, at the very least, keep up appearances. If you're not getting along, she's not going to make a scene. You should trust in the good advice of your Rabbit friend because her intuitive senses are strong. She'll be sincere when she recommends that you investigate another direction.

WITH A DRAGON

When you ask a Dragon for an opinion, her recommendation will be to make it bigger and better. By the same token, as a hostess born in the year of the Boar, you're most likely to say the more the merrier. Put these two personalities together and you can have a pretty grand wedding on your hand. If you're lucky enough for money to be no object, then have the time of your lives. Otherwise, one of you is going to have to be the brakes and maintain a realistic view. You two could easily run up some credit cards or finish too many cocktails before a brainstorming session is through.

× WITH A SNAKE

Hate to tell you this, but if you don't have a foundation of friendship or family obligation with a person born in the year of the Snake, you might find working with this person a little jerky. It's nothing to take personally, but people born in the year of the Snake are introspective Thinkers. You exercise no pretense in sharing your ideas openly and having people build on them or even tear them down. On the other hand, you'll find that your friend can be a brick wall about her thoughts. If a Snake person wants to help, she'll follow through, and with the highest of standards. She often prefers to work individually, so don't be hurt if she needs to be alone to collect her thoughts or finish a project.

WITH A HORSE

The Horse sign is tons of fun to be around. She's entertaining and armed with lots of great stories of adventure. However, working with someone is different from simply hanging out and shooting the breeze. Depending on the level of involvement, your Horse friend can test your patience. Horse signs are prone to sudden flare-ups in temper. Since the Unifier Bride is happiest when others are happy, you can find she adds more stress to your life when she's experiencing stress in hers. Fortunately, the Horse has a winning personality that makes her the most spirited of team players. As long as you do not saddle the Horse with too detailed an activity, she will follow through on anything you ask of her.

Δ WITH A SHEEP

You find quick friendships with people born in the year of the Sheep. Your friend or family member shares a tender heart and is a compassionate listener to your rants and raves about the wedding planning activities. When choosing people to take a very active role in your wedding, if you're considering a Sheep sign, you should consider what else is on her plate. Sheep signs do not deal with stress well, and you may end up doing some of the things that your friend volunteered for originally, just to keep the peace. It's best to avoid a situation like this, especially when there are probably a number of people who will be able to lend a helping hand.

WITH A MONKEY

The Unifier Bride can gain a fresh perspective from working with the Monkey sign. Clever and creative, the Monkey sign probably led the first brainstorming session. There's always a newer, better way to do something in the Monkey's eyes. She can inspire you to be vigilant in finding the best deals or discovering ways to make things yourself. Monkeys are good second opinions when you're shopping around.

They can sniff out a scheme easily because they're familiar with all the tricks. Some might take issue with the Monkey's enterprising ways. A Monkey could be recommending her friend the photographer for your wedding and be getting a referral fee on the side, but neither of you sees the harm in this. You need a photographer, and the Monkey's helping you get one. If she gets a bit extra, that's gravy. The Monkey would agree.

WITH A ROOSTER

Roosters can be quite the chatterboxes, but you'll find that these people are not all talk. They can deliver incredible results. A Rooster friend or acquaintance is committed to producing a quality product. A perfectionist at heart, this person believes to the core, "If it's got my name on it, it better be good." And you shouldn't be surprised to see and hear the Rooster make mention of her handiwork. Let's just say that people will know that she singlehandedly put together those lovely centerpieces. Well, there's pride in a job well done, and you're wise enough to not take issue with this person indulging in a little bit of self-promotion. Other friends may not see things as diplomatically, so be sure to thank them all for their contributions, small and large.

WITH A DOG

A member of the Protectors Affinity Triangle, the Dog sign is also known as the voice of reason, and a person born in this year will be a source of support and protection to you. Taking part in a wedding is a responsibility, and a Dog responds to the call of duty. She can be depended on to maintain fairness among a diverse group of people. An ideal judge, she's least likely to play favorites, so she makes a great choice for a maid of honor or other person with great responsibility. You can also depend on the Dog sign to be an elegant bearer of bad news—a role that you're very uncomfortable with.

Δ WITH ANOTHER BOAR

Working with another Boar can either be the best of situations or a power struggle. The deciding factor will be the nature of your relationship. By and large, Boars are jovial and don't mind compromise. However, Boars can butt heads when there's a fight for dominance. You're the bride now and should be making the final decisions. But an older Boar, perhaps a sibling, parent, or in-law, may assert opinions strongly and rub you the wrong way as a result. Most likely this person's intentions are sincere and may actually be built on habit. Boars do tend to take on extra responsibilities for the people they care about. If you've been letting this person guide you in the past, and you're deciding to step up now as a leader, that alone could be the game changer.

PART III

A Time and a Season to Get Married

A few years ago, couples around the world got into long lines and paid a king's ransom to be married on August 8, 2008. Why was this date all the rage? Was it the insurance of a wedding anniversary date that was virtually unforgettable? Well, 8/8/08 is seen as practically the Halley's Comet of perfect wedding dates to the Chinese and most of Asia. The day of triple eights was seen as one of the most auspicious days possible because of the symbolism of the number eight to the Chinese. Lucky number eight is the equivalent of the Western world's lucky number seven. The number eight gets its prosperous reputation from it being a homonym of sorts to the word "prosperity" when spoken in Cantonese. And when you rotate the numeral 8 ninety degrees, it becomes the sign for infinity. Put those two meanings together and you have a date that symbolizes prosperity forever. Thus, all the fuss—even though 8/8/08 really wasn't the traditional luckiest date for all the couples who chose it! Because of its general auspicious connotations, many couples threw the age-old customs used to choose a personalized wedding date out the window. This brings us to the fundamental truth of all things wedding planning: it always depends on the couple.

For those interested in following the traditional Chinese approach, choosing a wedding date is based on what is referred to as the couple's set of eight characters, or *ba zi*. The *ba zi* is the road map of a couple's compatibility. In the old days of matchmakers, a family would give an astrologer an eligible man or woman's set of characters, as determined by birth date and hour of birth. A zodiac animal governs each of these pieces of data. The matchmaker would create a compatible match based on the collective *ba zi*, as well as each family's social standing. Once the match was made, each family would consult their ancestors for approval. While formal matchmaking is far less common today, some families still practice the ritual of asking for the ancestral blessing through the altar test. The groom's family goes first, by taking a piece of paper with his future wife's four-character signature and placing it at his family's ancestral altar. If three days pass without any sign discouraging the match, then the process is repeated over the next three days by the bride's side. If those days pass without warning, the engagement is blessed. What constitutes a bad sign or a good sign is subjective and based on each family's interpretation.

The next step is choosing a wedding day and time. The dates recommended in *Wedding Feng Shui* are based on our methodology, which puts dominance on the animal year of birth. (If you are interested in strictly following the traditional *ba zi* method, we recommend you consult a Chinese astrologer who can chart you as a couple and choose a date and time in the Chinese Almanac. The number of possible *ba zi* combinations is so great that it could not be covered in one book!) Additionally, there are some commonly held Chinese beliefs about planning a wedding day, which have been marked on our set of recommendations. For example, the Chinese believe that it is inauspicious to get married in a blind year—a year with no first day of spring (*li chun*). It's believed that without the first day of spring a year has no eyes to guide a marriage or a new business. It is seen as a time where a person or couple is met with more challenges than other years, so it's a difficult time to conceive a child, start a business, or get married. That doesn't mean these things are impossible, but difficult. The years 2011 and 2012 both have the eyes of *li chun*, which we refer to as Bright years. In fact, 2012 has two *li chun*. A year with two *li chun* is called Double Bright and an especially auspicious time for couples to get married.

In addition to selecting the wedding date, Chinese astrologers consult the Chinese Almanac to pick the wedding and bed setting time. Here, you can use your knowledge of the animal hours from this book to guide yourself. There are two paths that you can take. The Chinese believe that marrying during the birth hour or ascendant of the bride or groom is prosperous. If one of your birth hours is a good time for a ceremony, this is recommended. The alternate method is to use the Affinity Triangle Relationships △ and Conflicting Relationships × marked throughout the chapters as a guide. You now know which signs have complementary relationships to each of your animals. Consult the table "Ascendants: The Twelve Animals and Their Birth Hours" on p. 16 to find an hour that is not challenging to either of your signs.

For example, if you were born in the year of the Rabbit and your fiancé was born in the year of the Rat, you would avoid the hours of 5–7 P.M. (Rooster) and 11 A.M.–1 P.M. (the Horse) because they are in opposition to your respective signs. A solution would be an evening wedding between the hours of 7–9 P.M., during the Dog's time interval. Both the Rabbit and Rat have positive relationships with the Dog, and it is therefore a suitable hour to wed.

The pages that follow recommend a set of wedding dates for each of the 144 wedding combinations. For each of your zodiac signs, we have provided you with the most auspicious days in each year. For practical planning purposes, we have recommended only weekend dates. For every sign, it is considered auspicious to start at the half hour, symbolic of an upswing.

The seventh month of the lunar year is known as the Ghost Month. The Chinese believe this is an unlucky time to get married because it coincides with the Ghost Festival, a time when ghosts are believed to return to Earth. This typically falls in the July to August time frame. The decision to marry during this time is a personal choice, but the most traditional Chinese families will not marry during this time of the year. The ghost months fall during the following times:

- 2011: August 1–August 28
- 2012: August 17–September 15

If you cannot get married on one of the days suggested, there are still ways to incorporate an auspicious date. You could get your marriage license on a recommended day, or plan an important wedding ceremony on one of these days, such as an engagement party or the gift exchange explained earlier (p. 40). A few final items to note:

* February 3, 2011–January 22, 2012, the year of the Rabbit, will be a challenging time for the Rooster.

** January 23, 2012–February 9, 2013, the year of the Dragon, is a more difficult year for the Dog, but it is a Double Bright year (possesses two *li chun*, first day of spring), which helps counteract the opposing forces of the Dog and the Dragon.

RECOMMENDED WEDDING DATES
FROM 2011 TO 2012

Bride's birth sign	Groom's birth sign	2011*	2012**
Rat	Rat	January 1, 2011	January 21, 2012
		January 2, 2011	February 19, 2012
		January 29, 2011	March 17, 2012
		February 26, 2011	
		February 27, 2011	
Rat	Ox	January 1, 2011	January 21, 2012
		January 2, 2011	February 19, 2012
		January 29, 2011	March 17, 2012
		February 26, 2011	
		February 27, 2011	
Rat	Tiger	February 26, 2011	January 21, 2012
		April 3, 2011	January 22, 2012
		May 7, 2011	May 26, 2012
		June 4, 2011	
Rat	Rabbit	February 26, 2011	January 21, 2012
		April 3, 2011	January 22, 2012
		April 10, 2011	February 19, 2012
		June 5, 2011	March 17, 2012
			April 22, 2012
Rat	Dragon	January 1, 2011	January 21, 2012
		January 29, 2011	January 22, 2012

Bride's birth sign	Groom's birth sign	2011*	2012**
Rat	Dragon	February 26, 2011 April 3, 2011	April 22, 2012
Rat	Snake	February 26, 2011 February 27, 2011 July 9, 2011 September 11, 2011	January 21, 2012 March 17, 2012
Rat	Horse	February 27, 2011 July 9, 2011 September 11, 2011	January 21, 2012 March 17, 2012
Rat	Sheep	February 26, 2011 July 10, 2011 September 11, 2011	July 1, 2012 July 29, 2012
Rat	Monkey	February 26, 2011 October 16, 2011 December 11, 2011	October 6, 2012 November 3, 2012 December 1, 2012
Rat	Rooster	February 26, 2011 October 16, 2011 December 11, 2011	January 21, 2012 October 6, 2012 November 3, 2012 November 4, 2012 December 1, 2012 December 2, 2012
Rat	Dog	February 26, 2011 December 11, 2011	February 19, 2012 October 6, 2012 December 1, 2012

Bride's birth sign	Groom's birth sign	2011*	2012**
Rat	Boar	January 1, 2011	January 21, 2012
		January 29, 2011	February 19, 2012
		February 26, 2011	March 17, 2012
		February 27, 2011	
Ox	Rat	January 1, 2011	January 21, 2012
		January 2, 2011	February 19, 2012
		January 29, 2011	March 17, 2012
		February 26, 2011	
		February 27, 2011	
Ox	Ox	January 1, 2011	January 21, 2012
		January 2, 2011	January 22, 2012
		January 29, 2011	February 19, 2012
		February 26, 2011	March 17, 2012
		February 27, 2011	
Ox	Tiger	February 27, 2011	February 19, 2012
		April 9, 2011	March 17, 2012
		May 7, 2011	March 25, 2012
		June 4, 2011	April 28, 2012
			May 20, 2012
			May 26, 2012
Ox	Rabbit	February 27, 2011	February 19, 2012
		May 8, 2011	March 17, 2012
		June 5, 2011	

Bride's birth sign	Groom's birth sign	2011*	2012**
Ox	Dragon	February 26, 2011	January 21, 2012
		February 27, 2011	January 22, 2012
		April 3, 2011	February 19, 2012
			March 17, 2012
			April 22, 2012
Ox	Snake	February 27, 2011	January 21, 2012
		July 9, 2011	March 17, 2012
		September 11, 2011	
Ox	Horse	February 27, 2011	January 21, 2012
		July 9, 2011	January 22, 2012
		July 10, 2011	February 19, 2012
		September 11, 2011	March 17, 2012
			June 30, 2012
			July 28, 2012
Ox	Sheep	February 26, 2011	January 21, 2012
		July 10, 2011	July 1, 2012
			July 29, 2012
Ox	Monkey	February 26, 2011	January 21, 2012
		February 27, 2011	March 17, 2012
		October 16, 2011	October 6, 2012
		December 11, 2011	October 7, 2012
			November 3, 2012
			November 4, 2012

Bride's birth sign	Groom's birth sign	2011*	2012**
Ox	Monkey		December 1, 2012
			December 2, 2012
Ox	Rooster	February 26, 2011	January 21, 2012
		February 27, 2011	March 17, 2012
		October 16, 2011	October 7, 2012
		December 10, 2011	November 4, 2012
		December 11, 2011	December 2, 2012
		December 17, 2011	
Ox	Dog	February 26, 2011	January 21, 2012
		February 27, 2011	January 22, 2012
		October 15, 2011	February 19, 2012
		December 10, 2011	March 17, 2012
		December 11, 2011	September 30, 2012
		December 17, 2011	October 7, 2012
			November 4, 2012
			December 2, 2012
Ox	Boar	January 1, 2011	January 21, 2012
		January 29, 2011	February 19, 2012
		February 26, 2011	March 17, 2012
		February 27, 2011	
Tiger	Rat	February 26, 2011	January 21, 2012
		April 3, 2011	January 22, 2012
		May 7, 2011	May 26, 2012
		June 4, 2011	

Bride's birth sign	Groom's birth sign	2011*	2012**
Tiger	Ox	February 27, 2011	February 19, 2012
		April 9, 2011	March 17, 2012
		May 7, 2011	March 25, 2012
		June 4, 2011	April 28, 2012
			May 20, 2012
			May 26, 2012
Tiger	Tiger	March 20, 2011	March 25, 2012
		April 23, 2011	April 21, 2012
		May 21, 2011	April 22, 2012
		May 22, 2011	April 28, 2012
		June 18, 2011	May 20, 2012
			May 26, 2012
Tiger	Rabbit	March 20, 2011	April 21, 2012
		April 23, 2011	April 22, 2012
		May 21, 2011	April 28, 2012
		May 22, 2011	May 20, 2012
		June 18, 2011	May 26, 2012
Tiger	Dragon	May 21, 2011	March 25, 2012
		May 22, 2011	April 21, 2012
		June 18, 2011	April 22, 2012
			April 28, 2012
			May 20, 2012
			May 26, 2012

Bride's birth sign	Groom's birth sign	2011*	2012**
Tiger	Snake	April 9, 2011	March 25, 2012
		May 7, 2011	April 22, 2012
		June 4, 2011	May 20, 2012
		July 10, 2011	June 30, 2012
		September 11, 2011	July 28, 2012
Tiger	Horse	April 9, 2011	June 30, 2012
		May 7, 2011	July 28, 2012
		June 4, 2011	
		July 10, 2011	
Tiger	Sheep	April 9, 2011	April 28, 2012
		April 10, 2011	May 26, 2012
		May 7, 2011	June 30, 2012
		May 8, 2011	July 1, 2012
		June 4, 2011	July 28, 2012
		July 10, 2011	July 29, 2012
		June 5, 2011	
Tiger	Monkey	April 3, 2011	April 21, 2012
		April 9, 2011	September 30, 2012
		May 7, 2011	October 6, 2012
		October 16, 2011	November 3, 2012
		December 11, 2011	
		December 17, 2011	
Tiger	Rooster	April 9, 2011	March 25, 2012
		May 7, 2011	April 22, 2012

Bride's birth sign	Groom's birth sign	2011*	2012**
Tiger	Rooster	June 4, 2011	May 20, 2012
		December 17, 2011	September 30, 2012
			October 7, 2012
			November 4, 2012
			December 2, 2012
Tiger	Dog	April 9, 2011	September 30, 2012
		May 7, 2011	December 1, 2012
		June 4, 2011	December 2, 2012
			December 16, 2012
Tiger	Boar	June 4, 2011	March 25, 2012
		June 5, 2011	April 21, 2012
		April 9, 2011	May 20, 2012
		April 10, 2011	May 26, 2012
		May 7, 2011	
		May 8, 2011	
Rabbit	Rat	February 26, 2011	January 21, 2012
		April 3, 2011	January 22, 2012
		April 10, 2011	February 19, 2012
		June 5, 2011	March 17, 2012
			April 22, 2012
Rabbit	Ox	February 27, 2011	February 19, 2012
		May 8, 2011	March 17, 2012
		June 5, 2011	

Bride's birth sign	Groom's birth sign	2011*	2012**
Rabbit	Tiger	March 20, 2011	April 21, 2012
		April 23, 2011	April 22, 2012
		May 21, 2011	April 28, 2012
		May 22, 2011	May 20, 2012
		June 18, 2011	May 26, 2012
Rabbit	Rabbit	March 20, 2011	April 21, 2012
		April 23, 2011	April 22, 2012
		May 21, 2011	April 28, 2012
		May 22, 2011	May 20, 2012
		June 18, 2011	May 26, 2012
Rabbit	Dragon	April 23, 2011	April 21, 2012
		May 21, 2011	April 22, 2012
		May 22, 2011	April 28, 2012
		June 18, 2011	May 20, 2012
			May 26, 2012
Rabbit	Snake	April 10, 2011	April 22, 2012
		June 5, 2011	April 28, 2012
		September 11, 2011	May 20, 2012
			July 29, 2012
Rabbit	Horse	April 9, 2011	April 28, 2012
		April 10, 2011	May 26, 2012
		May 7, 2011	June 30, 2012
		May 8, 2011	July 1, 2012
		June 4, 2011	July 28, 2012

Bride's birth sign	Groom's birth sign	2011*	2012**
Rabbit	Horse	June 5, 2011	July 29, 2012
		July 10, 2011	
Rabbit	Sheep	April 10, 2011	April 28, 2012
		May 8, 2011	May 26, 2012
		June 5, 2011	July 1, 2012
			July 29, 2012
Rabbit	Monkey	April 3, 2011	April 21, 2012
		April 10, 2011	April 28, 2012
		May 8, 2011	May 26, 2012
		June 5, 2011	October 6, 2012
		October 15, 2011	November 3, 2012
		October 16, 2011	December 1, 2012
		November 12, 2011	December 16, 2012
		December 10, 2011	
		December 11, 2011	
Rabbit	Rooster	April 10, 2011	April 22, 2012
		May 8, 2011	April 28, 2012
		November 12, 2011	May 20, 2012
		December 10, 2011	May 26, 2012
			October 7, 2012
			November 4, 2012
			December 16, 2012
Rabbit	Dog	April 9, 2011	April 28, 2012
		April 10, 2011	May 26, 2012

Bride's birth sign	Groom's birth sign	2011*	2012**
Rabbit	Dog	May 7, 2011	September 30, 2012
		May 8, 2011	December 16, 2012
		June 4, 2011	
		June 5, 2011	
		October 15, 2011	
		November 12, 2011	
		December 10, 2011	
Rabbit	Boar	April 9, 2011	February 19, 2012
		April 10, 2011	March 17, 2012
		May 7, 2011	April 21, 2012
		June 5, 2011	April 22, 2012
			May 20, 2012
Dragon	Rat	January 1, 2011	January 21, 2012
		January 29, 2011	January 22, 2012
		February 26, 2011	April 22, 2012
		April 3, 2011	
Dragon	Ox	February 26, 2011	January 21, 2012
		February 27, 2011	January 22, 2012
		April 3, 2011	February 19, 2012
			March 17, 2012
			April 22, 2012
Dragon	Tiger	May 21, 2011	March 25, 2012
		May 22, 2011	April 21, 2012
		June 18, 2011	April 22, 2012

Bride's birth sign	Groom's birth sign	2011[*]	2012[**]
Dragon	Tiger		April 28, 2012
			May 20, 2012
			May 26, 2012
Dragon	Rabbit	April 23, 2011	April 21, 2012
		May 21, 2011	April 22, 2012
		May 22, 2011	April 28, 2012
		June 18, 2011	May 20, 2012
			May 26, 2012
Dragon	Dragon	April 23, 2011	April 21, 2012
		May 21, 2011	April 22, 2012
		May 22, 2011	April 28, 2012
		June 18, 2011	May 20, 2012
			May 26, 2012
Dragon	Snake	April 3, 2011	March 25, 2012
		September 11, 2011	April 21, 2012
			April 22, 2012
			May 20, 2012
Dragon	Horse	April 9, 2011	March 24, 2012
		June 4, 2011	July 28, 2012
		July 10, 2011	
Dragon	Sheep	April 3, 2011	April 21, 2012
		April 10, 2011	April 28, 2012
		May 8, 2011	May 26, 2012

Bride's birth sign	Groom's birth sign	2011*	2012**
Dragon	Sheep	June 5, 2011	July 1, 2012
			July 29, 2012
Dragon	Monkey	April 3, 2011	April 21, 2012
		October 16, 2011	October 6, 2012
		December 11, 2011	November 3, 2012
			December 1, 2012
Dragon	Rooster	April 3, 2011	March 25, 2012
		October 16, 2011	April 21, 2012
		December 11, 2011	April 22, 2012
			May 20, 2012
			October 6, 2012
			October 7, 2012
			November 3, 2012
			November 4, 2012
			December 1, 2012
			December 2, 2012
Dragon	Dog	April 3, 2011	April 21, 2012
		April 9, 2011	September 30, 2012
		June 4, 2011	October 6, 2012
		December 11, 2011	December 1, 2012
Dragon	Boar	February 26, 2011	January 21, 2012
		April 3, 2011	January 22, 2012
		April 10, 2011	April 21, 2012

Bride's birth sign	Groom's birth sign	2011*	2012**
Dragon	Boar	May 8, 2011	April 22, 2012
		June 5, 2011	
Snake	Rat	February 26, 2011	January 21, 2012
		February 27, 2011	March 17, 2012
		July 9, 2011	
		September 11, 2011	
Snake	Ox	February 27, 2011	January 21, 2012
		July 9, 2011	March 17, 2012
		September 11, 2011	
Snake	Tiger	April 9, 2011	March 25, 2012
		May 7, 2011	April 22, 2012
		June 4, 2011	May 20, 2012
		July 10, 2011	June 30, 2012
		September 11, 2011	July 28, 2012
Snake	Rabbit	April 10, 2011	April 22, 2012
		June 5, 2011	April 28, 2012
		September 11, 2011	May 20, 2012
			July 29, 2012
Snake	Dragon	April 3, 2011	March 25, 2012
		September 11, 2011	April 21, 2012
			April 22, 2012
			May 20, 2012
Snake	Snake	July 9, 2011	June 30, 2012
		July 10, 2011	July 28, 2012

Bride's birth sign	Groom's birth sign	2011*	2012**
Snake	Snake	September 11, 2011	July 29, 2012
Snake	Horse	July 9, 2011	June 30, 2012
		July 10, 2011	July 28, 2012
		September 11, 2011	July 29, 2012
Snake	Sheep	July 10, 2011	June 30, 2012
		September 11, 2011	July 28, 2012
			July 29, 2012
Snake	Monkey	September 11, 2011	October 6, 2012
		October 16, 2011	November 3, 2012
		December 11, 2011	November 4, 2012
			December 1, 2012
			December 2, 2012
Snake	Rooster	September 11, 2011	November 4, 2012
		November 12, 2011	December 2, 2012
Snake	Dog	July 10, 2011	June 30, 2012
		September 11, 2011	July 28, 2012
		December 17, 2011	September 30, 2012
			November 4, 2012
			December 2, 2012
Snake	Boar	February 27, 2011	March 17, 2012
		July 9, 2011	July 29, 2012
Horse	Rat	February 27, 2011	January 21, 2012
		July 9, 2011	March 17, 2012
		September 11, 2011	

Bride's birth sign	Groom's birth sign	2011*	2012**
Horse	Ox	February 27, 2011	January 21, 2012
		July 9, 2011	January 22, 2012
		July 10, 2011	February 19, 2012
		September 11, 2011	March 17, 2012
			June 30, 2012
			July 28, 2012
Horse	Tiger	April 9, 2011	June 30, 2012
		May 7, 2011	July 28, 2012
		June 4, 2011	
		July 10, 2011	
Horse	Rabbit	April 9, 2011	April 28, 2012
		April 10, 2011	May 26, 2012
		May 7, 2011	June 30, 2012
		May 8, 2011	July 1, 2012
		June 4, 2011	July 28, 2012
		June 5, 2011	July 29, 2012
		July 10, 2011	
Horse	Dragon	April 9, 2011	March 24, 2012
		June 4, 2011	July 28, 2012
		July 10, 2011	
Horse	Snake	July 9, 2011	June 30, 2012
		July 10, 2011	July 28, 2012
		September 11, 2011	July 29, 2012

Bride's birth sign	Groom's birth sign	2011*	2012**
Horse	Horse	July 9, 2011	June 30, 2012
		July 10, 2011	July 1, 2012
		September 11, 2011	July 28, 2012
			July 29, 2012
Horse	Sheep	July 10, 2011	June 30, 2012
		September 11, 2011	July 28, 2012
			July 29, 2012
Horse	Monkey	October 16, 2011	June 30, 2012
		December 17, 2011	September 30, 2012
			November 3, 2012
			December 1, 2012
Horse	Rooster	July 10, 2011	June 30, 2012
		September 11, 2011	July 28, 2012
		December 17, 2011	September 30, 2012
			November 4, 2012
			December 2, 2012
Horse	Dog	July 10, 2011	June 30, 2012
		December 17, 2011	July 28, 2012
			September 30, 2012
Horse	Boar	July 10, 2011	January 22, 2012
		September 4, 2011	February 19, 2012
			June 30, 2012
			July 1, 2012

Bride's birth sign	Groom's birth sign	2011*	2012**
Horse	Boar		July 28, 2012
			July 29, 2012
Sheep	Rat	February 26, 2011	July 1, 2012
		July 10, 2011	July 29, 2012
		September 11, 2011	
Sheep	Ox	February 26, 2011	January 21, 2012
		July 10, 2011	July 1, 2012
			July 29, 2012
Sheep	Tiger	April 9, 2011	April 28, 2012
		April 10, 2011	May 26, 2012
		May 7, 2011	June 30, 2012
		May 8, 2011	July 1, 2012
		June 4, 2011	July 28, 2012
		June 5, 2011	July 29, 2012
		July 10, 2011	
Sheep	Rabbit	April 10, 2011	April 28, 2012
		May 8, 2011	May 26, 2012
		June 5, 2011	July 1, 2012
			July 29, 2012
Sheep	Dragon	April 3, 2011	April 21, 2012
		April 10, 2011	April 28, 2012
		May 8, 2011	May 26, 2012
		June 5, 2011	July 1, 2012
			July 29, 2012

Bride's birth sign	Groom's birth sign	2011*	2012**
Sheep	Snake	July 10, 2011	June 30, 2012
		September 11, 2011	July 28, 2012
			July 29, 2012
Sheep	Horse	July 10, 2011	June 30, 2012
		September 11, 2011	July 28, 2012
			July 29, 2012
Sheep	Sheep	July 10, 2011	June 30, 2012
		September 11, 2011	July 1, 2012
			July 28, 2012
			July 29, 2012
Sheep	Monkey	October 15, 2011	July 1, 2012
		October 16, 2011	July 29, 2012
		November 12, 2011	October 6, 2012
		December 10, 2011	November 3, 2012
		December 11, 2011	December 1, 2012
			December 16, 2012
Sheep	Rooster	September 11, 2011	July 1, 2012
		November 12, 2011	November 4, 2012
		December 10, 2011	December 2, 2012
			December 16, 2012
Sheep	Dog	July 10, 2011	June 30, 2012
		October 15, 2011	July 1, 2012
		November 12, 2011	July 28, 2012
		December 10, 2011	July 29, 2012

Bride's birth sign	Groom's birth sign	2011*	2012**
Sheep	Dog	December 17, 2011	September 30, 2012
			December 16, 2012
Sheep	Boar	February 26, 2011	July 1, 2012
		July 10, 2011	July 29, 2012
Monkey	Rat	February 26, 2011	October 6, 2012
		October 16, 2011	November 3, 2012
		December 11, 2011	December 1, 2012
Monkey	Ox	February 26, 2011	January 21, 2012
		February 27, 2011	March 17, 2012
		October 16, 2011	October 6, 2012
		December 11, 2011	November 3, 2012
			November 4, 2012
			December 1, 2012
			December 2, 2012
Monkey	Tiger	April 3, 2011	April 21, 2012
		April 9, 2011	September 30, 2012
		May 7, 2011	October 6, 2012
		October 16, 2011	November 3, 2012
		December 11, 2011	
		December 17, 2011	
Monkey	Rabbit	April 3, 2011	April 21, 2012
		April 10, 2011	April 28, 2012
		May 8, 2011	May 26, 2012
		June 5, 2011	October 6, 2012

Bride's birth sign	Groom's birth sign	2011*	2012**
Monkey	Rabbit	October 15, 2011	November 3, 2012
		October 16, 2011	December 1, 2012
		November 12, 2011	December 16, 2012
		December 10, 2011	
		December 11, 2011	
Monkey	Dragon	April 3, 2011	April 21, 2012
		October 16, 2011	October 6, 2012
		December 11, 2011	November 3, 2012
			December 1, 2012
Monkey	Snake	September 11, 2011	October 6, 2012
		October 16, 2011	November 3, 2012
		December 11, 2011	November 4, 2012
			December 1, 2012
			December 2, 2012
Monkey	Horse	October 16, 2011	June 30, 2012
		December 17, 2011	September 30, 2012
			November 3, 2012
			December 1, 2012
Monkey	Sheep	October 15, 2011	July 1, 2012
		October 16, 2011	July 29, 2012
		November 12, 2011	October 6, 2012
		December 10, 2011	November 3, 2012
		December 11, 2011	December 1, 2012
			December 16, 2012

Bride's birth sign	Groom's birth sign	2011*	2012**
Monkey	Monkey	October 15, 2011	September 30, 2012
		October 16, 2011	October 6, 2012
		November 12, 2011	November 3, 2012
		December 10, 2011	November 4, 2012
		December 11, 2011	December 1, 2012
		December 17, 2011	December 2, 2012
			December 16, 2012
Monkey	Rooster	October 16, 2011	September 30, 2012
		November 12, 2011	October 6, 2012
		December 10, 2011	November 3, 2012
		December 11, 2011	November 4, 2012
		December 17, 2011	December 1, 2012
			December 2, 2012
			December 16, 2012
Monkey	Dog	October 15, 2011	September 30, 2012
		November 12, 2011	October 6, 2012
		December 10, 2011	November 4, 2012
		December 11, 2011	December 1, 2012
		December 17, 2011	December 2, 2012
			December 16, 2012
Monkey	Boar	February 26, 2011	October 6, 2012
		October 15, 2011	November 3, 2012
		October 16, 2011	December 1, 2012
		November 12, 2011	December 16, 2012

Bride's birth sign	Groom's birth sign	2011*	2012**
Monkey	Boar	December 10, 2011	
		December 11, 2011	
Hen	Rat	February 26, 2011	January 21, 2012
		February 27, 2011	March 17, 2012
		October 16, 2011	November 4, 2012
		December 10, 2011	December 2, 2012
		December 11, 2011	
		December 17, 2011	
Hen	Ox	April 9, 2011	March 25, 2012
		May 7, 2011	April 22, 2012
		June 4, 2011	May 20, 2012
		December 17, 2011	September 30, 2012
			November 4, 2012
			December 2, 2012
Hen	Tiger	April 10, 2011	April 22, 2012
		May 8, 2011	April 28, 2012
		November 12, 2011	May 20, 2012
		December 10, 2011	May 26, 2012
			November 4, 2012
			December 16, 2012
Hen	Rabbit	April 3, 2011	March 25, 2012
		October 16, 2011	April 21, 2012
		December 11, 2011	April 22, 2012
			May 20, 2012

Bride's birth sign	Groom's birth sign	2011*	2012**
Hen	Rabbit		October 6, 2012
			November 3, 2012
			November 4, 2012
			December 1, 2012
			December 2, 2012
Hen	Dragon	September 11, 2011	November 4, 2012
		November 12, 2011	December 2, 2012
Hen	Snake	July 10, 2011	June 30, 2012
		September 11, 2011	July 28, 2012
		December 17, 2011	September 30, 2012
			November 4, 2012
			December 2, 2012
Hen	Horse	September 11, 2011	July 1, 2012
		November 12, 2011	November 4, 2012
		December 10, 2011	December 2, 2012
			December 16, 2012
Hen	Sheep	October 16, 2011	September 30, 2012
		November 12, 2011	October 6, 2012
		December 10, 2011	November 3, 2012
		December 11, 2011	November 4, 2012
		December 17, 2011	December 1, 2012
			December 2, 2012
			December 16, 2012

Bride's birth sign	Groom's birth sign	2011*	2012**
Hen	Monkey	October 16, 2011	September 30, 2012
		November 12, 2011	October 6, 2012
		December 10, 2011	November 3, 2012
		December 11, 2011	November 4, 2012
		December 17, 2011	December 1, 2012
			December 2, 2012
			December 16, 2012
Hen	Rooster	November 12, 2011	September 30, 2012
		December 10, 2011	October 6, 2012
		December 11, 2011	November 4, 2012
		December 17, 2011	December 1, 2012
			December 2, 2012
			December 16, 2012
Hen	Dog	February 27, 2011	March 17, 2012
		November 12, 2011	December 2, 2012
		December 10, 2011	December 16, 2012
Hen	Boar	February 26, 2011	January 21, 2012
		February 27, 2011	March 17, 2012
		October 16, 2011	November 4, 2012
		December 10, 2011	December 2, 2012
		December 11, 2011	
		December 17, 2011	
Dog	Rat	February 26, 2011	February 19, 2012
		December 11, 2011	October 6, 2012

Bride's birth sign	Groom's birth sign	2011*	2012**
Dog	Rat		December 1, 2012
Dog	Ox	February 26, 2011	January 21, 2012
		February 27, 2011	January 22, 2012
		October 15, 2011	February 19, 2012
		December 10, 2011	March 17, 2012
		December 11, 2011	September 30, 2012
		December 17, 2011	October 7, 2012
			November 4, 2012
			December 2, 2012
Dog	Tiger	April 9, 2011	September 30, 2012
		May 7, 2011	December 1, 2012
		June 4, 2011	December 2, 2012
			December 16, 2012
Dog	Rabbit	April 9, 2011	April 28, 2012
		April 10, 2011	May 26, 2012
		May 7, 2011	September 30, 2012
		May 8, 2011	December 16, 2012
		June 4, 2011	
		June 5, 2011	
		October 15, 2011	
		November 12, 2011	
		December 10, 2011	
Dog	Dragon	April 3, 2011	April 21, 2012
		April 9, 2011	September 30, 2012

Bride's birth sign	Groom's birth sign	2011*	2012**
Dog	Dragon	June 4, 2011	October 6, 2012
		December 11, 2011	December 1, 2012
Dog	Snake	July 10, 2011	June 30, 2012
		September 11, 2011	July 28, 2012
		December 17, 2011	September 30, 2012
			November 4, 2012
			December 2, 2012
Dog	Horse	July 10, 2011	June 30, 2012
		December 17, 2011	July 28, 2012
			September 30, 2012
Dog	Sheep	July 10, 2011	June 30, 2012
		October 15, 2011	July 1, 2012
		November 12, 2011	July 28, 2012
		December 10, 2011	July 29, 2012
		December 17, 2011	September 30, 2012
			December 16, 2012
Dog	Monkey	October 15, 2011	September 30, 2012
		November 12, 2011	October 6, 2012
		December 10, 2011	November 4, 2012
		December 11, 2011	December 1, 2012
		December 17, 2011	December 2, 2012
			December 16, 2012
Dog	Rooster	November 12, 2011	September 30, 2012
		December 10, 2011	October 6, 2012

Bride's birth sign	Groom's birth sign	2011*	2012**
Dog	Rooster	December 11, 2011	November 4, 2012
		December 17, 2011	December 1, 2012
			December 2, 2012
			December 16, 2012
Dog	Dog	October 15, 2011	September 30, 2012
		November 12, 2011	October 6, 2012
		December 10, 2011	November 4, 2012
		December 11, 2011	December 1, 2012
		December 17, 2011	December 2, 2012
			December 16, 2012
Dog	Boar	October 15, 2011	January 22, 2012
		November 12, 2011	September 30, 2012
		December 10, 2011	December 16, 2012
		December 17, 2011	
Boar	Rat	January 1, 2011	January 21, 2012
		January 29, 2011	February 19, 2012
		February 26, 2011	March 17, 2012
		February 27, 2011	
Boar	Ox	January 1, 2011	January 21, 2012
		January 29, 2011	February 19, 2012
		February 26, 2011	March 17, 2012
		February 27, 2011	
Boar	Tiger	April 9, 2011	March 25, 2012
		April 10, 2011	April 21, 2012

Bride's birth sign	Groom's birth sign	2011*	2012**
Boar	Tiger	May 7, 2011	May 20, 2012
		May 8, 2011	May 26, 2012
		June 4, 2011	
		June 5, 2011	
Boar	Rabbit	April 9, 2011	February 19, 2012
		April 10, 2011	March 17, 2012
		May 7, 2011	April 21, 2012
		June 5, 2011	April 22, 2012
			May 20, 2012
Boar	Dragon	February 26, 2011	January 21, 2012
		April 3, 2011	January 22, 2012
		April 10, 2011	April 21, 2012
		May 8, 2011	April 22, 2012
		June 5, 2011	
Boar	Snake	February 27, 2011	March 17, 2012
		July 9, 2011	July 29, 2012
Boar	Horse	July 10, 2011	January 22, 2012
		September 4, 2011	February 19, 2012
			June 30, 2012
			July 1, 2012
			July 28, 2012
			July 29, 2012
Boar	Sheep	February 26, 2011	July 1, 2012
		July 10, 2011	July 29, 2012

Bride's birth sign	Groom's birth sign	2011*	2012**
Boar	Monkey	February 26, 2011	October 6, 2012
		October 15, 2011	November 3, 2012
		October 16, 2011	December 1, 2012
		November 12, 2011	December 16, 2012
		December 10, 2011	
		December 11, 2011	
Boar	Rooster	February 27, 2011	March 17, 2012
		November 12, 2011	December 2, 2012
		December 10, 2011	December 16, 2012
Boar	Dog	October 15, 2011	January 22, 2012
		November 12, 2011	September 30, 2012
		December 10, 2011	December 16, 2012
		December 17, 2011	
Boar	Boar	January 1, 2011	January 21, 2012
		January 29, 2011	January 22, 2012
		February 26, 2011	February 19, 2012
		February 27, 2011	March 17, 2012

Glossary of Chinese Terms and Symbolism

an chuang (ān chuáng 安床): seating the bed for a newly married couple.

ba gua (bā guà 八掛): eight trigrams, a combination of broken and solid lines that comes from the I Ching.

ba zi (bā zì 八字): literally translated as "eight words," refers to the birth information of a couple, traditionally used for matchmaking and choosing a wedding date.

bai he: water lily, symbolizes a couple being together for a hundred years.

butterfly: symbolizes happiness and a long-lasting marriage.

cha: tea, symbolizes a closeness of family.

cheongsam (cháng shān 長衫): Cantonese word for *qi pao*.

circle: represents the Metal element, symbolizes unity, perfection, and femininity.

coconut: symbolizes continuity of generations and is a homophone for "son" in Mandarin.

cypress: symbolizes peace.

da ling jie (dà ling ji 大姈姐): wedding organizer, assists with traditions and ceremonies.

dragon: symbolizes masculinity.

feng shui (fēng shuǐ 風水): literally "wind" and "water," the art of balancing energy and environment.

fu (fú 富): prosperity, sign of good luck.

gan bei (gān bēi 乾杯): literally means "empty glass," a traditional wedding toast similar to "cheers!"

hao ming gong/po (hào mìng gōng 好命公; hào mìng pó 好命婆): person who has been lucky in life who performs the *shang tou* ceremony. *Hao ming* *gong* refers to a lucky man and *hao ming po* refers to a lucky woman performing the ceremony.

hong bao (**hóng bāo** 紅包): red envelope for lucky money given on special occasions.

hong gua (**hóng guà** 紅掛): Cantonese word for *hong pao*.

hong pao (**hóng páo** 紅袍): bride's red two-piece formal wedding outfit.

hou tian ba gua (**hòu tiān bā guà** 後天八卦): Later Heaven *ba gua* used for living environment.

kumquat (**jīn jú** 金桔): symbolizes gold or prosperity.

lai cee (**lì shì** 利是): Cantonese word for *hong bao*.

li chun (**lì chūn** 立春): first day of spring.

long feng tai (**lóng fèng tāi** 龍鳳胎): Dragon and Phoenix, used commonly to refer to a set of twins.

lychee (**lì zhī** 荔枝): symbolizes family.

mirror: symbolizes a bright and long-lasting marriage, also believed to ward off evil.

orange: symbolizes gold or prosperity.

palm fruit: symbol of fertility.

peaches: symbol of longevity.

peony: the royal symbol of elegance.

phoenix: symbol of femininity.

pomegranate: symbol of fertility.

qi (**qì** 氣): literally "air," meaning life force.

qi pao (**qí páo** 旗袍): fitted dress.

ruler: symbolizes abundance and plenty.

scissors: shape resembles the butterfly, which represents long-lasting love.

shang tou (**shàng tou** 上頭): hair-combing wedding ritual, which occurs night before the wedding ceremony.

square: represents the Earth element, a stabilizing force.

tang yuan (**tāng yuán** 湯圓): round rice dumplings. The dumplings' round shape represents wholeness and perfection.

xin tian ba gua (**xiān tiān bā guà** 先天八卦): Early Heaven *ba gua* used for final resting places and warding off evil.

yang (**yáng** 陽): the masculine, positive or active force.

yin (**yīn** 陰): the feminine, negative or passive force.

Acknowledgments

Kenneth Lau—For his gift of calligraphy, but most of all for his wisdom and guidance through the *Wedding Feng Shui* process.

Michele Fujimoto—Thank you for your beautiful drawings, and especially for your love and friendship.

Jonathan Lau—Thank you for your constant support and honesty throughout the writing of this book.

Janelle and Kai Chan—Thank you for welcoming us into every intimate detail of your wedding. We'll always be grateful.

Deanelle Gho—Thank you for your insights into traditional Chinese weddings.

Kwong Kai and Peggy Lau—Xiao Jiu Gong and Xiao Jiu Po, thank you for gathering such useful information about modern Chinese weddings for us and making our visit so productive.

Natalie Chin, Michele Fujimoto, Michelle Entezari, Sacha Kuo, Tamara Belkin, Uma Karmarkar, and Veronica Tiglao—Laura's lovely bridesmaids (and unofficial bridesmaid), thank you for your love and friendship through my wedding and beyond. My wedding and your gift of being there helped me write this book.

Stephanie Meyers—Our wonderful editor, who championed this idea from the beginning and provided enthusiastic support.

Harsh Karmarkar—For his love, honesty, and encouragement to write this book.

About the Authors

Kenneth Lau

Kenneth Lau

LAURA LAU is a second-generation author on Chinese culture and horoscopes. She is a coauthor of *Best-Loved Chinese Proverbs*, with her parents, Theodora and Kenneth. Born in Hong Kong, she divides her time between Los Angeles and Singapore with her husband, Harsh.

THEODORA LAU is the author of *The Handbook of Chinese Horoscopes*, *The Chinese Horoscopes Guide to Relationships*, *Chinese Horoscopes for Your Child*, and *Best-Loved Chinese Proverbs*. Theodora's books have been translated into more than seventeen languages and have introduced many topics of Chinese culture to readers all over the world. She was born in Shanghai, China.

About the Artists

KENNETH LAU

KENNETH LAU is a calligrapher and illustrator whose work has been featured in *The Handbook of Chinese Horoscopes*, *The Chinese Horoscopes Guide to Relationships*, *Chinese Horoscopes for Your Child*, and *Best-Loved Chinese Proverbs*. Born in Shanghai, China, Kenneth is fluent in multiple Chinese dialects and skilled in a variety of styles of Chinese calligraphy.

MICHELE FUJIMOTO

MICHELE FUJIMOTO'S artwork was featured in *Chinese Horoscopes for Your Child*. She is a Southern California artist whose work is in museums and private collections.

Wedding Feng Shui Worksheet

EXAMPLE

	BRIDE	GROOM
Birth Date:	February 1, 1981	January 2, 1977
Time of Birth:	3:30 A.M.	1:15 A.M.
Animal Year:	Monkey	Rabbit
Birth Year Element:	Metal	Wood
Ascendant (birth hour):	Tiger	Rooster
Western Sun Sign (birth month/day)	Aquarius	Capricorn
Animal Month of Birth	Tiger	Ox

NOTES: (Elements, Colors, Gemstones)

My birth animal's colors are white and metallic tones, but my ascendant and animal month are Tiger, which is green. Thomas also has green from being a Rabbit.

POSSIBLE WEDDING DATES:

2011: November 12, 2011

2012: November 3, 2012

Wedding Feng Shui Worksheet

	BRIDE	GROOM
Birth Date:		
Time of Birth:		
Animal Year:		
Birth Year Element:		
Ascendant (birth hour):		
Western Sun Sign (birth month/day)		
Animal Month of Birth		

NOTES:

_____

_____

_____

_____

_____

_____

_____

_____

POSSIBLE WEDDING DATES:

2011: _____

2012: _____

Wedding Feng Shui Worksheet

Name: _____

Role in Wedding: _____

Birth Date: _____

Time of Birth: _____

Animal Year: _____

Birth Year Element: _____

Ascendant (birth hour): _____

Western Sun Sign (birth month/day): _____

Animal Month of Birth: _____

NOTES:

_____

_____

_____

_____

_____

_____

_____

_____

_____

_____

_____

_____

Wedding Feng Shui Worksheet

Name: _____

Role in Wedding: _____

Birth Date: _____

Time of Birth: _____

Animal Year: _____

Birth Year Element: _____

Ascendant (birth hour): _____

Western Sun Sign (birth month/day): _____

Animal Month of Birth: _____

NOTES:

_____

_____

_____

_____

_____

_____

_____

_____

_____

_____

_____

Wedding Feng Shui Worksheet

Name: _____

Role in Wedding: _____

Birth Date: _____

Time of Birth: _____

Animal Year: _____

Birth Year Element: _____

Ascendant (birth hour): _____

Western Sun Sign (birth month/day): _____

Animal Month of Birth: _____

NOTES:

_____

_____

_____

_____

_____

_____

_____

_____

_____

_____

Wedding Feng Shui Worksheet

Name: _____

Role in Wedding: _____

Birth Date: _____

Time of Birth: _____

Animal Year: _____

Birth Year Element: _____

Ascendant (birth hour): _____

Western Sun Sign (birth month/day): _____

Animal Month of Birth: _____

NOTES:

_____

_____

_____

_____

_____

_____

_____

_____

_____

_____

_____

Wedding Feng Shui Worksheet

Name: _____

Role in Wedding: _____

Birth Date: _____

Time of Birth: _____

Animal Year: _____

Birth Year Element: _____

Ascendant (birth hour): _____

Western Sun Sign (birth month/day): _____

Animal Month of Birth: _____

NOTES:

_____

_____

_____

_____

_____

_____

_____

_____

_____

_____

_____

_____

Wedding Feng Shui Worksheet

Name: _____

Role in Wedding: _____

Birth Date: _____

Time of Birth: _____

Animal Year: _____

Birth Year Element: _____

Ascendant (birth hour): _____

Western Sun Sign (birth month/day): _____

Animal Month of Birth: _____

NOTES:

_____

_____

_____

_____

_____

_____

_____

_____

_____

_____

_____

_____

Wedding Feng Shui Worksheet

Name: _____

Role in Wedding: _____

Birth Date: _____

Time of Birth: _____

Animal Year: _____

Birth Year Element: _____

Ascendant (birth hour): _____

Western Sun Sign (birth month/day): __

Animal Month of Birth: _____

NOTES:

_____

_____

_____

_____

_____

_____

_____

_____

_____

_____

_____

_____

Wedding Feng Shui Worksheet

Name: _____

Role in Wedding: _____

Birth Date: _____

Time of Birth: _____

Animal Year: _____

Birth Year Element: _____

Ascendant (birth hour): _____

Western Sun Sign (birth month/day): _____

Animal Month of Birth: _____

NOTES:

_____

_____

_____

_____

_____

_____

_____

_____

_____

_____

_____

Wedding Feng Shui Worksheet

Name: _____

Role in Wedding: _____

Birth Date: _____

Time of Birth: _____

Animal Year: _____

Birth Year Element: _____

Ascendant (birth hour): _____

Western Sun Sign (birth month/day): _____

Animal Month of Birth: _____

NOTES:

_____

_____

_____

_____

_____

_____

_____

_____

_____

_____

_____

_____

Wedding Feng Shui Worksheet

Name: _____

Role in Wedding: _____

Birth Date: _____

Time of Birth: _____

Animal Year: _____

Birth Year Element: _____

Ascendant (birth hour): _____

Western Sun Sign (birth month/day): _____

Animal Month of Birth: _____

NOTES:

_____

_____

_____

_____

_____

_____

_____

_____

_____

_____

_____

Wedding Feng Shui Worksheet

Name: _____

Role in Wedding: _____

Birth Date: _____

Time of Birth: _____

Animal Year: _____

Birth Year Element: _____

Ascendant (birth hour): _____

Western Sun Sign (birth month/day): _____

Animal Month of Birth: _____

NOTES:

_____

_____

_____

_____

_____

_____

_____

_____

_____

_____

_____

_____

Wedding Feng Shui Worksheet

Name: _____

Role in Wedding: _____

Birth Date: _____

Time of Birth: _____

Animal Year: _____

Birth Year Element: _____

Ascendant (birth hour): _____

Western Sun Sign (birth month/day): _____

Animal Month of Birth: _____

NOTES:

_____

_____

_____

_____

_____

_____

_____

_____

_____

_____

_____

Wedding Feng Shui Worksheet

Name: _____

Role in Wedding: _____

Birth Date: _____

Time of Birth: _____

Animal Year: _____

Birth Year Element: _____

Ascendant (birth hour): _____

Western Sun Sign (birth month/day): _____

Animal Month of Birth: _____

NOTES:

_____

_____

_____

_____

_____

_____

_____

_____

_____

_____

Wedding Feng Shui Worksheet

Name: _____

Role in Wedding: _____

Birth Date: _____

Time of Birth: _____

Animal Year: _____

Birth Year Element: _____

Ascendant (birth hour): _____

Western Sun Sign (birth month/day): _____

Animal Month of Birth: _____

NOTES:

_____

_____

_____

_____

_____

_____

_____

_____

_____

_____

Wedding Feng Shui Worksheet

Name: _____

Role in Wedding: _____

Birth Date: _____

Time of Birth: _____

Animal Year: _____

Birth Year Element: _____

Ascendant (birth hour): _____

Western Sun Sign (birth month/day): _____

Animal Month of Birth: _____

NOTES:

_____

_____

_____

_____

_____

_____

_____

_____

_____

_____

_____

Wedding Feng Shui Worksheet

Name: _____

Role in Wedding: _____

Birth Date: _____

Time of Birth: _____

Animal Year: _____

Birth Year Element: _____

Ascendant (birth hour): _____

Western Sun Sign (birth month/day): _____

Animal Month of Birth: _____

NOTES:

_____

_____

_____

_____

_____

_____

_____

_____

_____

_____

_____

How'd it go?

After your wedding, we'd love to know how it went. Please send us digital pictures and your story by following the directions on the book's Web site, www.weddingfengshui.com, so we can post them and share with our growing community. We'll be posting updates and new content regularly, and we'd love to have you join the conversation to give other brides ideas and inspiration.

MORE FROM
LAURA LAU & THEODORA LAU

THE HANDBOOK OF CHINESE HOROSCOPES, 7th EDITION

ISBN 978-0-06-199091-5 (paperback)

Now in a fully revised and updated seventh edition, *The Handbook of Chinese Horoscopes* remains the definitive, classic work on this fascinating subject and artfully combines the Eastern lunar calendar with Western solar-based astrology.

This seventh edition has a refreshed design and contains brand new predictions for all signs for the upcoming years, as well as updates throughout the text.

BEST-LOVED CHINESE PROVERBS, 2nd EDITION

ISBN 978-0-06-170365-2 (paperback)

A timeless collection of the most profound and meaningful Chinese proverbs on fate, honor, love, knowledge, success, and much more.

In addition to collecting and translating more than 300 ancient Chinese proverbs, Theodora Lau and Laura Lau have included notes on interpretation wherever necessary to help a modern American audience discover the subtleties and depth of the original language.